THE

Bond

BETWEEN

Women

A
JOURNEY TO
FIERCE COMPASSION

THE
Bond
BETWEEN
Women

CHINA
GALLAND

RIVERHEAD BOOKS
a member of
Penguin Putnam Inc.
New York
1998

RIVERHEAD BOOKS
a member of
Penguin Putnam Inc.
200 Madison Avenue
New York, NY 10016

Library of Congress Cataloging-in-Publication Data

Galland, China.
The bond between women : a journey to fierce compassion /
China Galland.
p. cm.
Includes bibliographical references and index.
ISBN 1-57322-088-4 (alk. paper)
1. Galland, China. 2. Spiritual biography—United States. 3. Women
and religion. 4. Feminist spirituality. I. Title.
BL73.G34A3 1998   97-37796 CIP
291.4'092—dc21
[B]

A list of permissions appears on pages 335–36.
Title spread and pages 1, 153: Taleju Bhavani, a form of the Goddess Durga,
Bhaktapur, Nepal (*China Galland*)

BOOK DESIGN BY DEBORAH KERNER

For my daughter,
Madelon,
and for my mother,
Ruth,
for my sons,
Matthew and Benjamin,
and for my husband,
Corey

ILLUSTRATIONS

*[People] can apprehend and know their own being
insofar as they can make it visible in the image of their gods.*

— ERNST CASSIRER,
The Philosophy of Symbolic Form

Contents

1

WHAT IS BEAUTIFUL

I want to begin with what is beautiful. I want this because what follows is hard for me to tell you. It is a small part of a much larger story, but it is the thread that drew me through the eye of the needle.

The waters were rising, flooding this constricted place inside myself. I had to swim for my life to get to where the way opened, to make my way to a broader shore. To safety. I could no longer stay in the narrows, handless, voiceless. But this is not what I want to write.

I want to write about what is beautiful, about how wisdom—the principle of enlightenment—is within each one of us, about how it is unavoidable.

I want to write about a passionately happy, blissful source of wisdom, a dynamic, fierce female divinity who awaits our discovery—awaits the sun and water of our attention—to transform our life. About how pure and unpolluted our nature is, how our basic mind is like water; though like water it may be dirty and full of mud, "... its nature remains just clear—its nature is not polluted...." the Dalai Lama, Tenzin Gyatso, tells us. He goes on to write that no matter what disturbing emotions arise, no matter how distressing, our primordial nature, our "basic mind ... remains unaffected by defilement, beginninglessly good."[1] Goodness without beginning, goodness without end.

The journey I took was not the one I planned. This is in the nature of a pilgrimage. I went to the places I intended, met the women whom I set out to meet, but over time it became apparent that another story was unfolding, underneath, one that at first I did not fully recognize except for an intermittent sense of dread, a periodic nightmare, and a paralyzing backache that I pushed aside. I stayed focused on the fact that this story is about coming to understand "fierce compassion," about transforming anger into compassion, about spiritual practices, faith and action, and about women of action who each can show us a different face of fierce compassion. It includes some of the sacred stories, myths, and tales that tell us the divine feminine will rise up when the world is in danger, that help comes from forgotten quarters, from what's been cast out, lost, rejected, and marginalized, and that what we have cast out is what saves us, what becomes the cornerstone for a new foundation.

This journey is also about that point where the spiritual and the political intersect. It is about discernment, about taking action. About love and water and forests. My task is to take you with me to Asia and Latin America, to invite you to accompany me on this journey to find the waters of fierce compassion so that together we might rise up and be able to contribute more fully to the world. So that we might save it.

It wasn't until I went to Argentina, until I was able to see and hear first-hand how corrosive silence is, how it engenders complicity, that I began seriously to consider including more of my own experience in these pages. The intrepid Brazilian Catholic theologian of liberation Ivone Gebara—despite being "silenced" by the Vatican—wrote to me during her exile in Belgium about the story of Susanna in the Old Testament. Gebara says that women have to resist silence, that women have to speak up, to cry out like Susanna, who spoke out against the elders even though she knew she would not be believed, and that it could cost her her life.

In the end, I resisted the comfort of silence. I included certain episodes from my own life in order to tell the story of this journey as fully and as truthfully as I could, for I now see how they shaped this journey in ways I could not have known beforehand and how they led me to this unfolding. I could not face the world's pain until I faced my own. Paradoxically I could not pass through that narrow place until I was willing to attend more deeply to the pain of others. Most important, certain experiences are included in order to show—in ways that I have only begun to discern—that we are always guided, always cared for, always healing, moving inevitably toward wholeness, even when we cannot yet see it for all the pain and difficulty that surrounds us.

There is a goodness, a Wisdom that arises, sometimes gracefully, sometimes gently, sometimes awkwardly, sometimes fiercely, but it will arise to save us if we let it, and it arises from *within* us, like the force that drives green shoots to break the winter ground, it will arise and drive us into a great blossoming like a pear tree, into flowering, into fragrance, fruit, and song, into the wild wind dancing, sun shimmering, into the aliveness of it all, into that part of ourselves that can never be defiled, defeated, or destroyed, but that comes back to life, time and time again, that lives—always—that does not die. Into the Divine.

THE GODDESS DURGA SLAYING THE BUFFALO DEMON
(Durga Mahisasuramardini), CA. LATE EIGHTH CENTURY, SANDSTONE,
EASTERN INDIA (*Philadelphia Museum of Art*)

2

THE STORY OF DURGA

The world stood poised on the brink of destruction once before.

Rivers dried up, plants refused to grow. People starved. There was war everywhere. Slaughter prevailed. Dancing stopped, even singing was forgotten. The demons, known as the *asuras*, were loose in the world, raging unchecked across heaven and earth, drunk with destruction. No one could stop them, not even the gods, who had been defeated, one by one.

Humiliated, the gods withdrew to the heights of the Himalayas and took counsel amongst themselves, to no avail. Their dilemma was insoluble. They had lost all power against these demons and could only leave the world to its inevitable destruction. Then it was remembered that this time had been foretold—a demon would come to destroy the world, and only a woman could defeat this demon—only a woman could save the world.

At this, the gods shot forth streams of fire, and their fiery streams converged into a towering pillar of flames, as high as the Himalayas themselves. Out of this fire came the Great Goddess Durga herself, blazing with the light of a thousand suns, radiating her splendor throughout the universe. Riding a lion, wearing the crescent moon, smiling serenely, Durga had ten hands and arms, powerful and ready with weapons given to her by the gods themselves.

The Great Goddess Durga, the Warrior Queen, whose very name means "Fortress," "Unassailable," "Beyond Reach," rose up to fight Mahisasura, the Great Demon, and all his forces. She rode into battle with a roar that shook the earth.

The war between Durga and Mahisasura and his demons raged across heaven and earth, day after day. Oceans boiled, the sky stretched thin, the mountains shook. Every time Durga sighed, legions of female warriors sprang to her side. Demons were slain by the hundreds in the hail of weapons from the Goddess and her forces. The battlefield was choked with bodies. The Goddess consumed the army of demons like a great fire devours a forest. When the battle was over, Durga had won.

Mahisasura, enraged by defeat, now took the form of the Buffalo Demon and began the battles anew. Each time Durga killed the Buffalo Demon he would spring back to life in a more ferocious form. In what seemed to be the final struggle, Durga cut off the Buffalo Demon's head. Victory was in her hands. The gods praised her and worshipped her, and she retired to her throne in the Himalayas, riding her lion. But this was not to be the end.

This time the Lord of the Demons himself, Sumbha, and his younger brother, Nisumbha, sought out Durga. They did not confront Durga in battle; they tried to seduce her. They proposed that she marry Sumbha. Durga thanked them for the proposal, but reminded them of a vow she had taken, to marry only the one who could defeat her in battle. Since Sumbha was clearly unable to defeat her, she had no choice but to refuse his hand.

Sumbha was infuriated. He and his brother commanded their forces to attack, but Durga reduced their troops to ashes with a glance.

Sumbha sent in more demons and commanded them to drag Durga to him by her hair. Durga was enraged by his insolence. Her face grew as dark as a storm cloud, and the Goddess Kali sprang full-blown from her forehead—armed, black, enormous, terrifying, and ready for battle.

Kali strode out onto the battlefield laughing, filling the skies with her terrible cry. Bloodshed and death followed her every turn. She roared with pleasure as she devoured her foes. With each step she trampled entire battalions. Chariots and riders, troops of elephants, soldiers, one and all were swept up and swallowed in her enormous, howling maw. Her long teeth gleamed, her sword slashed everything in her path. She laughed and reveled in the fury of demolishing the Demon's forces.

Sumbha's army was put to flight and now only the Demon Raktabija remained. He was a hideous demon. Every time a drop of Raktabija's blood fell to the ground, a thousand more demons would spring up for battle. Rather than attack directly, to defeat him, Kali licked up the blood of his wounds until no more remained. Raktabija was routed. Finally even Nisumbha was killed, leaving Sumbha alone. Sumbha scoffed at Durga, railed at her, challenging her to prove herself and to fight him without the help of Kali and all her female warriors.

But Durga could not be trapped. She accepted his challenge and in an electrifying moment absorbed Kali and all her female warriors back into herself. She rode out onto the battlefield on her lion, alone. Serene and smiling, she challenged Sumbha to attack. The struggle for the fate of the world itself began.

Time stopped as the Goddess and the Demon embraced in their fight, turning and pitching, rolling across the sky. The cosmos groaned with the enormity of their encounter. At the last moment, Durga pierced Sumbha's heart with her dagger and he fell tumbling out of the heavens. The world was safe at last.

A great cry of victory rang throughout the world. All the gods assembled to honor Durga and to crown her Queen of the Universe. Rivers returned to their courses; music, dance, and song returned to the world. Plants grew, trees blossomed, joy could be found again. Being itself seemed to rejoice. The gods and all her followers begged her to stay and rule the world, but Durga would have none of it. She assured them that there was no need to fear further, she would feed her devotees with her own body, but she would not stay and rule the world. She put aside all adulation, put away the vast display of her powers, and withdrew from the world at the height of her victory with a promise:

3
SAVING THE WORLD

Travels to Nepal and India, and ongoing study, had led me to the *Devi-Mahatmya*, the fifteen-hundred-year-old classic Sanskrit text of Hinduism from which Durga's story comes. *Devi* means "Goddess" and *Mahatmya* can be translated as her "Greatness" or "Virtue," so the *Devi-Mahatmya* can be understood as the story of the Greatness or Virtue of the Goddess.[3] It tells us that, at least once before, the world was on the verge of destruction by "demons."

Demons are traditionally understood in Hinduism and Buddhism as symbols for our most serious human failings, for greed, hate, and delusion, or what in Christianity might be called the deadly sins. These are our real enemies. Read with this understanding, despite the unfamiliar names, Durga's story suddenly becomes timely. For is this not what threatens the world today? Think of the insatiability of human greed, the fires of hatred, the deluded thinking that tells us that we can poison the air and water upon which all life depends and remain unharmed ourselves. Have not the horrors of twentieth-century warfare made many think that whatever or whomever we had called God in the past had itself been defeated and fled the world, abandoning us to our own destruction?

This is what gives this ancient story such a contemporary ring. It tells us that the demons can be defeated, that the world can be saved—but not by traditional solutions, and not until defeat has been acknowledged. It was only after the gods had been beaten and humiliated that they withdrew to the Himalayas, admitted their defeat, and remembered Durga, remembered that this time had been foretold. The solution would come from unexpected quarters, from a place they had not thought to look—from the Goddess, from the power of the feminine. The stone that had been cast out had to become the foundation. But it is important to remember that even the "feminine" is ultimately a metaphor—a metaphor for that aspect of being human which has been considered weaker, inferior: a metaphor for the other-than-rational, the feeling, the emotive side of experience, which men have as well. And in continuing this commentary, it is important to note that it is the final scene of the battle that is the most telling.

Durga had killed the Demon Mahisasura many times in the earlier battles in this story, and though she cut off his head, he would come back to life in another form. He was not decisively defeated until his heart was pierced. This is the crucial element in what the story tells us. These human failings, these "demons" who threaten us can be defeated only when we go beyond reason, when we pierce the heart.[4]

When I thought of Durga's promise to return if the world was ever again threatened, I began to see her promise fulfilled everywhere that people—especially women—are standing up and defending life in all its fullness. For the divine comes to us through the human, we are the matrix. The divine exists in the world only insofar as we make its presence real. Even God had to become human, the story of Christ tells us. The human is the divine manifest. Hinduism, Buddhism, and the Western mystical traditions tell us this: Our task is to purify our hearts and minds so that we can see through what appears to be our separateness.

It was with the story of Durga that I began this journey to understand the fierce female deities and to find their gift: a new understanding of compassion, of its fierceness. Would a fresh look at this subject help strengthen the bond between women, could it help reconnect women of faith and women of action, help inspire us to rise to the tasks we face now?[5]

In 1994, I resolved to go back to Nepal in time for Durga Puja, the nine-day celebration of Durga's victory that takes place throughout Nepal and India every October. There I would be able not only to attend the festival but also to consult with Buddhist teachers, take further teachings, and deepen my understanding of fierce compassion, or compassionate wrath as it is sometimes called. Further, I would begin to seek out women who lived with fierce compassion. I would start with Mother Teresa's Sisters in Nepal, then go to her Sisters in Calcutta. I knew they were compassionate, and though they might not ordinarily be thought of in this way, I trusted that they were also fierce, or they could not face the human suffering they did and survive.

During the celebration of Durga's victory, the sacred text the *Devi-Mahatmya* is recited, chanted, reenacted, danced, and proclaimed aloud as it has been for generations.[6] I would hear it and see it reenacted again and again in Kathmandu during that nine-day celebration. I had read the story and studied it, but I needed to know it in context, in the world that it came from. I had to begin in Asia, though it was ten thousand miles away from where I wanted to end, in Latin America. That was all I knew. The rest I would find out in the course of this pilgrimage. Now I had to begin.

P ART

O NE

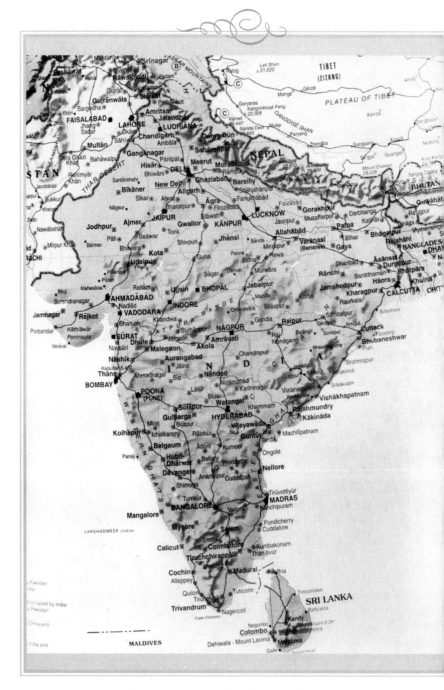

NEPAL AND INDIA (*Rand McNally*)

CHAPTER I

THE RETURN OF
THE FIERCE GODDESS

The Festival of Durga
Bhaktapur, Nepal

Wherever you are is called Here,
And you must treat it as a powerful stranger,
Must ask permission to know it and be known.

—DAVID WAGONER, "LOST"

Thousands pour through the narrow streets to the blare of trumpets and the beat of drums in the ancient village of Bhaktapur, in the Kathmandu Valley of Nepal. *Sarangis* soar like violins, cymbals clash, triangles and bells ring, while *tablas* keep the heart-pounding rhythms of Nepali music. We follow the music, snaking our way slowly in the late-afternoon sun to the Hindu temple of the Goddess Durga, the Warrior Queen.

The annual October celebration of Durga's victory, called Durga Puja or Navaratra, the Nine Nights of the Goddess, goes on throughout Nepal and India. Here in the Kathmandu Valley, signs of the feast are everywhere. Women and girls walk along the rutted roadway carrying trays of food adorned with brilliant red hibiscus and green rice sprigs for the temples. Feeding the deity is part of worship in Hinduism, where people are as at home with the divine as one is with a beloved family member.

Bhaktapur, the most medieval of the villages in the Kathmandu Valley countryside, is famous not only for its temples and shrines but also for the masked dances I've come to see. Here, I am told,

Durga returns at the moment the dancers pull her masks down over their heads during tonight's celebration.

I press through the moving crowd, making my way slowly, in a cycle of losing and finding the new friends I've come with. There are few Westerners here. Fortunately, one of the friends is a young Nepali woman, Tsering Gurung, who patiently answers my questions. The distinctive black saris with brilliant red borders that I admire are worn by women from a traditional caste, she explains, the Jyapu, farmers, who are Newaris, the indigenous people of the Kathmandu Valley. The Newaris gave Bhaktapur and Kathmandu a spectacular medieval artistic and architectural legacy, examples of which we pass on our way to the river—elaborate temples with carved wooden stories rising as high as one hundred feet off the cobbled street, aged red-brick houses with tiled roofs built in rectangles around courtyards called *chowks*. To the Newaris, the family was the focal point of life, and the shrines, temples, and water were placed in the center of the *chowks* while family life bustled around them, as it still does. Our path winds through a series of squares, twisting past temples, crumbling stone palaces, carved doorways into more *chowks,* and an elaborately sculpted water tank guarded by a bronze cobra that rises out of the center to show the presence of the *nagas,* the serpent deities who have control over water and who guard against evil spirits. I keep stopping to look, then fall behind, then catch up. Tsering manages to appear, laughing, just at the moment when I think I've lost our group altogether.

"Over here," she says, tugging my day pack, pulling me aside, out of the river of people into a tea stall. Inside are two of the women from our group, Marcia Anderson, a trim fifty-year-old American, and Federica Mastropaolo, a tall young Italian woman. Faces familiar only for days seem suddenly to have been known for much longer. I breathe a sigh of relief at being reunited.

Slipping into the crowded stream of celebrants and devotees, I feel the subtle presence of *shakti,* that powerful energy traditionally considered feminine, with its "kinetic," vibrational quality, as the Hindu scholar Diana Eck puts it.[1] I had been told that Bhaktapur is full of *shakti,* but now I feel it—in the living faith in the crowd, in the tempo of music, in the growing excitement as we draw nearer the temple. The word *shakti* itself means "power" or "energy," and its root means "to be able," Eck explains. It is his Shakti, his divine female counterpart—her energy—that gives the Hindu god Shiva, the Lord of the Universe, his power. In the fluid Hindu cosmology, the Trimurti, a threefold form of God, contains Brahma, the creator; Vishnu, the sustainer; and Shiva, the destroyer. Of Shiva it is said that he is *shava,* a corpse, unless he is connected to his *shakti,* that dynamic, surging, radiating, activating, sacred, feminine life energy, personified as the Goddess in her myriad forms. Here her energy is palpable.

In the Hindu cosmos, time is cyclical, the world born anew and destroyed time and again, over and over, in the never-ending divine play, the cosmic dance of dissolving and becoming. The gods and goddesses are numberless, but behind them all is the divine unity of the One in the many.

We pass dark-eyed young men with coal-black mustaches tossing down *rakshi,* the local alcoholic brew, while girls and excited young women in saris the color of jewels stand by shyly on the sidelines, watching with their big kohl-lined eyes, their bodies swaying to the rhythm of the music. I want to burst into dance, but I contain myself, slipping in and out of the crowd, darting ahead of the musicians, taking pictures, hiding behind the lens of my camera.

The mass of people thickens and surges, growing larger and larger over the more than two hours it takes us to reach the one narrow bridge to the temple that we all must cross. The air cools as the light fades and darkness softly billows. The light of lanterns being struck flickers at first, then glows steadily. Electric streetlamps come on at distant intervals, their harsh glare punching holes in the dark. By the time we reach the Hanumante River it is nightfall.

On the other side of the river, inside the small Durga temple, nine male dancers whirl and move in a trance, unseen by the crowd, nearing the end of their ritual, when they will put on the masks of Durga and become possessed by her presence. I have been told that it is dangerous to watch this ritual. I was also told not to photograph the dancers once they emerge from the temple with the masks, after Durga has come over them. Last year a Westerner was beaten to the ground for breaking this rule. In Hinduism, the image is considered to be a form of the deity itself; gazing at the image of the divine, one receives divine energy and is seen by the deity. Called *darshan,* this being in the presence of the deity and gazing, this "seeing," is the central act of devotion in Hinduism.

I have been warned to stay out of the temple, told that the moment the dancers put on Durga's masks, her presence is so charged, so heightened, that I would be harmed, as if struck by lightning, that I would die. Though I did not take this warning literally, I resolved not to go inside the temple, not to photograph the dancers. There is a parallel belief in Western culture that the unprepared soul cannot see God face to face and survive the encounter.

"Sight" and "seeing" are as crucial to understanding the Hindu and Buddhist worldviews as are the "Word" and "hearing" to Judaism, Christianity, and Islam.[2] In Hinduism, this world is ablaze with divinity, inseparable from it, completely interpenetrated by it.

The crowd has become so dense, so frenzied as we near the bridge, Tsering decides not to cross. She has been here many times. The way narrows. I want to see the dancers, the masks—so do Marcia and Federica—we keep going. Tsering promises to wait on the other side.

When we near the river's edge, just before the bridge, we are picked up and tossed in the sea of bodies like corks, and jammed between people's shoulders, I float across, my feet barely able to touch the ground. This is not a place to fall down. Many of the men are drunk by now.

I look around for my friends Marcia and Federica. Did they make it? We can no longer move independently, we are packed in so tightly. The crowd pulses like the irresistible drums. Federica and I struggle to stay within sight of each other. We've lost Marcia. Suddenly a wave of moving bodies pushes us into an area closer to the temple doorway. A Nepali man shoves his way up to us with a menacing look, staring at the cameras over our shoulders. Once he sees that they're behind us with their lens caps on, he breaks into a big smile and holds up red-and-white strings, drawing circles in the air in front of us. I don't understand what he wants. The people around us grin, the women smile reassuringly, the men hold up their cups of *rakshi* as if they're offering a toast. Suddenly the man with the strings grabs my hand and pulls me closer to the temple. Federica and I grab on to each other, following him as best we can through the stream of people shouting, drinking, and singing. The dancers will appear at any moment. The air swells with music, almost bursting with the sound of drums; the heavy sweet smell of incense fills the air. One more tug on my arm by the man with the strings, and Federica and I are popped out into a sliver of an opening at the bottom of the temple steps.

There in front of me is the enormous hairy black head of the water buffalo I had seen grazing earlier on the bottom floor of a village temple. He was decapitated only hours ago in the ritual reenactment of Durga's defeating the Buffalo Demon. Now as his head lies resting on the bottom temple steps—a candle burning on top of it and green sprigs of rice shoots tucked behind his ears—he looks curiously peaceful, astonishingly calm compared to the wild liveliness of the crowd. His large dark eyes are still open wide, unblinking and clear. People press in on either side.

Someone motions us to step up to the buffalo head and touch it to show our fearlessness and willingness to participate in the defeat of the Buffalo Demon. I watch the woman in front of me step forward, bend down, and touch the crown of his head. The crowd surges again—there's a way through. Nervous, I step into the opening, lean down and dip the fingers of my right hand in the thick red *tika* paste that lies on top of his head by the candle. I place it in the middle of my forehead and lean over again to touch the top of his broad, smooth head. This act feels strange, almost dangerous, but I have done it now, there is no going back. Federica follows suit. As soon as we move aside, the man with the red-and-white strings comes up, takes my arm, his face beaming, and begins to wrap his strings around first my wrist, then Federica's. Now we are part of the celebration, not just bystanders: we have helped "kill the demon" and assured Durga's victory. My mind is reeling—the image of this powerful Goddess Durga dressed like a queen, riding a lion, sailing serenely into battles, her ten hands armed, is in such contrast to the Catholic Mary I grew up with that I stand there shaking my head and begin to laugh.

"Hurry, hurry! The dancers are coming, the dancers are coming!" A young man bursts out of the temple, flying past me, nearly hurling himself down the steps as he staggers under the weight of the ornate, resplendent, and bright-colored three-foot-high mask of Durga and headdress that he wears. The crowd bursts into a roar! People encircle him, handing him small clay cups of *rakshi*, which he quaffs with abandon, one after another. He reels around wildly, then continues his dance, barely able to move through the crowd, people are so crammed together. Then comes the next masked dancer, blasting out from the temple door, reeling to catch his balance, running more than he is dancing. More shouts, then another dancer, louder shouts, then another, then a roar. They come more quickly now, more forcefully, one after another, running down a gauntlet of men who protect them from the chaos of the crowd, which becomes more unrestrained at each dancer's appearance. The shouts grow deafening, the chanting becomes a steady roar, "*Jai Ma*, Victory to the Mother, *Jai Ma*, Victory to the Mother, *Jai Ma*, Victory to the Mother!"

The world is safe again, the Buffalo Demon has been defeated. Durga has returned.

The world is safe again, the Buffalo Demon has been defeated.

Tired but wide awake on the long, bumpy ride back to Kathmandu, I sit next to Marcia. She has come to Nepal from the States to work in a clinic and to make a spiritual retreat with her teacher, a woman yogi. When she asks why I've come and I tell her that I am on the trail of "fierce compassion" and the sacred feminine, she becomes very excited.

"Fierce compassion!" she exclaims to my surprise, seeming to understand that phrase instinctively. "Do we need that now! Do you know what's happening in Nepal?"

I don't know what she means. I have been in Kathmandu for only a week.

"There's been an explosion in child prostitution," she says. "More and more parents are selling their children, particularly their daughters. Selling them," she repeats slowly for emphasis. "It's terrible."

This is the third time in the week that I've been here that someone has brought up the subject of child prostitution. A few days ago at lunch, I was joined by a woman who also talked about the problem and gave me a booklet entitled "Red Light Traffic, the Trade in Nepali Girls." She too was concerned about the problems of children, especially street children and child trafficking, now complicated by AIDS. I took the booklet, but had not read it. I wanted to avoid the subject, I had my agenda set.

The following evening, I was walking down the street in the Thamel district with a friend when a Nepali man stopped us and handed us a magazine on development in Nepal that he'd just published. He explained that he was trying to make contact with Westerners, especially Western women, because he thought we could help. He felt that unless the women of Nepal received help, there was little that could be done for the country. Helping women was his mission. Women were the key to real growth and development, not the million-dollar projects that were called "development." I didn't know what to say, I was so dumbfounded by the directness of his approach. Would we let him interview us, he asked.

I took the magazine and his phone number and said that I had work to do in Kathmandu, but that I would think about it and call him. One of the feature stories of his magazine was on the girls in Nepal and how some are forced into "religious" prostitution. Given to the temple when very young, between the ages of five and seven, kept illiterate and unskilled, these girls are taught to believe that they can refuse no man because all men come from God. Though the practice has been outlawed and the women are now allowed a traditional marriage, this is a comparatively recent development, and is still a problem in certain districts, though not all of them.[3]

Now Marcia's talking to me about this problem. We discover that we both have daughters the same age, as do the other women who brought this to my attention. "A lot of people sell their daughters because they're so poor. Villagers up in the mountains. They're told their daughters will have a husband or a job here in Kathmandu and so they let them go, sometimes out of ignorance, sometimes out of greed."

As we bounce along, jarred by the pot-holes in the road, my stomach tightens and my pulse races. I feel frightened. This is not what I came to Nepal to find out about. I am relieved when Federica and Tsering take over the conversation and talk about the Buddhist teachings we've been attending together.

By the time we get back into Kathmandu my spirits are sinking. What did I expect? I think for a moment of the powerful energies I want to understand: Durga, the fearless warrior goddess and the fierce form of compassion. Did I think I was coming to a tea party in Nepal, with gloves and lotus blossoms?

Like the poet Ramprasad, I began this journey calling for Durga,
I will take what she gives me.

. . . .

I've peddled my bones in the marketplace
Of this world and bought up Durga's name.
I'm rooming in the house
Of the good soul living in this flesh.
So when Death enters, I've made up my mind
To open my heart, to show Him all.
Tara's name is the best remedy.
I've tied it to my topknot.
Ramprasad says: I have begun
My journey calling on the name
Of Durga.[4]

—RAMPRASAD, EIGHTEENTH CENTURY, BENGAL
(*translated by Leonard Nathan and Clinton Seely*)

Before Marcia and I part, she tells me that she has friends who are
working to fight child prostitution. She offers to introduce me to
Dr. Aruna Uprety, an activist on child prostitution and the related
issues for women and children. Aruna Uprety is virtually the only
female general practitioner addressing this area, Marcia says, from
educating the police force about rape, domestic abuse, and AIDS to
training people in women's health issues, and doing advocacy work
from the grass-roots to the policy-making level. Very few women in
Nepal will speak publicly on these matters, but Aruna does so—in
person, on television, on the radio. She cofounded the nongovernmental organization (NGO) called Rural Health Education Service
Trust (RHEST), which focuses on health and education for women
and children. She and her friends have opened halfway houses for

11

women with AIDS, women's clinics, and village maternity centers; she conducts Traditional Birth Attendant trainings (TBAs)—the maternal mortality rate here is unbelievably high—no one can keep track of all she does. She is very dedicated to stopping child prostitution, Marcia tells me, but it's an uphill battle. It will take a legion of female warriors to help fight the trafficking in women and children.

The next day I visit the great stupa, the sacred monument, at Boudhanath, on the eastern side of Kathmandu, the famous gleaming white rounded tower over relics of the Buddha, with a squared roof and a pyramid on top, the Buddha's eyes painted on each side, overseeing the four directions. It is said that when this stupa was consecrated, hundreds of years ago, one hundred million Buddhas dissolved into it and filled it with their relics, making it a powerful place for prayer and meditation. Pilgrims come from hundreds of miles around to circumambulate this sacred site and pray. I, too, have come to circumambulate the stupa saying my beads to Tara, the female Buddha in the Tibetan tradition.

As I make my way clockwise around the circle, I hear the rhythmic clip-clop of wooden clogs behind. I turn around to find a wild old pilgrim with a sunburnt face and wearing a leather apron doing full body prostrations. Down on his padded knees, wooden handcovers strapped to his palms hitting the ground, clip-clop, the sound of wood sliding across cement, then sliding back, then up on his knees, then to his feet again, a small bow, then down again, clip-clop. This is the way he does his *kora*, his circumambulations of the stupa. This pilgrim's long silver hair is in dreadlocks, loosely tied into a topknot with a bright red-orange strip of cotton. He gives me a knowing look, as though we've met. His face is beaming. He's come all the way from Tibet, more than five hundred miles over the

Himalayas, doing full prostration bows, stretching out the full length of his body, touching his head to the ground, standing up, then bowing down, stretching out again. Cement, mountains, rocky trails, streets, it makes no difference to him. It's how he travels, chanting his mantras, singing, praising. He is free.

It elates me just to see this pilgrim; nonetheless, I am not free. I still can't forget the conversation with Marcia Anderson and her offer to take me to meet Dr. Aruna Uprety. The pull to follow up with Marcia is strong. It may take days to track down the busy Dr. Uprety, Marcia warned me, but I will call and take Marcia up on her offer. I'm not sure what I'm setting in motion, but the process is no longer in my control. I don't know where it will lead, this unexpected direction—if I'm being led or being taken—but there is an inevitability to it that propels me forward.

CHAPTER 2

HER SONG IS
CARRIED ON THE WIND

Indramaya's Devotion
Kathmandu

he meeting with Dr. Aruna Uprety is set. Marcia and I
will meet with her, but not for a matter of days. In the
meantime, I go back to spend more time with Chökyi
Nyima Rinpoche, the Tibetan teacher who first gave me meditation
instruction on the Goddess and female Buddha Tara, years ago.
(*Rinpoche* means "precious jewel," a title accorded an honored
teacher.) Tara is best known in her peaceful forms of White Tara for
long-life and healing, and Green Tara for removing fears and obstacles, but she has numerous forms, at least one of which is black and
looks fierce like Kali. I want Chökyi Nyima to help me understand
Tara's fierceness now. He is a respected and reliable teacher. I know
he can help. His large monastery at Boudhanath bustles with
monks, students, and visitors, especially Westerners. I've been fortunate enough to attend parts of the annual fall teachings that he's
giving on Buddhism with his father, the Venerable Tulku Urgyen,
one of the last great meditation masters from Tibet. On the way into
the monastery I run into Federica and Tsering, my fellow students
with whom I went to Bhaktapur.

Tsering says she has a treat in store for Federica and me this afternoon. We can see a *living* embodiment of the Goddess, a woman
named Kusali Devi, if I'm free. By midafternoon, Federica, Tsering, and I have crammed ourselves into a *tempo,* an auto-rickshaw,

gathered offerings of silk scarves, flowers, and bottles of San Miguel beer, and are off to see the Devi at her house in Doubhichaur, the laundry-washers' district of Kathmandu.

Kusali Devi is a local Newari Buddhist teacher and healer. Newari Buddhism is a unique blend of Tibetan Buddhism, the ancient pre-Buddhist shamanistic Bon tradition of Tibet, indigenous Newari beliefs, and Hinduism, especially Shaktism, the intense devotion to the Goddess that is so concentrated in the Kathmandu Valley.

Kusali Devi is a spiritual leader known primarily to the local community; they consult her for spiritual direction and guidance as well as problems with heartbreak, enemies, and illness. To her followers she is a treasured vessel whose spirit possessions transform her into living manifestations of a variety of goddesses, including Durga, Tara, Kali, and Ajima, her primary deity, one of the fierce female deities and the protector of children. Today it is not only the celebration of the last day of Durga Puja, it is the thirtieth anniversary of the Devi's possession by Ajima, a very auspicious occasion.

I hear people chanting and singing, and bells ringing in the room above as we wait in the dark stairwell of the Devi's small two-story traditional Nepali house. There is the sweet, heavy smell of incense burning, garlic and onions simmering, meat cooking. When we climb up and finally reach the opening, my day pack snags and I have to back down two steps, start up again, then lean closer into the stairs to get through the narrow passage at the top.

Thirty people are crammed tightly into this room that might comfortably hold twelve. We stand in back, looking for a place to sit. Afternoon sunlight streams in through the open windows, the sills of which people are using for seats. Devotees have come to see Kusali Devi, with her laughing dark eyes and her striking open face; they fill every available inch of floor space.

The Devi sits on a raised brass throne in the front of the room, singing. To her left is a picture of Durga riding her lion, smiling serenely as she defeats the Buffalo Demon. To her right is a large picture of a Green Tara, the Mother of All the Buddhas, with long black hair unbound and flowing freely down her back. Next to the Devi's throne is a small altar to Ajima laden with flowers, oil lamps burning, coins, incense, and fresh whole turnips. The back of her bright brass throne is shaped like a cobra, its hood open to protect her, as was the cobra's hood at the Buddha's enlightenment, when the Buddha sat under the bodhi tree in sixth-century-B.C.E. India and realized the way to relieve the world's suffering.

I draw in my breath when I look at the Devi, she is so beautiful, sitting there on her vermilion cushion, smiling, her legs tucked under her red-and-gold brocade dress. The Devi is a woman in full blossom, a full woman, not young, not old but mature, a woman ripe like a deep red pear. She wears a gold-colored crown tied onto her head with red strings, and smiles often, her eyes shining. A hot pink blossom dangles on her forehead from underneath her crown, a tear-shaped rhinestone just below it. Garlands and garlands of bright yellow marigolds have been placed around her neck as offerings, making a living collar of gold.

The Devi is tossing rice pellets and giving blessings to her devotees. An attendant brings out a small plate with a braided cord on fire on it. The Devi takes the flaming cord and tosses it into her mouth with gusto. Nothing is made of the fire-eating. No one gasps or seems to take note, they just keep singing as I stand there bursting with delight.

We have arrived near the end of the ceremony but not too late to pay our respects by giving the Devi our *khatas*, the ceremonial scarves, some small gifts, and to receive *tika* and blessings from the Devi while she is still possessed by the living Goddess. Her smile is radiant, her eyes warm and clear, her gaze direct as Tsering nudges Federica and me to step up in front of her. She puts thick, wet, red *tika* paste on our foreheads, and hands us sprigs of green rice shoots, flower petals to put on the top of our heads, and strips of rough red cotton gauze to tie around our necks. I feel a catch in my throat. I am unexpectedly moved.

Space opens up and we are seated. The Nepali man next to me whispers a welcome in English and assures me we have come on a very auspicious day. His name is Pushpa. He's been coming to the Devi every afternoon for twenty years on his way home from his work, he confides in a soft, cultivated voice. There is one more round of singing, then several people get up to leave, thinning out the crowd, chatting as they go. I use this lull to ask Pushpa to tell me more about the Devi and about Ajima.

The Devi has had no human teacher, only the Goddess Ajima, who instructs her in dreams and in meditations. *Ajima* means "grandmother." The puja today is for both Durga and the Devi. Ajima takes over the Devi's body in a trance and speaks through her. The possession began when the Devi was a young girl—she would feel light, she would tremble, her cheeks would turn red. Later it broke up her marriage, when Ajima told the Devi to leave her husband, and it paved the way for possession by other deities such as Tara, to whom she has a great devotion, Durga, and Kali, among others.

Does the Goddess really possess the Devi? In Nepal it is hard to sort out fact from fiction. This is the landscape of belief, where what Westerners might call magical events are accepted as part of every-day life, by even the most rational people. It is a different way of being in the world. Time and reason bend here, break out of their molds, reshape themselves into remarkable stories, like the one Pushpa tells me about Ajima.

Ajima liked children so much that she stole five hundred of them. People got so upset with her that they complained to the Bud-dha and asked him to stop her, she was causing so much suffering. So the Buddha stole one of Ajima's children. Now it was Ajima's turn to be grief-stricken, to look for her lost child everywhere. She was broken-hearted. Beside herself, she went to the Buddha to ask

KUSALI DEVI (*left*), PRIESTESS OF AJIMA, PROTECTRESS OF CHILDREN,
KATHMANDU, NEPAL (*China Galland*)

for his help. The Buddha sat patiently and listened to her woe. Then
he spoke.

"Now you know what it feels like for someone to steal your
child," said the Buddha. "It breaks your heart, doesn't it? Now you
have felt that in yourself, the kind of suffering you have caused.
And think, you have stolen five hundred children, I took only one of
yours. You must vow never to steal a child again, and to become the

protector of all children. This is the only way I will give you your child back."

Ajima agreed to the Buddha's terms and vowed never to steal a child again. In that moment, she was transformed into the protectress of all children. Ever since, people have prayed to her to protect their children.

As Pushpa finishes his story, an old woman in a pink cotton sari appears in the doorway. She stands still for a moment surveying the room, then suddenly moves into it, singing in a rich, full voice, clapping her hands and stamping out a complicated rhythm with her feet. Talk falls away, conversations stop. Though she is a small woman, perhaps only four feet, ten inches tall, she has the presence of someone with an enormous body. She moves spontaneously and naturally, suffused by a tremendous spirit of ardor, for to her, a devotee, the possession that the Devi undergoes is real, transforming the Devi into a living incarnation of the Mahadevi, the Great Goddess. Her presence is electrifying and palpable. The Devi smiles serenely at her from underneath the red canopy. I am riveted by the old woman's entrance.

"Indramaya is her name," Pushpa tells me, "she comes every month or two."

Indramaya has limp gray hair pulled back off her neck into a bun. She is an old woman like many I have seen on the streets of Kathmandu. She is a woman whom I might otherwise overlook—an old woman selling vegetables, a grandmother sweeping a doorway—but in this moment, she is an electrical current, white-hot and crackling. Those of us left in the room move back against the walls as the old woman dances slowly toward the Devi's throne, clapping her hands to the rhythm of her song, capturing everyone's attention. A swath of pink fabric slips off her shoulder, revealing a pale gold bodice covering her small torso. The pounding beat of her feet continues, never missing, while she circles and moves into the center.

Indramaya sings the story of Durga and her battle with the Buffalo Demon. She is inside the story, living it. It moves through her. Her voice is strong and full, the rhythm of her clapping punctuated by the drumming of her bare feet on the wooden floor. I begin to keep time, clapping with her. Soon others follow. Everyone claps now as she dances in the center of the circle. Finally Indramaya stops. No one seems to think anything of it. Some people drift off to the kitchen to attend to dinner, others leave, some stay to talk, and new people continue to arrive. I can't understand what is happening.

"Pushpa, will she dance again, will you translate for me, can I talk to her?" I ask earnestly, barraging the patient man with questions. I want her to sing her song of Durga and Kali again, I want to record it if she will let me, but everyone seems intent on taking a break, including Indramaya.

"Wait," he tells me gently, "wait. I will help you. Don't worry."

Yes, Indramaya tells him, she will sing her song again and let me record it. She sits down beside me on the floor after I retrieve the tape recorder from my bag in the hallway. She turns a copper bowl upside down in front of her and immediately begins to bang out a complicated tempo. She beats out the rhythm on the wall, claps it with her hands, then drums it on the bowl again, all the while continuing to sing. She sings with great verve, but it's a different song, it's not the song of Durga and Kali that she sang when she came in. Sitting next to her listening is so energizing that finally I have to move and begin to sway from side to side and clap again. Others join me. When that song is done, I ask her again if she will sing the first song she sang when she came in. She nods affirmatively, and then sings a different one. I ask again, and she sings yet another different one.

Indramaya sings song after song. Half the people in the room are dancing now, but she never sings the song she sang for the Devi at the beginning. I let go. No moment is repeatable. Suddenly, Indramaya stops and asks me to play back the tape. She bursts into sobs when she hears her own voice.

"Pushpa, what's happening?" Have I offended her? I reach my hand out to her, but her face is buried in her palms. I put my arm around her shoulders. She looks up at me with tears streaming down her face, her hair slipping out of its knot. Tears well up in my eyes, seeing hers. Federica chokes up and coughs. Tsering blows her nose. I still can't understand why she's weeping, why I'm suddenly about to cry.

"She's not crying because she's sad," Pushpa explains gently. "She's crying out of happiness. She says that now her voice will be carried on the wind and other people will hear her. That's what's making her cry. She never thought anyone would hear her."

CHAPTER 3

PAGES ON FIRE

*Learning About the Trafficking
in Young Women*

Marcia Anderson calls. We can see Aruna Uprety, the doctor, this evening. Finding Aruna's house after dark is complicated by the Kathmandu evening power cut-off that usually lasts from six to eight P.M. Kerosene lamps are struck and hung in the vendors' stalls. We walk through a maze of unmarked streets.

"This is it, I'm sure," Marcia tells me, indicating an unpaved road back to a street of large houses behind high walls. We get as far as the front door of the building, but the darkened hallway proves to be a formidable corridor of turns, side rooms, and passageways to other apartments. Aruna lives up three flights and we can't find the stairwell. We bump into each other, then find ourselves in an open courtyard. Marcia calls out, "Aruna? Aruna Uprety?"

In a moment we hear footsteps, then see the strong beam of a flashlight from the stairwell above.

"I am here. This way," Aruna calls, pointing the light to the stairwell.

We sit down in the apartment, still dark but for a low table bright with candles. Aruna is small and slender, a woman in her mid-thirties and the mother of two girls, five and eight years old, who run in and out of the room as we talk. Though she has hair cut short like that of our friend Tsering, another modern Nepali woman, she wears traditional Nepali clothes, the long tunic dress over pants.

Aruna has invited Agnes Jacquemin, a colleague from Belgium who has been helping her in her work to fight child prostitution in

Nepal for the last four years. Agnes is a clothing designer and has gone back and forth between Nepal and Belgium for nearly twenty years. Agnes explains that few really knew about the sale of Nepalese girls until the Nepalese people revolted against the ruling monarchy and established a democracy. Then the word began to get out. Since then she has been working with Aruna, bringing clothes, medicines, and funds to help support the work and the children in Nepal, making a film called *Angels of Nepal,* and writing articles on the subject of child labor and trafficking. Agnes and Aruna also help Child Workers in Nepal (CWIN) support different homes for children whether trafficked, at risk, or seeking escape.

From this first moment we plunge directly into a startling conversation on child prostitution in Asia, especially in Nepal. Formalities are dispensed with. Agnes has postponed another appointment to make our meeting, Marcia has to leave early, there is no time to waste. Aruna pulls her red wool cardigan sweater around her shoulders, then smooths back a lock of her silky straight dark hair behind her ear. The air is chilly, I scoot in closer to the low table, hold my hands over the candles for warmth.

"Tell her about Gita, Agnes."

"Gita!" Agnes says, letting out a sigh and leaning closer. "She's the one who prompted Aruna and another doctor to form the Women's Rehabilitation Center [WOREC], another NGO they started. It was their first halfway house. Gita has full-blown AIDS. She was sold into prostitution when she was thirteen years old—by her mother. She lived in a Bombay brothel for several years.[1] When Gita first arrived in Bombay she was kept in a dark room, beaten with iron bars, and burned with cigarettes, on top of the repeated rapes to break her.

"In the end, she couldn't work anymore—AIDS. She was always in bed, losing so much blood. The madam sent a message to Gita's family that they should come visit her. The madam was from the same village as Gita. Her father had come three times before to collect the money Gita had made. It is difficult to imagine the first time this man living in the middle of a remote village in Nepal was able to find his way four thousand kilometers down to Bombay when he had never been away from his village before. There are twelve million people living in Bombay," says Agnes, shaking her head, "but he found her. He made it to his daughter's brothel to get the money. He did it that first year and then came two more times to Bombay to get her money.

"The fourth time he was called, it was because Gita was dying. The madam wanted him to take her back to the village. Her father was angry because the lady of the brothel insisted on keeping all the money Gita had made for the trouble she had caused her.

"Gita's father brought her back to the village and immediately put her to work in the fields. But Gita was dying. Her mother wouldn't let her in the house or even give her a cup of water, she was so afraid of AIDS and so ignorant about it. Gita was so sick that finally one of the neighbors took pity on her. That's when ABC [Agro-forestry, Basic Health and Cooperative] found her. That's how she came to Aruna's attention. I videotaped a one-and-a-half-hour interview with her telling her story for UNICEF, the story of what she went through in Bombay. Remember, this was a thirteen-year old girl.

"When Gita worked in the brothel, she might have up to thirty customers in a day. She could not take more than five or ten minutes with a customer or she would be beaten with iron bars again. She explained this to me in detail. You cannot believe that she did that for so many years when you see her. After being found and cared for now, though she still has AIDS, Gita's smile has returned. She lights up the room, she radiates, she is so full of life."

Aruna tells us about a recent demonstration against child prostitution in a nearby district of the Kathmandu Valley. "The demonstrators wanted to make people aware of prostitution, but the people wouldn't allow them into the village.

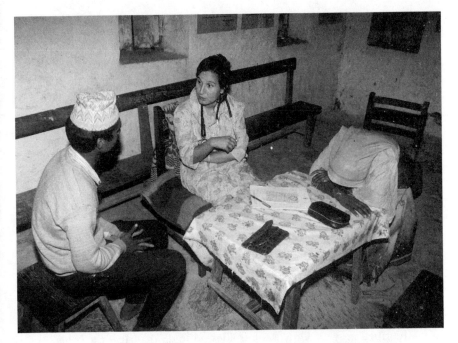

DR. ARUNA UPRETY (*center*) WITH VILLAGE HEALTH WORKER AND
PATIENT, DEMIMANDU, NEPAL (*Thomas L. Kelly*)

"The villagers told them, 'We will kill you if you come into our village and say that prostitution is bad. What we do with our daughters and daughters-in-law is none of your business. We send them to work. If people go outside of Nepal to work, it doesn't matter. So our girls are going outside the village. If you come into our village, we will kill you,' they shouted. This isn't the first time this has happened."[2]

"It was unbelievable!" Agnes adds as I sit there wide-eyed, jotting notes as fast as I can. "It is very difficult for me to understand. Some people excuse it because of poverty. Yes, that is a big problem, it's true, but the mother-daughter relationship," she says, shaking her head, "the love between mother and daughter—it gets twisted by all the pressure here to have sons."

Aruna nods her head in agreement. She explains that it's not that mothers don't love their daughters, only that, unless a family has a lot of resources, right from the beginning, from infancy, girls get less food, they do more work in the house, and they frequently are not allowed to go to school. They are seen as a drain on the family since once they are grown they will go to live in their husband's home and work for their mother-in-law. To a Westerner, it might seem like a lack of love, but it's more a result of cultural pressures and tradition, intensified by the weight of poverty. Mothers in Nepal love their daughters as mothers everywhere love their children, but the emphasis on having sons has been debilitating.

"You have to understand," Aruna says, "in Nepal many people believe that if you don't have a son, then you will fall certainly into hell. You have to have at least one son. It doesn't matter how many daughters you have, ten, twelve—you have to have one son, because when you die, it's the son who will light the cremation fire and say the ritual prayers. Only a son is allowed to do that. It is the belief. Then instead of hell, you'll go to heaven. But without a son to perform the ritual, you are condemned to hell."

"But the sale of daughters is not everywhere," Aruna says, "please, this is not all over Nepal. Trafficking goes on primarily in certain districts—problem districts. Some are worse than others."

Trafficking, as Aruna and Agnes call it, whether of girls, women, or boys, is one of the problems that has grown with Nepal's development. Westerners use the term "child prostitution," but this gets into the challenge of defining childhood, Aruna points out. Girls younger than fourteen are taken from Nepal to brothels in India. Is this considered child prostitution in Nepal or in India? How does one count and keep track of such a phenomenon? It is difficult. In Nepal, girls over fourteen are not considered children, so they are not included in discussions and statistics on child prostitution.

My heart sinks as they summarize the problem. It is complicated by numerous other issues, such as the literacy rate for women—75 percent are illiterate—and ownership of property, to mention two. Women were not allowed to own property until democracy was established, in 1982, but because most of the population is rural and most women poor and illiterate, they have few ways to establish themselves or gain any kind of economic foothold. Add the deeply embedded cultural disdain for women in the caste system—like racism in the United States, outlawed but still operative and oppressive—to the problems of literacy and poverty, and one begins to understand how the situation continues.

Increased poverty, deforestation in the mountains, in part from tourism—the trekking boom—and erosion of arable land drive growing numbers of able-bodied young people into the city, where there are too few jobs, inadequate housing and services, which leaves growing numbers of people homeless in the streets, an increasingly dangerous place for women and girls. Street children are especially vulnerable to traffickers. Aruna explains that most of the trafficking is done with India, where a large percentage of the sex workers are women and girls from Nepal.

Human Rights Watch Asia estimates that "hundreds of thousands, and probably more than a million women and children are employed in Indian brothels."[3] Nongovernmental organizations estimate that half the women and girls in the brothels of Bombay alone are Nepalese. And Bombay has among the highest number of sex workers diagnosed as HIV positive in the world. This has led to predictions that Nepal will have the highest rate of HIV in Asia by the year 2000.[4] Though it is difficult to get reliable statistics on the subject, no statistics are needed to convince me that this is a tragedy.

The power is still out. Aruna's daughters are giggling, running in and out of the candlelit room while we're talking, flicking my flashlight off and on. They are a joyful antidote to the distress I feel listening to Agnes and Aruna outline the complexity of this subject. My back hurts, my foot is going to sleep, still I am riveted by this conversation.

Sitting in the monastery this morning, listening to Buddhist teachings, while beautiful and fortifying, is in strong contrast to what I'm feeling now. At the monastery I'm removed from the sheer weight of everyday life. Here at Aruna's I've crossed over from the world of contemplation into the world of action. In coming to meet Aruna, I find a place to put my feet down. She is grappling with a level of human suffering I've never encountered, and she isn't just meditating on the causes of suffering, she's taking action to remove them.

Many of the women and girls in Bombay are trafficked by brokers who deliver them to brothels for anywhere from five hundred to thirteen hundred dollars. The brokers buy them from "recruiters," who go to the poorer areas of Nepal and distant hill villages. Elaborate promises of jobs or marriages are made. With the average Nepali family's annual income being less than two hundred dollars a year, and nearly 90 percent of the population living in rural areas, the economics of the situation can be difficult to resist.[5]

On some occasions the girls are married off and then delivered by their "husband," who is really an agent, to a brothel.[6] Sometimes the family is involved in the deceit it often takes to procure a girl—at times out of ignorance, at other times out of despair at their own poverty, and sometimes out of greed.

Children don't take to rape easily, Agnes tells me as Aruna nods her head vigorously. Brothel owners, pimps, and madams break the children's spirits once they get them to the brothel—lock them in a room, torture them, beat them. I hear story after story. Hardest to hear are the stories of the young children, six, seven, and eight years old.

"The problems are getting worse because the age of the girls they are selling is going down. They are taking girls younger and younger. Because of AIDS, they need fresh meat. Now it goes down to six years old. More and more children are missing, boys too." Aruna explains that there is a belief in India that if you sleep with a young virgin, you will be cured of AIDS, so now younger and younger girls are getting AIDS.

As a Nepali woman medical doctor, Aruna seems very much alone in this fight. It takes great effort on her part to keep going, not to become discouraged. The fierceness of Aruna's commitment to women, and Agnes's passionate support of her and the cause of women and girls are tangible. The bond between these women is strong.

"The carpet business," Agnes goes on to say, "is one of the primary points of procurement of girls for sale into prostitution."

The carpet business. Working conditions in many of the factories are widely known to be appalling, the use of child labor is endemic, and many of the children are in an arrangement called "debt bondage," in which they receive no wages and have for all practical purposes been sold, or apprenticed as it's deceptively called, to factory owners.

Reports are common about young girls working in the carpet factories of Nepal being subjected to sexual abuse and rape. Moreover, promises of wages and better working conditions make it easy to entice young workers to leave the carpet factory with brokers, who often abduct them to India. Some carpet factories in Nepal seem to function as underground brothels.[7] This part of the expansion of global trade's exploitation of children we hear less about: the underbelly of sexual exploitation of children, especially of girls.

And yet the carpet business in Nepal has helped build the economy, and carpets have become one of the country's most important export products. Ironically the Tibetans too have been especially successful in the carpet business, owning many of the factories, and contributing to the building and support of the Tibetan monasteries. I think of a young Tibetan lama I recently met. He offered to sell me carpets from the factory he owns to help support his monastery. I liked him very much. He was dedicated and energetic. He comes from a respected family. His cell phone was always by his side, he was so busy. I assume that he runs a clean shop, that he wouldn't allow abuse of children. But suddenly the question has been introduced and I can't take it back: Are some of the Tibetan monasteries indirectly being supported by the growing trade in child prostitution? I am glad Agnes interrupts my train of thought.

"In certain villages you can tell which families have sold their daughters. They are the only ones who have tin roofs and glass windows in their houses. There is no other way to earn money.

"The traffic now is not only between Nepal and India, it's international. Only days ago, a Chinese man was arrested. The police found out that he was issuing fake passports and telling girls that they had wonderful jobs waiting for them in a department store in Hong Kong. The traffic between Hong Kong and Nepal used to be gold and drugs. Now it's girls too. Young, uneducated women being promised work outside of Nepal can easily end up in prostitution. Certain families specialize in the trafficking. They started with gold and drugs during the Vietnam War. Now they are wealthy, very wealthy.

"It took me sixteen years of blindness to see these things," Agnes says. "Sixteen years I had been living here, going back and forth, and I did not know these things were going on.

"Since democracy we are finding out so much, we have so many stories, there is an explosion! Remember the time we went to the police together," Agnes says, turning to Aruna, "to find out about that girl who had been raped?"

Without waiting for her to answer, Agnes turns back to Marcia and me, explaining, "As we walked into the station Aruna was saying to me, 'Oh, my God, I hope they don't remember me!' No sooner were we inside than a man behind a desk in the corner looks up and says, 'Aren't you Dr. Aruna Uprety?'"

Aruna picks up the story. "I was in jail for demonstrating three times during the democratic movement in 1989: prodemocracy, against development, always demonstrating. But every time, they had to let me out because I am a doctor—people need me. Everyone was making noises.

"This one daughter," she continues, pointing to the younger girl, who has just run out of the room again with my flashlight, "I was still breast-feeding her and my breasts were full, but I was in jail and she was at home crying. The police wouldn't let me telephone and no one knew where I was. My husband was worried to death. He told me the next day after I got out, 'If you demonstrate again, I'll cut your feet off!' he was so upset."

"Did you stop?" I ask, shocked, not knowing what to think, because she is laughing so hard as she tells this.

"Oh, no, of course not!" she assures me with her enormous smile. "Next time I took my husband. We went to jail together," she says, now doubling over with laughter. "No problem."

Marcia takes advantage of this moment of levity to say good night and be on her way. Now I know why I've come to Nepal—I've come to meet these women. They *are* fierce. The energy of Durga is rising through them. They are on the battlefield. Aruna is indomitable.

Agnes insists that Aruna tell me the mantra story. "The Gyatri mantra is considered to be very sacred, and it is to be learned only by Brahmin men. If a woman or other low-caste person were to learn it or say it, they would supposedly go mad or die. So I learned it and said the mantra publicly on TV. Some of my relatives were angry—but I am not mad or dead yet!" Aruna tells me, laughing again, her eyes merry. Then she grows serious and quiet.

The story Agnes told me of Gita is emblematic of the problem in Nepal. There are thousands more. Child prostitution—trafficking in women and children—is not a problem limited to Southeast Asia; it is a growing global problem, Agnes assures me, affecting the United States, Europe, and Russia as well. There is hardly a country in the world untouched by it. Increasing numbers of women are trafficked into the United States not only from Southeast Asia but also from Latin America, from whichever countries are poor, repressive, or politically unstable.[8] That's when it becomes economically attractive for families to sell their daughters or female members. Many girls and women think they are going to legitimate jobs, only to find themselves trapped behind locked doors in a foreign country as part of the international sex trade, unable to get out.

There is much that needs to be done, from enforcing existing international laws against trafficking, slavery, and debt bondage to getting legislation passed so that travelers who participate in organized tours for sex can be prosecuted in their own countries. Governments, the police, the military—from border patrols to immigration services—have to be held accountable. Too often they're corrupted by the money involved. But there is one point which Aruna emphasizes as crucial: "Above all we need to educate women. Education is key. This is a monumental problem. If we can make a dent in education, the rest will follow."

The hour is late. Still no electricity. I do not know what to say. I'm exhausted, in a state of shock.

Agnes offers to take me back to Boudhanath. When we get ready to leave, Aruna tells me, "Sometimes I want to give up. I get so discouraged. But tonight has been wonderful. You don't know how much it means to find out that other people are disturbed by this. I am so happy you and Marcia came, it gives me hope."

When Agnes and I arrive back in Boudhanath, we sit in the car in front of Boudha Gate, the entrance to the enormous stupa. The flat I'm staying in is between this pilgrimage site and the Bhutanese monastery. Red-robed Tibetan monks of all shapes, ages, and sizes pour in and out of the gate, not many tourists at this hour. The shops are closed. It's mostly monks going to do *kora*, circumambulating the stupa, turning the prayer wheels with one hand as they walk clockwise, and counting their *malas,* prayer beads, with the other. The driver has killed the engine. The windows are up to keep out the evening chill, the noise, and the beggars. I am about to get out of the car when Agnes puts her hand on my arm and asks me to wait. She needs to tell me one more story, about my own country.

A businessman from Italy telephoned a clandestine network operating in Los Angeles to procure a child. American, Mexican, Chinese, he didn't care, he just wanted a girl ten years old or younger, as young as six, if need be, for—as he called it—very hard sex, and he wanted to film it. Once he had used her he would kill her and would need help getting rid of the body. That was the hard part, getting rid of the body. He didn't want to do that. He would be happy to pay for the service.

Fortunately, the man taking his "order" was an undercover agent from the Los Angeles Police Department (LAPD), and their conversation was surreptitiously recorded. It became part of a film that Agnes had seen and was telling me about now.[9]

When the man arrived in Los Angeles he was met by the police, not someone with a child, as he had expected. He was arrested, held in custody, and finally brought before a judge. He was sentenced, but for reasons beyond understanding, his sentence was somehow suspended and he was released. He returned to Italy and, for all we know, Agnes says, is loose in the world today.

I am stumped, undone. Does he comparison shop? What's the current market rate? Is there an index? Do they accept Visa or American Express? Is a child for sex and murder cheaper in Brazil or Thailand, India or America?

I say good night to Agnes, but I can't begin to think of sleeping after everything I've heard. I join the beggars and the monks, circling the great stupa, doing *kora*, grateful for the murmured sounds of prayer, the smell of incense, and the click of prayer wheels turning.

I dream of pages on fire. I am jumping up and down on the burning pages, trying to put the flames out. I wake from the dream at 3:00 A.M., unable to fall back asleep. I sit bolt upright in bed, pull my sleeping bag up around me. The evening has ignited my own memories, the flames I am trying to stamp out.

When I was four years old I was raped by a friend of the family, a man in our neighborhood, "Jim" I will call him. I had tried innumerable ways to make peace with this event. After more than ten years of not drinking, I reached a point where I knew that in order to continue to stay sober—that meant to stay alive, in my mind—I would have to speak up and look this man in the eye. The residue of shame was threatening to kill me. Confronting Jim directly was the final attempt I would make to put the matter to rest.

Jim was a man I hadn't seen or spoken to for many years. Well into his sixties when I went to see him, he was slow-moving and stout, suffering from lupus and chronic alcoholism curtailed only by esophageal cancer.

"Haven't had a drink in twelve years," he announced with a jovial guffaw, attempting to make conversation as he sat down on his green Naugahyde lounger. In the course of my phone call about seeing him in person I had told him that I was sober. He knew that I credited my abstinence to the community of recovery. It was certainly nothing I had done on my own. As for him, "Hey, I didn't need any help. It was no big deal for me," he added just to be sure I knew how tough he was.

Jim had lived in our neighborhood during World War II. My father was stationed in other parts of the country and overseas from time to time, as part of the Army Air Corps. Sometimes my mother and I stayed at home, at other times she and I joined my father and lived at the various bases where he was stationed. Sometimes she went to be with him alone and I was left with members of our traditionally large extended family. We lived in a big, close neighborhood full of friends, a safe community. Children wandered freely in and out of neighbors' houses, people covered child care for one another. If someone in my family wasn't available, there was always a neighbor or two to leave me with from time to time, or someone who would come over. It was a different era, another time, and it was the South.

I had no sooner asked Jim if he remembered any episodes in particular from my childhood than he launched into a detailed, vivid description of an event of which I had no memory. He explained that he had often been one of my baby-sitters when I was three and four years old. He carried me around on his hip whenever he was with me, he said. "I loved to take care of you."

A chill ran through me. This was new information. I didn't remember him as a caretaker. I decided simply to listen until he was through. When I asked him what he was doing that left him time to baby-sit at twenty-three, he explained that he worked only sporadically at that time, off and on, in the Louisiana oil fields.

"I was crazy about you. You were a beautiful child," he went on, smiling. "I had to watch you closely though," he explained with a chortle, "you were always trying to run away from me. You were quick!" My breath grew short.

One day stood out in his mind. He said that I was playing in the front yard, close to the street, down in the gravel driveway, but where he could still see me. He had brought a chair out onto the lawn so that he could watch me. He said that I slipped in the gravel and cut myself on the brick driveway border, below the left knee. It bled profusely.

He astonished me with the preciseness of his memory. He leaned over in his chair and touched his left shin four inches below the knee to show exactly where I had been cut. He said he rushed me upstairs to the second floor, to a bedroom in the back of the house where I was staying. He said that he put me in "the trap"—a Murphy bed that had to be pulled down out of a closet to open—got some ice out of the refrigerator, and put it on my cut to stop the bleeding. He said that I wouldn't stop screaming and crying, that he kept telling me to cross my legs. I don't understand why he is telling me this. Why would I have had to cross my legs if it was only my shin bleeding? He is so precise in these details, right down to the place in the driveway where the red bricks fanned out into a curve. It was the bricks that I cut myself on, he says. The dark red bricks. I don't remember this, and yet, from the age of four, I do remember him, but not this. What he is telling me makes a terrifying kind of sense. From the edge of my chair, I feel pieces of memories that had never fit line up together and begin to fall into place with what I already knew. Click, click, click.

He said the cut wouldn't stop bleeding, and that no matter what, I wouldn't stop crying. The ice was melting and the sheets were wet and bloody and I was screaming, and the family whose house we were in came home and heard me crying and ran to see what was happening. When they found him with me, they were furious, he said, he had had hell to pay.

I sat quietly for a moment, dumbfounded at his revelation and his implicit denial of what had happened. Then I told him, "What I remember is that you raped me when I was four years old."

His brow furrowed for a moment, then he denied it vehemently, said, "I never would have done such a thing to you, you were the apple of my eye. I'll swear on a stack of Bibles, take a lie-detector test, and by the way, how are your children? Haven't seen them since they were just about that age. They must be all grown now."

My children are fine, I tell him, but they are not what I came to talk about. There is no need for him to take a lie-detector test. I tell him that I feel sure that he is telling me the truth as he remembers it.

It's just that I had a different experience. I am astonished at the calm I feel. I knew that it was extremely unlikely that he would acknowledge what had happened from my perspective. I had spent years coming to understand this event myself, questioning myself, not wanting it to be true, being horrified, denying that it could be true, feeling ashamed that this had happened to me. Above all I had remained silent.

I had come to confront Jim because I had discovered that there was a part of myself that cowered from the knowledge of what had happened. A part of me felt permanently damaged. I was unable to conceive of being whole. Now I not only had to cut off the head of this demon of shame and negativity inside myself, I would have to pierce its heart. It was crippling me, invisibly, silently, in ways that no one else could see but that I recognized and felt. When it began to threaten my desire to stay sober, I finally accepted the fact that I would have to face this man and tell him that I remembered what happened. I could no longer be silent.

But before I can say more, he's asking, "How is your momma? She was the prettiest woman," and trying to make small talk about people we knew from the neighborhood. Then he zigzags and shifts subjects again. "No, no, it's impossible. I never would have done a thing like that."

When I tell him that I don't see the point in talking further by ourselves, he doesn't understand. "You mean you won't speak to me?" he asks.

That's not what I mean, but we have come to an impasse. With a patience beyond my own, I explain that I had not said that I wouldn't speak to him, only that my experience of what happened was so different from his that it seemed that there was little point in talking further. I tell him that I think we need someone trained to help people communicate when they are so far apart. I ask him if he would be willing to sit down with me with a third party.

"Over my dead body," is his reply.

I pull out my beads and pray to Tara, who removes all fears, and to the Black Madonna, who absorbs all suffering. It has been a long night. Finally the sky begins to pale outside the gauzy curtains. The long low moan of Tibetan horns sounds from the large adjacent Bhutanese monastery, calling monks to prayer. A great teaching is being given, for which thousands of Tibetans have gathered, traveling all the way from India and Tibet. A young monk who was robbed of all his belongings by Chinese border guards sleeps on a mattress in the stairwell of this house so that he can attend the teaching. His companion was shot in the leg as they slipped across the border.

I hear him rolling up his sleeping bag. The woman whose flat I am renting met him while traveling in Tibet. I open the door and call to him. Though he speaks no English and I have no Tibetan, he stands in the doorway in his robes, tall and very thin, and bows, greeting me, giving me such a smile when he looks up that I am filled with gratitude for his reminding me of the sweetness of men. Still I have to steel myself to offer him a cup of hot tea and the use of the bathroom. He is too shy to accept, and this morning, I am relieved.

CHAPTER 4

"Whose Anger Is It?"

A Teaching on Fierce Compassion

The evening smell of onions being cooked for Chökyi Nyima Rinpoche's dinner wafts through the gauze-covered kitchen door. I'm sitting in the reception hall on the third floor of his monastery. Outside, firecrackers for Durga Puja whistle, then explode like tiny machine-guns—*rat-a-tat-tat*. The ever-present sound of Tibetan chants rises and falls, amplified by the powerful sound system of the nearby Bhutanese monastery, where the month-long teaching ceremony continues. Dogs bark as another round of firecrackers goes off. The Kathmandu air is chilly, crisp, and fetid with the sour odors of pollution.

Thomas Doctor, a young translator from Norway, hurries across the hallway to meet me. We have an appointment to meet a young abbot, Khenpo Choga, in a few minutes. Chökyi Nyima insists that Choga is the one who can help me with my research on the wrathful female deities, though now, after the meetings with Aruna, Agnes, and Marcia, and what I've read, I'm not sure who can help me, I'm so stirred up.

We go down three flights of stairs, out into a courtyard, and then up another flight of stairs, to where the young monks live. There we find Khenpo, lying down on the rim of a thick ledge around the perimeter of the roof, watching the firecrackers and the stars.

"Tashi delek." He calls out the traditional Tibetan greeting as we approach, not moving from his restful position. He turns back to talk with the other monks nearby. I stand awkwardly by Thomas, waiting to be introduced to this curious monk. Finally Khenpo rolls

off the ledge, stands up, smooths out his robes, adjusts his sleeveless yellow silk shirt, throws his wide red wool shawl over his left shoulder, and reaches out his hand to shake mine.

Khenpo is a cheerful, stocky man of medium height, with a thick black mustache, coal-black hair, and the dark brown eyes of many Tibetans. He is not given to formalities. He holds out a handful of cookies that he insists Thomas and I eat. It's food from the feast offering, he explains. Having been blessed, it is now *prasad,* food from the buddhas and bodhisattvas, the Enlightened beings and saints.

"This way," Thomas says, as Khenpo sets off at a brisk pace across the stucco portico to his corner room. We stop at the doorway to leave our shoes outside, then enter into his one-room quarters lined with bookcases, statues, and pictures of buddhas, bodhisattvas, and his teachers. Khenpo seats himself on his Tibetan carpet–covered bed and pulls his legs up under his capacious robes. He indicates that we are to sit down on the floor in front of him as he chats merrily with Thomas, rattling on in rapid-fire Tibetan, laughing and making jokes.

I sit down on the soft blue carpet and pull out my tape recorder and notebook. I don't know how to begin to talk to this young monk about how disturbed I am by what Aruna and Agnes told me. Talking to him about my own experience would be unthinkable. I am still intent on putting the fire out, stamping out the flames, being quiet. Just then half a dozen monks, old and young, file in, smiling shyly, whispering among themselves. They bow and sit down close to the door, clearly intending to listen to whatever Khenpo, the scholar, might have to say to me. This only compounds my feelings of discomfort: This was to be a private interview. I am put off by their presence, but again I say nothing.

Thomas explains to Khenpo that Rinpoche sent me to him to deepen my understanding of fierce female deities in Tibetan Buddhism. Khenpo responds, Tibetan style, with a story.

"There was a monstrous child born to a demoness," he begins. "The mother demon died in childbirth. The child had four legs and two heads. It was so ugly and terrible that it was left on its dead mother's body to die. But it wouldn't! Instead it suckled its dead mother's breasts and it grew larger and larger, into a powerful, terrifying, gigantic demon itself.

"Eventually this demon became so powerful that he was on the verge of ruling the entire world. He made a great show of letting everyone know that he was the most powerful being on earth, that he had the largest army, the greatest army, and that no one—*no one*—could defeat him. He didn't need anyone, and he didn't need to be afraid of anyone.

"The Buddhas Tara and Chenrezig, the Bodhisattvas of Compassion, appeared to him and told him to give up his ways and take refuge with them, but he refused. He assured them that he was the most powerful being in the world. They didn't help him become powerful. Teachings and spiritual activities were not necessary! He was beyond that.

"But then Tara and Chenrezig went inside him, and he became very frightened. Just as human beings on their deathbed cry out for their mothers when life is ending, this demon started crying and shouting, 'Mother! Mother, help me! Help me!' He was terrified.

"Suddenly his consciousness was shot out of his body, and in that moment he realized all his terrible mistakes. His mind was transformed. He was filled with deep regret for his past deeds. Now he had only love and compassion for all beings. He became very teachable, and everything the Buddhas had to teach him came very easily. In no time at all he became a fully realized being and was transformed into Mahakala, a great Wisdom deity."

Thomas stops translating for a moment to explain that Khenpo tells this story to show how even one such as this terrible demon can be transformed into something or someone who can benefit others. How? Because his consciousness was transformed and his motivation was purified. Mahakala became filled with loving-kindness and compassion, despite his terrible, frightening visage.

"So too tanks and war machines could be turned into agricultural instruments," Khenpo tells me. "They might be shaped very strangely to us, not necessarily attractive, but they could be transformed into machines that could help grow food instead of killing people, animals, and plants," Khenpo continues.

"This demon had a partner just as terrible as he was. She was a huge female demon, a great demoness. But Tara and Chenrezig got inside her too. Her consciousness was shot out of her body, and she was completely transformed as well. She was turned into the Wisdom being Mahakali.

"These terrible, frightening, huge, black bodies of the demons became the property of Chenrezig and Tara. Even though they were frightening to look at, they were used by Tara and Chenrezig, the Bodhisattvas of Compassion, to help sentient beings attain enlightenment."

Khenpo's story irritates me. I know that it conveys a deeper teaching, but tonight I don't have the patience for the fantastic Tibetan tales that have so often delighted me. I want the inner core, the undiluted wisdom that would help me look child prostitution and my own rape in the eye. But still I say nothing. I sit politely, respectfully, nodding, listening for nearly an hour, as he covers point after point on how Mahakala only looks angry his real motivation is compassion. I know this, but tonight it makes no difference. I finally boil over.

"Khenpo, I came all the way from America because I think these images embody an essential understanding of something that we need in the West now. They are important. I want to graft this concept of compassionate wrath—the fierce deities, especially the female deities—from your culture onto ours. We need their help! We have problems in the West—degradation of the environment, exploitation of children—many people, good people, are trying to help, but often they—we—end up making more demons.

"Does he understand?" I ask Thomas, who's now translating

with great earnestness. "Yes, yes, I think so," Thomas says. "Very interesting, go on."

"We need the image of an enlightened fierce feminine like you have in Tibetan Buddhism. I need it. 'Compassionate wrath,' you call it. We need to understand how to be fierce *and* compassionate. *I* need this. But how to do this?"

He laughs. I grow more earnest, freed by having broken through my silence. I feel more myself as I reveal my concerns and frustration.

"We have to stop the exploitation, but we don't—I don't—know how to do it without getting angry. I get furious! I know there's a difference between being angry and being fierce. I know the difference is in the motivation, that it has to be compassion, not anger or hatred. But how to tame the demons?"

"Do you understand what I'm saying, Khenpo? Can you help me develop this understanding?"

At this Khenpo bursts out laughing. The floor feels suddenly hot underneath me. I am flushed with anger. What is so funny? How is Thomas translating this? I know that he's a good translator. I like Thomas and I trust him instinctively. I know that as a Westerner he has some sense of the world I'm talking about.

"Khenpo, wait. Let me be specific. I am talking about child prostitution here in Nepal. I came back here for Durga Puja, to understand more about fierce compassion, the female deities, and activism. I was going to Mother Teresa's, I didn't come to find out about child prostitution. I've tried to ignore it, I wasn't looking for this, but I cannot seem to avoid these stories." I tell him about Agnes and Aruna, the man who stopped me on the street, the woman who spoke to me unbidden at lunch.

"I've started informing myself, talking to others. The number of Nepali girls being sold and sent to brothels in Bombay or Calcutta is shocking. Girls as young as six and seven, on up through early teens."

Khenpo looks a little more thoughtful as Thomas translates this, but on the whole he remains irrepressibly cheerful. I press him for a personal response.

"Tell me, Khenpo, if you saw a man taking a child off to sell her, not just a girl, maybe a young boy—this is happening to boys too—and you knew that child was going to be sold into prostitution and raped, and that maybe the man was even the child's father, what would you do?"

He's smiling, his eyes twinkling. Without missing a beat, he replies, "It's her karma."

A jolt of adrenaline races through me like lightning. My heart pounds, my palms get sweaty. My jaw drops in disbelief, and before I can say anything, he goes on.

"Maybe it's better if it's her father. Then at least there may be some kind of feeling that otherwise wouldn't be there. He might not be as cruel to her as a stranger."

I'm speechless, my head is spinning, I can't believe what I am hearing this celibate monk say to me. His words set off an explosion inside me. It feels like the floor is on fire, my scalp prickles. I am dumbfounded and outraged and, above all, silent.

I turn to Thomas. His face is red. His lank blond hair falls from behind his ear. He sweeps it back again. He is caught between Khenpo and me: We are both completely dependent on Thomas for our understanding of each other.

"Are you sure about your translation?" I ask him in disbelief. He nods yes. My forehead is damp and hot. I had forgotten that the experience of anger could be so strong physically.

Khenpo is laughing again now, but I see nothing funny about this topic. I think we're about to have a horrible misunderstanding.

Before I can gather more words, Khenpo continues. "You must have compassion for the little girl, for her karma—for the ripening of the karma that is bringing this pain on her, *and* you must have compassion for the man for the karma he is bringing upon himself by inflicting this kind of suffering."

Measuring my words very slowly, I ask, "Are you telling me that if you saw this and you knew what was going on you would just stand there and 'have compassion'? You wouldn't do anything?"

I wait heatedly as Thomas translates my question back to Khenpo. This is the worst of Buddhism, I think to myself, this is how karma can be used to justify passivity and silence. Out of respect for Chökyi Nyima and his insistence that I consult this young Khenpo, I bite my tongue. Thomas continues softly, completely neutral, his voice uninflected.

"Khenpo was just saying that he finds your example very interesting. In fact he says that maybe all the fathers in Nepal could sell their daughters to Bombay."

I bend over as though I've been hit in the stomach. I take a moment to adjust my crossed legs and calm myself. But my outrage pulls me bolt upright.

"Khenpo, you can't mean this. You would do nothing?" I ask, refusing to accept his answer. He won't let up, he repeats his outrageous statement, taunting me. Now I won't let up. "Nothing?" I repeat.

Finally he relents. "No. We must do what we can to try to stop such a thing. We must take whatever action we can. But no matter what, even if we fail, what action we take has to be taken out of compassion."

I begin to be relieved. Thomas continues.

"Also, Khenpo says that you should take care that you don't have any anger toward the man or attachment to the girl. Just compassion, knowing that both of them suffer."

"No anger?" This doesn't seem possible to me. It's made me so angry even to have this conversation.

Khenpo explains patiently. "If you are angry at the man, and if you have some fondness for or attachment to the girl, then it will be difficult for you. It is difficult for those two, and it will also become difficult for you. It will actually end up so that the one who sells his daughter and you are both equally at fault."

I have another surge of anger. How could the observer be guilty if he or she has tried to stop it? I write this out on a yellow pad in disbelief so that I can read it aloud. Meanwhile, Thomas and Khenpo are continuing to speak in Tibetan.

"If, if . . ." I manage to sputter out, looking at the notepad.

"If you have anger toward the man . . ." Thomas fills in.

"If you're angry, whose anger is it?" Khenpo cuts through and asks me suddenly. His question brings me up short, forces me back in on myself.

"If I am angry, it's my anger," I say slowly. I acknowledge this reluctantly. I know that this means that even now, in this moment, no matter how understandable my reaction, no matter how justified I might feel, *I* am the one responsible for all the heat and discomfort and fury I've been feeling off and on during this interview, no one else.

"If you were really compassionate," Khenpo says, leaning toward me, "you know what you would do?" I shake my head, waiting for his answer. "You would turn yourself into a terrible demoness and you would kill all the people doing this and you would stop them." Suddenly he's become very serious. "Are you compassionate enough to do this?"

"If I had compassion, I would turn myself into a demoness?" I repeat slowly, struggling to follow.

"A huge demoness," Khenpo says. "Fathers who abuse their daughters, fathers who sell their daughters, mothers, everyone who goes to prostitutes—you should take their lives in a single instant, such a big and powerful demoness you should become. Do you have enough compassion to do this?"

I look at Khenpo. I look at Thomas. They are perfectly calm. Does he mean that if I were truly compassionate I would be like Tara and Chenrezig and be able to transform the demons from the inside, to change their hearts and minds, to "kill" them figuratively by annihilating their egos, their greed, their clinging, and to ignite their compassion? Or is he referring to a story of the Buddha in a former lifetime, as a merchant, before he was enlightened, when out of compassion he chose to kill one man on board a ferryboat because that man was going to kill 499 other passengers? It is said that the Buddha's motivation even in his former lifetime was so pure, so loving, and so selfless that he deliberately took on the painful and unavoidable karma of killing the man out of compassion rather than have that man take on the horrendous karma of killing 499 people. No one, not even one who became the Buddha, can avoid the inexorable laws of karma, the consequences of thought and action. To put it in Western terms, in this legend the bodhisattva had such pure love and compassion that he regarded this potential murderer as his own child and was willing to go to hell and back in the most literal sense, in order to save this man and spare him the unspeakable consequences of killing 499 other people.[1]

This story has always made me uncomfortable. It seems easily misunderstood, the kind of story that gets usurped and corrupted by dictators and zealots. They want to drop the part about consequences, about the implacability of fate when one harms another, even for a great saint. It would take nearly a buddha to have such pure compassion, with the full knowledge of the suffering, to commit such an act out of loving-kindness unmixed with even a faint suggestion of any other emotion such as anger or fear or jealousy or greed. My motivation is certainly mixed, my emotions wild and conflicted, not pure like the bodhisattva's in the story.

"No, Khenpo," I say slowly, "I don't have enough compassion." All my recent fury begins to heave and break up like an ice floe.

"Okay, then, I'll do it," Khenpo says, suddenly looking earnest, no longer laughing.

Now I'm the one who bursts out laughing, at this unlikely reply. This man teaches by being a trickster, I see. Suddenly I feel Khenpo completely with me instead of against me.

"When?" I shout, slapping my palms down on my thighs. "When will you do it? When?" Khenpo's laughing now too.

"Unfortunately," Khenpo says, "I am not really ready to do this either. I need to build up more compassion myself."

The three of us double over with laughter now. The other monks twitter and chuckle, speaking softly among themselves in Tibetan, the conversation being so strange to them. They've come to ask Khenpo to buy them socks too, not only to hear him lecture. They want to get down to monastery business. Khenpo pulls the money they need out of a hanging basket, and they're off.

I left Khenpo and Thomas that night exhausted. The evening ended with a sense of friendliness and goodwill. I wasn't yet clear what I was taking away from it, I knew only that it had been a roller coaster full of twists, surprising turns, and plunges at high speed that ended well. I was still in one piece, though my heart was pounding.

Khenpo Choga had engaged me on a very deep level, rocked me, helped me begin to see how hard it was for me to speak up. He helped me begin to calculate the cost of silence. It would be a long time before I understood the depths of the teaching he gave me. I was alternately angry, pleased, and mystified about our meeting.

I think of the man who tried to buy a child to rape and kill in Los Angeles. What color demoness would I become if I could do what Khenpo Choga suggested? Would I be black? Red? No. I would be white, white with fury, the white of knuckles clenched, the white of a face drained of color, blanched, bloodless, and without mercy.

In my interchange with Khenpo, I also stumbled over my own anger. He has helped me see what is missing.

What am I angry about? In part, I'm frustrated by my ingrained habit of assuming that men are the experts. I know better, yet here it is again. I go to male teachers to learn about the sacred feminine. It's an involuntary response. What Aruna and Agnes have given me is a teaching of another kind. It is equally valuable.

I do not know where the path I am on will lead, but I have begun to see the dangers: the amazing ease with which I can become embattled. I come out of the corner swinging. I was a tomboy and grew up fighting, literally. The love of struggle can be a subtle seduction. It's so familiar. One can fall in love with the struggle and lose sight of the peace one struggles for.[2]

"ONLY IN A WOMAN'S BODY"

The Buddha Tara's Vow

*O*nce there was a woman named Yeshe Dawa, "Wisdom Moon." She lived in a time long ago when people believed that in order to be enlightened one had to have a man's body.

Wisdom Moon was so developed in her understanding, her compassion, her wisdom, her patience, her concentration, and her generosity—in all ways—that people came from all over the kingdom to seek her counsel. Crowds sat at her gate. Finally all the monks and holy men in the kingdom gathered around her and told her, "Wisdom Moon, you are so close to being enlightened that if only you had the male form, you would be fully and completely enlightened. You must pray to be magically transformed into a man. Please, for the sake of everyone, pray either to be transformed in this lifetime or to be born again in a man's body, for the moment you have the male form, you will be a buddha!"

Wisdom Moon was quiet for a moment. She knew that the monks and holy men meant well but that their vision was limited. Finally she addressed them. "Thank you very much, but I have thought about this matter for a long time. Worldly beings are always deluded on this account.

"Nowhere can I find what is male, nowhere can I find what is female. These are simply forms, no more separate from one another than a wave is from water. But since most buddhas have chosen to come as a man, perhaps it would be more helpful if I became enlightened in a woman's body.

"Therefore," she said slowly, looking at them each lovingly, directly, "I vow for all time, until all suffering is ended, in all worlds, for all beings, in all universes, I will become enlightened only in a woman's body."

Wisdom Moon did not achieve her enlightenment overnight. Some people are enlightened instantly, spontaneously; for others it is a long and arduous process. For Wisdom Moon it was a process that occurred over a period of time beyond calculation. Once she had vowed to become fully and completely enlightened, nothing could stop her or diminish her desire to be of benefit to all beings. She would not eat breakfast until she had "saved" a million beings, that is, until she had taken the anger or the greed or the hatred in their hearts and transformed it to loving-kindness and compassion. Then she wouldn't eat lunch until she had saved another million beings, and the same with dinner. So every day, lifetime after lifetime, for thousands and thousands of years, she saved millions and millions of beings.

Then one day she was fully and completely enlightened. She was no longer Wisdom Moon or Yeshe Dawa, she was Tara. She had burst fully into bloom, imperceptibly, like a flower. People came to know her by many names. Her Tibetan name is Drolma, Mother. In Chinese, she is Kwan Yin. Her Sanskrit name is Tara, which means "Liberator," "Saviouress," and "Star." Of all the buddhas and bodhisattvas, she is the quickest and most compassionate, the one who rushes to your aid the moment you think of her, even if you have never believed in her or called on her before.

Called the Mother of All the Buddhas, the Goddess of Compassion, the Bodhisattva of Compassion, the Womb of Enlightenment, Prajnaparamita—Wisdom—and the Buddha herself, this Buddha Tara has at least twenty-one forms, some say a hundred and eight, some say the number of her forms is beyond counting. Her forms are both peaceful and fierce. Though she can enter a state of complete liberation now—bliss, nirvana—she chooses instead to stay in the world to relieve the suffering of others. Avalokiteshvara (Chenrezig in Tibetan), the Lord and Bodhisattva of Compassion himself, had to be saved by her. He had taken a vow to save all beings from suffering, but he had given up. For every being he saved, he lost another. Finally he began to weep in despair. Tara arose, Green Tara this time, from the tears of one eye, and White Tara from the other. She told Avalokiteshvara not to worry, she had come to help him. Together they would save all beings.

Tara comes in whatever form you need to see her in order to believe in her. She is like Wisdom in the Old Testament, Sophia, she comes to you as you go to her.[1] She is known especially for removing great fears and for granting long-life and healing. They say that she even "cheats death." And she is swift.

When I first heard of Tara's vow to be enlightened only in a woman's body, I felt liberated. I was standing on the deck at San Francisco Zen Center's Green Gulch Farm having tea after Sunday lecture. A friend knew that I was discouraged by my growing suspicion that Zen Buddhism wasn't as far from Catholicism as it first looked, that I had heard traditional stories about how only men could be enlightened, about how inferior and full of defilements a woman's body was. Though this misogynist aspect of Buddhism has been downplayed in the West, it is in the texts and can permeate and distort Buddhism as it can any tradition. When he told me the story, the hot teacup almost jumped out of my hands, I was so excited. There had been a woman who said, "Thank you very much, but I will become a buddha as a woman. I don't have to become a man to be enlightened." That such a woman lived thousands of years ago made the story that much more remarkable and instructive. Tara— as Yeshe Dawa—stood against all received tradition and relied on only what she knew to be true from her own experience. This is precisely what the Buddha taught and what drew me to his teachings: Don't take anyone else's word as "the truth"—even his, the Buddha's. He told his followers to test the truth of his teaching against their own experience the way a goldsmith examines gold—heating

GREEN TARA (*Andy Weber*)

it up, pounding it, hammering it, biting it. Only then does she declare that it's real, *after* she has verified by her own experience that it
is truly gold.

Tara made her vow lovingly, out of her vast compassion and her
commitment to save all beings, because she thought it would be
more useful and instructive for people to see a woman become a
buddha. After hearing her story, I began years of studying and writing about Tara, making my first trip to Nepal, in 1980, to find her.[2]
She transformed my life.

CHAPTER 5

EARTH'S HEART BEATING

Tara's Shrine
Pharping, Kathmandu Valley

O ur taxi takes off from Boudha Gate in a swirl of road
dust from a big blue Indian Tata truck. Christina Lundberg, a young filmmaker, and I slide back and forth
across the slick vinyl of the backseat as the car speeds around a
corner. We met at Chökyi Nyima's teachings. This afternoon
we're taking off to go to Pharping, a village in the countryside, to
see the legendary figure of the Buddha Tara "growing" out of a
rock.

Today is a reprieve from the stories of child prostitution.
Christina, twenty-nine, has been untouched by this subject. No one
has approached her with information as they have approached me,
nor has it been brought up in conversations. She knows little about
it, and I am relieved not to discuss it. I resolve to put aside the troubling stories and the feelings they stir up.

The afternoon sky overhead is a gun-metal gray, so full of smog
and exhaust fumes that we put on "greenscreens" for the drive into
the countryside, masks like the ones bicyclists wear in big cities. The
air pollution in the Kathmandu Valley has grown to the point that a
cheap Nepalese version of the greenscreen masks is sold in neighborhood grocery stores. Not just Western tourists but increasing
numbers of local people, even the Tibetan monks, use these masks
or pull up shawls over their noses.

Our taxi driver wears nothing to keep from breathing the raw
fumes through the open windows, unlike some who pull a ban-
danna up over their face when it's bad like this. He coughs and darts

through the thick black exhaust smoke of the Tata trucks and buses, weaving through traffic with such speed that I decide it's better not to look. To look means to see an accident looming at every moment—whether with another taxi, a bus, a water buffalo, a tractor, an auto-rickshaw, or a pedestrian with a bale of straw on his or her head. Either we will make it or we won't.

It's been nine years since I last made this drive to Pharping, when my friend Tara Doyle took me much the same way I'm now taking Christina, bouncing along in a taxi, conversing in shouts. Christina has spent the last nine months in Asia, most recently in Tibet, where she worked on a segment of her documentary film on women spiritual teachers, *On the Road Home.*

Christina and I have an immediate, strong connection. Driven by a thirst for women's wisdom and spiritual teachings, she reminds me of ways in which I have been and am driven on the subject of fierce compassion and the sacred feminine—beyond reason. Increasingly it's connected with the bond between women. Further, we share a background in wilderness travel, mine on rivers, hers in the mountains, and an awareness of the fact that spiritual traditions arise from specific landscapes. We share a sense that Buddhism will have to meet the Native American traditions to come to fruition in the Americas.

On the drive Christina tells me stories of her travels in Tibet, about climbing up a steep scree slope and inching her way around jagged rock spires at nearly eighteen thousand feet, into an ice-roofed cave, the Assembly Hall of the Dakinis. The dakinis are female Wisdom beings in Tibetan Buddhism, roughly parallel to saints in Christianity, only wildly different. Called "Sky-Dancers" because they emanate out of the vastness of space, many are considered female buddhas. To reach the cave itself, she had to make the last part of her climb up an ancient ladder of wood planks fastened with yak intestines, then crawl on her stomach to get through the opening.

Once inside the cave she made offerings to the Wisdom beings and meditated to purify her motives for making her film. She spent the night alone, sleeping on a tiny pallet called "Yeshe Tsogyal's bed," covered with yak hides left for pilgrims, feeding herself by boiling up stinging nettles that grew outside the doorway.

Yeshe Tsogyal is one of the most famous women teachers in the Tibetan Buddhist tradition, a great holy woman from the eighth century who was the consort of Padmasambhava, the patron saint of Tibet. She is also a dakini, a "Sky-Dancer." Padmasambhava, also known as Guru Rinpoche, brought Buddhism to Tibet from India and transformed the demons who opposed the protectors and guardians of the Buddha's teachings. As his consort, Yeshe Tsogyal is widely credited with originating the *terma* tradition, the form of the Buddha's teachings that have been hidden in rocks, or in the sky, or in water, or in the mind itself, to be found only when the time is ripe and the need is present. The rare person who has the ability to find a *terma*, to extract it from its hidden place, and to reveal its teaching is called a *terton*. According to legend, Yeshe Tsogyal meditated in this cave, this is why the pallet is named for her.

Five-feet-nine, lean and lovely, with soft green eyes, Christina laughs as she tells me about folding up her long frame to fit on the tiny bed of Yeshe Tsogyal, then being startled awake just before dawn by the clatter of rocks. Who would be climbing at eighteen thousand feet in the dark? Wild mountain goats—silhouetted in the palest dawn light—just as surprised to see her as she was to see them.

Christina adjusts the rumpled green felt fedora she found in Lhasa to keep it from blowing out our taxi window and tells me of her good fortune in meeting the elusive Khandroma, believed to be an emanation or living embodiment of Yeshe Tsogyal. She's tucked her long brown hair under her hat, hair that usually falls halfway down her back loose or braided. She wears earrings that she made and threaded through her earlobes herself with a needle and dental

CHRISTINA LUNDBERG, ANI PHUNTSOG DROLMA, AND KHANDROMA,
IN TIBET (*Christina Lundberg*)

floss, seed pearls in front of the lobe and a small chunk of turquoise
suspended from the back, Tibetan style.

Once we arrive at Pharping, our plan is to measure the image of
the Buddha Tara that has been "growing" out of the limestone rock
there, miraculously, according to local Buddhist lore. The Tibetans
call this phenomenon *rangjung,* which means "self-arising" or "self-
manifesting." This kind of event is well known, revered, and un-
questioned. Tibetans believe that the power of the human mind
when concentrated with devotion is so great that it can call a deity
out of a substance as hard as rock. The Dalai Lama himself assured
me of this phenomenon. In Buddhism, the world of the mind and
the world of matter are not separate but completely interpenetrated,
a reality that Western medicine and science are only now beginning

to seriously explore. *Rangjung* is considered a breakthrough phenomenon by the Tibetans, something that comes about because of deep interior activity. It represents a passageway between worlds and is considered a very precious occurrence. Paradoxically, *rangjung* is also held to be a natural event, not something to be amazed about, for in truth there are no other worlds for it to be a passageway to, there is only the co-dependent arising of all phenomena, complete interpenetration of mind and matter. When *rangjung* occurs, it is believed that all the blessings of the deity are present in concentrated form.

Though I will measure the image again today, I've always taken the "growth" of Tara's form in the rock to be a metaphor, not a literal truth. I encourage Christina to do the same, not to expect anything but to find that the size will be the same. The numbers seven and three-quarter inches stay in my mind from reviewing the measurements I took in 1985 with a geologist. I have a tape in my pack today to see if there's any difference. "Think of this Tara as analogous to the way she's appearing in people's hearts. What could be harder than the human heart? That's where she is growing," I tell Christina. "That's what's important."

Still, Christina is excited, and although the idea that Tara could be measurably growing is delightful, I think it's far-fetched and wishful. I discourage her.

The first time I visited this Tara shrine, there were reports of the Virgin Mary growing in the barks of trees in Poland and appearing out of thin air in the former Yugoslavia, a Western form of *rangjung* that is still reported to be going on in Bosnia. As far as Catholics and others who follow these phenomena go, we are living in an age of apparitions, at least of Mary, in the Christian tradition. Reports of apparitions of the Virgin abound from around the world, whether in the form of actual bodily appearances, or in weeping statues, bleeding icons, seeping stones, shapes in trees, in shadows on the walls, or in brilliant light. Yet while many pursue the miraculous, it seems that Mary's messages—to be reconciled with one another, especially with those from whom we are estranged, to pray daily, to fast, to undergo a conversion, a change of heart, to follow her path of loving-kindness toward all—seem to be ignored no matter where, how often, or in what form she appears. One of my favorite stories is from Syria, I tell Christina, where a statue of the Virgin was reported to be seeping holy oil. There the Virgin's message was to take her out of the church, she belonged in people's homes—another way to say that she belonged in people's hearts, in daily life. Her messages are simple, down-to-earth. For people to live them, really to follow them, now that would be miraculous.

I think of these reported appearances of the Divine Mother as holographic phenomena, interior images issuing forth, projected out from the collective human psyche, archetypal code in iconographic form, showing us what we need to honor, to include, to bring home, in order to redeem the world: the sacred feminine. To me that means according women and girls full partnership in the world, it means acknowledging the depth of intimacy in our relationship to the world of nature, our constant feeding and suckling, the wealth of riches the natural world provides, the right of all creatures to live in her, the sacredness of her body, to extend the metaphor. Perhaps Marian apparitions are a Western way of glimpsing what the world's mystical traditions and the East have always known: Creation, nature, is the body of God. Not for our dominion but for our communion, our common union.

The Divine Mother comes when the world is in trouble, these stories tell us, whether the ancient story of Durga, the appearances of the Virgin Mary the world over, or this Tara in the rock at Pharping. The ways in which she comes, the forms in which she reveals herself, this is what is different, the outward manifestation, the cultural context, not the inner reality.

Christina has listened carefully, patiently, her eyes crinkling as her smile widens. She says, "Yes, China, but what if it really *is* growing?"

Finally we are high enough outside of the city and far enough to see green fields open out below us, carved and sculpted by centuries of labor on the hillsides. Pharping is in the foothills of the Kathmandu Valley, green with ancient curved terraces of rice plants heavy for harvest. Pale yellow-husked corn is stored on teepee-style structures for drying. The taxi stops where the foot trail to the shrine picks up. The air is cleaner here; we've gained elevation from the valley floor.

We hike up a narrow, dusty path through the brush. When we reach the small shrine, I pause in the doorway surprised by the strength of the feeling that comes over me, the sense that I was here only yesterday, not years ago. The room looks so intimate, so familiar that I want to cry.

Suddenly I see the *ani* sitting in the corner of the shrine room chanting Tara's mantra, the same little Tibetan nun I met nine years ago. She was chanting then just as she is today. Her brilliant smile, her dark eyes, her misshapen jaw—everything looks the same—her maroon robes, her silvered, nearly shaved-bald head, the red shawl wrapped around her waist, the beads she's telling in her hand, her joyful spirit.

I enter, going first to the *ani* to show her the photograph of Tara that I took in 1985. She smiles up at me and continues chanting. She takes the photograph and puts it on top of her head as a sign of respect for Tara, then she looks at it again, compares it to the Tara in the rock a dozen feet away, looks at the photo, and breaks out laughing, rocking back and forth in her seat, never missing a beat of her chanting.

I bow and offer her the traditional Tibetan sign of respect, a long white silk *khata,* my hands extended. She takes it, throws it around my neck, and ties the long ends in three large, loose knots as I stand, still bowing. This *ani* does little but sit in this corner of the shrine saying her beads, chanting Tara's mantra, *"Om Tare Tu Tare Ture Soha, Om Tare Tu Tare Ture Soha, Om Tare Tu Tare Ture Soha."* I am flooded with feelings for this small room, the rock it contains, the nun's chanting, and with gratitude for Tara the revolutionary, and her vow to be enlightened only in a woman's body.

I step in front of the rock to face the *rangjung,* "self-arising" Tara. Only a physical gesture can begin to acknowledge how deeply this piece of stone has affected me. I raise my hands, place my palms together over my head, touch them to my throat, my chest, and then kneel down and bend over, sliding my hands out in front of me across the dusty, cold cement floor until I am fully extended toward the stone Tara in the traditional prostration, offering body, speech, and mind to the Buddha, and in so doing I am transported.

This earthy rock Tara is my great teacher. I have a sense of waking up in her presence, and it grows stronger as I think of how this Tara transfigured my life. Searching for Tara brought me to the brink of death from dysentery, only to live and discover that it was alcohol that would kill me. Tara taught me that it was possible to be fully and completely enlightened as a woman; she gave me back my own culture, took away the contradictions and the conflict, showed me that Mary could be Tara in my tradition. I feel great reverence for what a stone can do and for the story it carries.

When I began to look for the Buddha Tara, I had only the smallest fragment of Tara's story. I did not know that this rock was actually a seed that would grow the story of Tara's vow. I did not know that it would take root and grow into an ancient flowering tree. The tree that grew from this stone seed sprouted ten thousand leaves, each one a different name for the Great Mystery.

"Now I am laying a stone in Zion, a precious cornerstone, and no one who relies on this will be brought to disgrace," "Be living stones," the New Testament tells us.[1] This stone is a living cornerstone, the foundation of what has been cast out, the tradition of a

TARA IN THE ROCK, PHARPING VILLAGE, KATHMANDU, NEPAL
(*China Galland*)

fully empowered, enlightened form of female Wisdom, the divine
feminine. This stone also challenges me to face what it is that I
would cast out, reject, and marginalize.

Adhi Rinpoche, an older lama, who had just come out of Tibet
after twenty-one years in a Chinese prison, gave the Buddhist teachings that Christina and I attended this morning before leaving for
Pharping. Tortured by his Chinese guards, nearly stabbed to death,
he bore no trace of anger, resentment, or ill will. I knew these details
only because his translator told them to me. Rinpoche never mentioned them.

He told us to visualize the Tree of Refuge in bloom, that source
of guidance and consolation, flowering with buddhas and bodhisattvas. He told us to imagine our parents on either side of us, and
our enemies in front of us, all facing the Tree together, taking
Refuge, placing our confidence in and seeking consolation from the

Enlightened beings, trusting and knowing that our enemies want peace and happiness just as much as we do. Can I imagine Jim in front of me as I face this Tara, wanting peace and happiness for all beings? Christianity tells me to love my enemies, but Buddhism and the community of recovery show me how. The thought crosses my mind, then vanishes; it is so hard for me to hold on to.

Adhi Rinpoche wrote out these teachings on cigarette papers in the Chinese prison and passed them on to the other monks and lamas to remember. His gentle, warm presence was a testimonial to the transformative capacity of Buddhist teachings. He said that the Ground of Refuge is gold, a gold so soft under your feet that it gives with each step and your foot leaves an imprint when you walk.

I stand up again and bow, stretching out on the vast gold floor of this Ground of Refuge. The altar in this room is stone. Inside this stone is the earth's heart. I can hear it beating, steadily, *Om Ta-re Tu Ta-re Tu-re So-ha, Om Ta-re Tu Ta-re Tu-re So-ha, Om Ta-re Tu Ta-re Tu-re So-ha.*

I stand and light twelve butter lamps on the ledge in front of the rock. Then, pushing as many of them as possible carefully to one side, I lean over the tiny flames and pull out my tape measure. I measure from the semicircular band over Tara's head to the bottom of her extended right foot, the iconographic clue that this is the Green Tara of the Khadiravani Forest, the main form of Tara. Then I stretch the tape across the width of the image, take a piece of paper, and with a pen trace the outline of the image as best I can.

Seven and one-half inches high, I note. How can this be? It's a quarter of an inch *smaller* than it was in 1985? This is a possibility I had not even considered. Both the geologist and I took the measurements in 1985.

"It hasn't grown, Christina," I tell her as I turn around, shaking my head. "I'm not surprised. I would have been surprised if it had. Still, I don't understand. Something's off, or else it's getting smaller."

This is what I get for trying to measure a deity—nonsense. The idea is preposterous in the first place. I walk over to the meditation bench under the window by a large green *damaru,* a drum for meditation and chanting that hangs suspended from the ceiling. I need to sit and be quiet, to meditate. This is the measure to take, the measure of the breath, of mindfulness.

Christina joins me. Moments pass in silence, with only the steady sounds of the *ani* chanting Tara's mantra and the click, click, click of prayer beads in the room. I pull out my text with the Praises to the Twenty-one Taras. The *ani* signals her approval, and now Christina and I chant aloud together:

"I salute the Powerful one, the supreme, noble, exalted Tara.... I salute her who is the Saviouress, the swift one without fear, whose eyes are like lightning ... whose face is fashioned from a hundred full-moons of Autumn, who gleams with the revealing light of a thousand stars.... Salute her, the swift one, greatly fearsome, defeater of the boldest demon, whose beautiful face frowns so fiercely that all foes are slain without remnant." [2]

I look up for a moment and the *ani* gives me such a smile that it seems that I could stay here chanting like this forever.

"Salute her whom the king of the Gods, all deities, and every other being serve and attend, the joyful beauty whose form is an armor against all evil and contention."

As darkness falls the little *ani* gets up to gather her belongings and leave. She lives in a cave in the hills above the shrine. Now we have to leave too. I get up to pay my respects and say good-bye. She takes my hand, puts her forehead to mine, saying the Tara mantra all the while, then backs away smiling, just as she did when Tara Doyle and I were there. I think of Tara Doyle now and the strong bond that was created between us by coming to Pharping and by receiving Tara initiations from Chökyi Nyima—meditation instruction—just the two of us. Becoming dharma sisters—performing ceremonies, taking teachings from him together—created a special tie between us. Christina and I met at Chökyi Nyima's, now we're at

Pharping together, how far will this connection go? She joins me to bid the *ani* farewell.

To our surprise, the *ani* breaks out laughing and makes a fist in the air and shakes it vigorously. "Drolma, Drolma!" she says, the Tibetan word for Tara, as though she was saying, "Keep chanting, keep practicing!" to us. This *ani* is fiercely devoted to Tara, passionate, ardent. Then with her big toothless grin, she gives us a thumbs-up sign. Christina and I laugh and make the gesture back. The butter lamps flicker; a dog sets up a row in the distance; the crickets start up. I stop in the doorway for one last look, then turn away, still not understanding all the emotion that this shrine brings up, knowing only that I'm grateful to have been here.

We walk back down the dusty trail, through a tunnel of bushes full of tree frogs and crickets, their night sounds washing us as we pass. Fireflies flit and twinkle in the dark. The air is as soft as on a summer night even though it's fall.

Christina tells me that at one point she was outside while I was still in the shrine, and she saw a monk standing in the doorway give a swift, hard kick to a dog that had the misfortune to walk past him.

"I was so shocked I scolded him!" she tells me. "Do you know that story in *Words of My Perfect Teacher*?[3] I wish I could have been like the lama in that book. He was giving a teaching outside under a tree when a dog wandered by. One of the monks listening picked up a rock and threw it at the dog, hard. He wanted to hurt the dog and drive it away, just like this monk, but at the moment that the rock hit, the lama cried out, not the dog!

"The lama took off his robes and turned his back to his students. There was a welt showing the impact of the rock on his back. Now that's fierce compassion. The dog had no mark on him. The lama had absorbed his suffering."

CHAPTER 6

MOPPING THE FLOOR

*Mother Teresa's Home
for the Elderly, Kathmandu*

*The beauty of youth is like a flash of lightning in the sky and
wealth is unstable like dew on the tip of a blade of grass.
Friends and relatives are inconstant like customers at the market place.
Bestow your blessings so that I may be able to understand
the true nature of impermanence.*

—PRAYERS OF REQUEST TO THE LADY TARA
(translated by Carol Savvas)

Tibetan drums announce the beginning of the day in Boudha. The drone of chanting swells the air, forming a cushion around the dog barks and blare of horns from nearby streets. Raucous crows call from the veranda. Federica and I are going to work at Mother Teresa's Home for the Elderly in Pashupatinath this morning. Mother Teresa is a well-known example of this fierce, no-nonsense, protective spirit that I seek. I remember an early story I heard of how Mother Teresa, when she first went out into the streets of Calcutta to begin her ministry, picked up a dying woman, took her to the hospital, and refused to leave until the woman was cared for. Her commitment to compassion for the poor and the cast-out is fierce. However, I am interested in her Sisters, in the Missionaries of Charity, the little-known women in the background who, day after day, are carrying out Mother Teresa's ministry. What are they like? I'm sure that her Sisters will show me another face of the compassionate fierce feminine. The bond between Mother Teresa and her Sisters is legendary, and the strength of it forms the basis of the success of her order. Mother Teresa might have been a wonder, but without her Sisters, her work would not be the internationally recognized phenomenon that it's become. This is why I want to be with her Sisters. Though they may be quiet nuns, they would have to have a kind of fierceness in them to face the suffering that they do, day after day. And I'm apprehensive, grateful that Federica's coming with me.

I heat up rice and *dahl* for breakfast, prepare to make a cup of tea. Getting ready for the day, even just making a cup of tea, requires a kind of thought that I'm not used to as a Westerner. In the back of my mind as I bustle around the kitchen, putting on the water to boil, I wonder if I'm being initiated into our future as water pollution and shortages continue. I stop myself, remembering suddenly that I have to turn on the electric water pump.

The water supply in Kathmandu has been drained so low that water is pumped into the system only once or twice a day. Everyone tries to draw water during the few hours it's available, creating an even greater shortage. Sometimes there is no water whatsoever, like in the small, elegantly crumbling former palace where I first stayed, in a friend's apartment. There we pumped drinking water by hand every morning. In order to prevent dysentery and the other water-borne diseases so common here, one boils the water for twenty minutes, cools it, then pours it through a charcoal filtering system. Any Nepali home that can afford it uses this filter system in addition to boiling the water. Living in one of the poorest countries in the world, most Nepalis cannot. Water-borne diseases plague the populace, putting millions of lives at risk every year, especially those of women and children. At home, where I am blessed to be able to drink water out of the tap, the reality of the loss of clean water barely penetrates. Here, where the limits of clean water have been breached so severely, the madness of this is unavoidable.

The third-floor flat I've rented at Boudha is equipped with not only the manual filtering system but also an electric pump, a luxury here. If I remember to turn on the pump and the neighbors aren't using theirs at the same time, there is water in the tap, water to boil and filter, a process that takes roughly two hours. One has to think ahead, prepare beforehand. No going into the kitchen in the middle of the night to get a drink of water out of the tap.

Even the cup holding the tea made from boiled and filtered water is not to be taken for granted, my host explained, for dishes are washed with tap water. Cups, dishes, silverware, everything at least has to have boiled water poured over it and then be dried off. Having nearly died of amoebic dysentery from the water here before, I take all precautions.

There'll be no bathing this morning, as not only does the water pump have to be turned on for ten minutes to fill the hot-water heater, the water also has to be heated, and that takes at least two hours. The hot-water tank takes so much electricity, very expensive here, that it is turned on only two hours beforehand. Tonight, I tell myself, I'll bathe tonight, as I turn down the propane fire under the rice and *dahl*. The propane tank is low. Forget the stove. Time to go! I have to meet Federica at the north end of the stupa.

Mother Teresa's sisters maintain the only home for the elderly in the entire country of Nepal, in one wing of Pashupatinath, the most revered Hindu temple complex in the country. Situated on the Bagmati River, Pashupati is known for its burning *ghats,* steps into the river, and the platforms just above them, where devout Hindus are cremated in the open on crackling funeral pyres, as on the Ganges in India. After meeting Aruna, Agnes, and later Olga Murray, who works with street children and orphans, sometimes rescuing them from jail, where they may be confined with their mothers, I view the clamoring street children who swarm around me now differently.

I visited Olga and many former street children at J House, one of the orphanages Olga started with her colleague Allen Ailstrop. An attorney in her seventies, retired from more than thirty years with the California State Supreme Court, Olga started the Nepalese Youth Opportunity Foundation (NYOF) to educate and provide for as many of these street children as possible. I met Devi-Maya, a blind girl who at five had her arm broken in three places by a drunken father so that she would be a more effective beggar. Devi-Maya now lives happily at J House and is the first in her class at the school for the blind. I met Ganu, a little girl who had been badly burned but who also advanced rapidly in school and could now dance, thanks to the medical care NYOF provided. Without Olga's passion for these children, hundreds would have been left on the street with no way to receive an education or the medical care many need. A great many would have been lost, kidnapped, stolen, sold into debt bondage or prostitution.

Street children are especially vulnerable to the dangers of child trafficking. When Federica and I climb out of the taxi they rush us. It is hard simply to be with what I now know about the life of these children. There are so many of them, at least fifteen around us now, that it is clear that I can do nothing, at least not in this moment, not by myself. My respect for these women for taking on the problems they have grows each day.

Federica and I refuse all the children. I shake my head, no, I don't want to buy jewelry, I say to one; no, I don't want to see burning bodies today, to another, who wants to walk me to the *ghats* to view a cremation. No. Federica and I duck through an open gateway into the temple complex to find the Sisters.

The main building at Pashupati is a large rectangular structure around a large open courtyard filled with small shrines. Mother Teresa's Sisters have a wing to themselves for the elderly. A tall, broad-shouldered woman named Sister Edwin greets Federica and me as we walk in. Wiping her hands across her blue-and-white-checked apron before she extends them, Sister Edwin is a large woman, substantial, cheerful, and efficient. There is little wasted time or motion around Sister Edwin. There's another volunteer here this morning, a young woman from Denmark who's spending three months working with the Sisters.

"We're mopping the floors, and they need drying. The section on the right has been done. Dry that first," Sister Edwin says to me, handing me a small clean towel. She tells Federica to help the other woman finish mopping the long room on our left. Drying a wet cement floor with one small towel? It's not much bigger than a washcloth. I'm not sure how this can be done, much less how helpful it is. I do it anyway. An old man sits cross-legged on the bed next to the one under which I'm drying. He's weak and cold and struggling to pull a shawl around his shoulders. I dry my hands on my skirt and stand up to help him. He must be in his nineties. He could have been my grandfather, I think as I bend over, pulling the shawl up around his shoulders. No, he wants it over his head too, he lets me know.

Sister Raissa comes along and pours warm milk into the cup he holds out. I kneel back down to continue drying under the bed. Suddenly I'm being splattered with warm milk. It's the old man sprinkling me. He does it again while I'm looking right at him. His eyes twinkle and he laughs, pleased at the surprise on my face. Just what he wanted. I am flooded with inexplicable delight.

Looking up past the old man, I see on the wall a well-known saying from Mother Teresa, "Christ needs our hands, our eyes, our hearts. . . ." It reminds me of what a Tibetan lama said when he first visited the Benedictine shrine of the Black Madonna at Einsiedeln, in Switzerland. Yes, the Madonna was very beautiful and her temple impressive, he thought, but he was more curious about what the people who were devoted to her were like. The divine feminine needs our hands, our eyes, our hearts too. Mary, Christ's mother, is the Western counterpart of Tara, the Mother of All the Buddhas, that's why he had been taken to see her shrine.

"It's the practitioner who brings the deity through," the lama explained. It's through the practitioner, the one who is devoted to her, that the power of the Madonna will show herself. The beaten gold backdrop of her altar, the drawers full of jewels given to her, her exquisitely embroidered robes, the ex votos in the back of the church—paintings of the miracles she had performed, visual thank-you notes—the importance of the centuries-old Benedictine monastery that housed the shrine were undoubtedly noteworthy and impressive, this Tibetan monk thought, but what were her devotees like? Had she tamed their minds and hearts, helped rid them of destructive impulses, made them more generous, more compassionate, more loving, as followers of Tara are taught in Tibetan Buddhism? This is what he wanted to know. Had she destroyed the demons of greed, hate, and delusion in her followers, like Durga and Kali, had she pierced their hearts, could she save the world?

As I continue drying the floor I think about Mother Teresa and the Sisters working here, and I encounter a paradox. What we imagine about God, Tara, the Buddha, Jesus, Durga—whatever or whomever it is we might call the divine—can be made up only of what we have seen people doing as they live out their lives. What Gandhi, Martin Luther King, Jr., Harriet Tubman, Dorothy Day, Mother Henriette Delille, the Dalai Lama, and countless others did and do is where my ideas of compassion, charity, patience, wisdom, love, and generosity come from, not from any text or teaching. Henriette Delille was a nineteenth-century New Orleans free woman of color who founded the Sisters of the Holy Family, an African-American order of Sisters, in 1843, during a time when African-American women were not allowed to be nuns and people could be put to death for teaching people in slavery to read. Henriette taught anyway. She fed and educated the poorest of the poor, the children, the old slaves, the discarded. I think of her now because she was an early Mother Teresa, too little known, though her Sisters are promoting her cause for canonization as a saint. Mother Henriette's life

71

inspires me time and time again. She will be the first African-American woman saint, when and if she is canonized.[1]

The floors here are washed every morning and swabbed down with disinfectant. This long room of beds doubles as an open hospital ward. I am drying the floor so that no one will slip and fall. A woman in the section Federica mopped had terrible open bedsores when she was brought in a few weeks ago. Sister Edwin is cleaning one just as I finish the floor and go to find her for further instructions.

I wince as Sister Edwin cleans. Sister Raissa sees me and says cheerfully in her British clip, "Oh, this is much better. She is really healing. When she first came, this sore was ten inches across and you could see the bone." The woman moans softly as Sister Edwin deftly and quickly swabs it with sterile cotton soaked with disinfectant. I gasp under my breath. The woman's husband stands at her feet, looking gently at his wife, who is quietly bearing her pain and the curiosity of the day's volunteers. They have four children and are very poor. He comes to feed her three times a day.

Nepali radio blares, horns honk, and a sitar drones in the background. Suddenly a group of tourists walk into the infirmary and begin taking photographs, even though there are signs that say clearly "No Pictures." I walk up to them and inquire if they read English, pointing to the sign. They apologize, in English, and retreat, snapping more pictures as they move backward out the doorway. Sister Edwin finishes up with her patient

"Outside!" she announces. "It's ladies' bathing day. Please come and help," she says as she turns toward the courtyard, and signals to an old man to fetch more water for warming. Federica and I follow.

We move outside to an aging green hand pump as the old women gather for their weekly bathing. The sky is clear and sunny this morning, no smog. The air is mild. The Sisters pumped water earlier this morning and heated it in big tubs now set out on the courtyard stones. Sister Edwin hands me a cup and a bar of soap, throws a towel over my shoulder matter-of-factly, and says, "Like this," as she begins to chat and vigorously soap up a partially dressed old woman. With quick, sure movements, always careful to preserve the woman's modesty, she washes and rinses her in no time and moves on to the next woman.

The women wear saris even as they are being bathed. The woman Sister Edwin bathes moves deftly out of her dirty clothes, simultaneously wrapping herself with swift movements that leave no private part exposed. No matter how old and arthritic the person, each maintains a remarkable dignity. Sister Edwin motions me over to a blind woman she wants me to bathe. My charge suddenly squats down a few feet away and begins to urinate.

"Sister, Sister, what do I do?" I ask, flustered, as my first assignee sits urinating all over her feet.

Sister Edwin laughs and dips her large cup into one of the tubs of water and swishes the urine away. "Nothing to do." She giggles, and says in her clipped English, "She must be out of those clothes anyway. Help her finish undressing and throw them in the laundry pile. They'll all get washed and boiled tomorrow. Everyone gets fresh clothes once a week with their bath. No harm."

"Sister, you wash all those clothes by hand?" I ask after seeing the growing size of the already three-foot-high pile of washing in the little laundry hut in the courtyard.

"Prayer makes everything easy, if we are doing it for God," Sister Edwin assures me. She has been a nun for twenty-two years. "All this that we are doing here at Mother Teresa's—all over the world—Mother started with only five rupees. That is all. She just started teaching the children. The first school was so poor that she had to draw the letters on the dirt floor.

"Five rupees. That's how she started. Doing it for God."

The blind woman stands up now, relieved. She must be four-feet-ten. Like all the women here, her head has been shorn, for lice, for ease of care, I don't know which. Her eyes are half closed in her blindness, but she smiles as I begin to pour warm water over her. She turns her face up like a flower to the warmth of the sun and streaming water, clearly enjoying it. Gently I soap her bare shoulders, her arms, and then reach down the back of her sari as far as I can with my soapy cloth and warm water. Then I do the same with her front; this isn't half as terrifying or difficult as I imagined the moment it was announced that it was time to help with the bathing. This is not a person who cannot move or do anything for herself. Though old and blind, she is ambulatory and lively. Between the two of us, we get her respectably clean and well rinsed.

Next comes the drying, toweling her off and then pulling a rough cotton green-and-white-checked dress over her head as she lets her wet sari drop. Now she is bathed, clean, and dressed, her silvery head shining in the morning sunlight. I help her into a purple sweater as she lets me put first one arm, then the other, into the sleeves, and then pull it up over her shoulders.

Marigolds bloom in the courtyard. An old man comes out to help with the hand pump, for the Sisters need more water. A young retarded man with a limp, wearing a bright green turban, teeters past on his uneven legs, his empty tin plate in his hands, ready for lunch to be served.

"We can't serve food to the elderly because we are low caste," Sister Edwin explains with a hearty laugh. "We are not Brahmin. Brahmins can only be served by Brahmins. They won't take food from our hands even if they're hungry. Yours either. Brahmin volunteers come in to serve them."

"Sister," I call back to her, now bathing her third charge in the time it took me to wash this one, "what is this woman's name?"

"Oh, that's Tara," she says, as the old blind woman smiles at me in the sunlight.

"Tara?" I repeat, taken aback.

"Yes," Sister says as she briskly towels off another woman. Federica laughs as she overhears our interchange. I had told her about my trip to Pharping to measure the Tara with Christina. She looks up and gives me a broad grin, raising her eyebrows and nodding her head knowingly, "Tara, eh-h?" then goes back to carefully trimming the toenails of the old woman she has just finished bathing.

I accompany this Tara with chipped pink fingernails to a place where she can sit down and enjoy the warmth of the morning sun, and then I begin to bathe the next woman Sister Edwin points out.

I have to laugh out loud as I think to myself, So this is it. Tara *is* growing, maybe not in the rock at Pharping but in the form of the joyful old blind woman who stands before me. This old Tara is a complete renunciate. Whether by intention or not, she has given up worldly possessions. She has only the one clean set of clothes she is given to wear weekly after her bath. She has only the food she is served, only the care she is given. She can initiate little or nothing by herself, and yet she seems quite happy. Did she always have simple wants and needs? I wonder as I turn and look at her again, sitting with her face turned toward the sun. Or could she have once known luxury and lost everything? Had she known the warmth of a family or had she always been alone?

What a teaching on acceptance this living Tara is giving me. Perhaps we have no more choices about our situation than this woman, only we labor under illusions that old age strips away so starkly here. We are dependent, deeply dependent upon the kindness of one another and the bonds between us.

Finding myself bathing Tara is a sweet consolation. I've always thought that the story of Tara growing out of the rock was a metaphor. Finding this Tara at Mother Teresa's confirms that intuition. She reveals herself through service, not only devotion. Mother Teresa's Sisters and this aging Tara remind me that the divine manifests itself in the person in front of me and that service can help me see that.

TARA GROWS

*A*wake at 3:30 A.M., I search for a copy of the 1985 measurements of the Tara in the rock at Pharping. Instead I find a list of the fierce forms of Taras.[1] Not all are dark blue or black. Some are red; some are black, or blue-black; others are gold; another white. The forms of fierce compassion defy stereotyping. I read the list, this litany from another world, an assurance that she will manifest herself in whatever form is necessary.

The central Tara is the great Green Tara of the Khadiravani Forest. From this form emanate all others. It is no accident that the main Tara is dark green, for she is Nature herself. She controls wild beasts, taming and subduing them. Bears, tigers, stags, leopards, all run and leap, play in her presence. Jackals sing, parrots call in the trees. Thousands of fruits grow in the trees, the odor of nutmeg and cloves fills the air in her forest.

Adorned with flowers, her breasts swollen with milk, the Khadiravani Tara sits on a lotus blossom in the lake of compassion, her face shining like the full moon high in the Khadiravani Forest, the forest full of *khadira* trees. This Tara contains all other Taras. This is the Tara who comes to help in whatever form you need her. This is the Tara who relieves the Great Fears,[2] known, like Durga, for dramatic rescues, who, like Durga, is called "Saviouress," only you may not recognize her, her forms are so varied.

At least one of these Taras is strikingly similar to Kali, the Tara who is called the Fierce Summoner. She wears a necklace of skulls and a tiger-skin loincloth, has a long protruding tongue and multiple hands holding objects such as a sword and a hook, and stands on a corpse. She is a black Tara with three faces.[3] The multiplicity of

Taras, peaceful *and* fierce, is reassuring. Her many forms are similar to the different Virgin Marys or Madonnas in the Christian tradition that one prays to for different needs: one to remove poverty, one to grant a child, another to remove blindness.

There is a laughing, joyful red Tara, the thirteenth Tara, one who charms and tames the entire world, defeating its demons through her laughter at the foolishness of "greed, hate, and delusion." I imagine demons disarmed by her laughter, tumbling helplessly at her feet. This buddha is slightly mischievous and known to have a sense of humor. Famous for her disguises, she can blaze up suddenly, red like fire, "slightly fierce." This is the Tara who appeared directly to Atisha, the great eleventh-century Indian Buddhist master, and told him to go to Tibet to save the Buddha's teachings.[4]

The fierce Tara Who Crushes All Demons is gold. Another Golden Tara, She Who Perfects Wisdom, has ten hands and arms, like Durga. The Tibetan Tara is not described as destroying demons even though she may crush them. She "tames" them, she "pacifies," she "averts," she "overcomes." This clarifies Khenpo Choga's story about Tara and Chenrezig "taking over" the ferocious bodies of Mahakala and Mahakali, not destroying them but helping even demons awaken their innate love and compassion. The fierce divine feminine is not about literal destruction. She is a symbol of the power of the forces of transformation, a transformation in which our "demons"—the forms in which our ego clings to the world— die to their old ways, like the people involved in child trafficking turning into thousands of versions of Ajima, the goddess who stole children and was transformed into a divine protector. With Tara's help, anything is possible.

I will be up the rest of the night if I don't put these papers aside and keep looking for the measurements of the Pharping Tara. I find them, photocopied from the original sheet of paper from 1985. Rather than clarify, they complicate. There are two sets of measurements on the page, one made by the Nepalese government geologist who accompanied me and one made by me. One notes that the image was six and three-quarters inches high, whereas the measurement I took with Christina at Pharping is seven and one-half inches, three-quarters of an inch taller.

I look again. Yes. The measurement has changed. But does this mean Tara is growing in the rock, or that nine years ago I measured from a different place on the image? I have no way to know. The more I compare the sets of numbers, the more questions and explanations for the variation come to mind.

I sit up in bed, half out of my sleeping bag, blankets around my shoulders, papers laid in piles all around me; I'm smiling. Maybe Tara growing isn't only a metaphor. Perhaps this is an extraordinary moment. Perhaps this is merely in the nature of things, as the Tibetans maintain. Perhaps this is human error. Perhaps . . . Then I have a wild thought: If the image *is* growing, is three-fourths of an inch in nine years fast or slow?

I hear the soft sound of bells ringing two floors below. The two old lamas who live downstairs are up doing their morning prayers. It's four-thirty in the morning now. The Sufis say that the prayer made in the dark of the night is the prayer heard by God. May it be so, I think to myself as I finally turn off the light and slide back down in my sleeping bag, saying my beads to Tara.

May all the fierce forms of Tara come to the protection of children everywhere, may compassion burn a hole through the night. Dear Tara Buddha, dear Mary, Mother of God, dear God the Mother, Wisdom herself, may it be so.

CHAPTER 7

NAKEDNESS IS
THE HARD PART

Healing the Wound Between Women

Two hundred people crowd inside a hilltop *gonpa,* a small temple, in the foothills above the Kathmandu Valley floor. Sitting on woven straw mats on a bare floor, we have come to hear the renowned teacher Tulku Urgyen, Chökyi Nyima's father, who escaped during the 1959 Tibetan uprising against the Chinese invasion. He is eighty-two years old, recuperating from surgery, and continuing to teach, against his doctors' orders. Those who couldn't fit inside stand at the open windows to listen. We sit knee to knee, bumping into each other with every turn and move. Rice pellets and bright marigolds are passed hand to hand to toss in the air upon Tulku Urgyen's arrival.

Peeling frescoes of the patron saint of Tibet, Padmasambhava, Yeshe Tsogyal's consort, smile from the front wall. Huge, fierce black deities—protectors of the teachings—are painted on either side of the entry to guard the doors. The doors are also the doorway into the room of enlightenment; the protectors are the ones who destroy deluded thinking and transform the mind. A young monk comes in bringing an offering of tall white, pink, yellow, and orange gladiolus, a signal that teachings are about to begin.

When Tulku Urgyen enters, everyone struggles to their feet to stand and bow. There is barely a path left for him to get to his seat. He moves slowly, looking at us with the great pleasure of one who is returning to health. Chökyi Nyima steps forward to help his father climb up on his teaching throne, an elevated, brocade-covered seat. Young nuns with newly shaved heads line up before him to make a traditional Tibetan offering of rice and flowers and song as he sits down. Their low, rhythmic chant is haunting. It is the sound of Tibet, which, like this old lama, may soon die. The Tibetan Buddhist way of life, the culmination of untold lifetimes of direct transmissions of teachings from teacher to student, has been ripped apart, destroyed like the ancient books in the six thousand Tibetan monasteries leveled by the Chinese. More than 1.2 million Tibetan people have been killed, a fifth of the population. Many Tibetans, including lamas, monks, and nuns, languish in Chinese prisons today, subject to forced labor, rape, and torture. Tulku Urgyen comes from another world, a time before the great sorrow that is Tibet today.

Tulku Urgyen wears a brilliant orange-gold silk shirt that fairly glows in the afternoon sunlight streaming through the window. Behind him on the wall is a faded, peeling orange fresco of two great lamas on a gold background. "Our confusion lies in believing something to be separate from ourselves," he begins, explaining the Buddhist view that sees mind and matter as one continuum, continually arising and falling back into itself, like waves into water. When one grasps this view, it becomes difficult, if not impossible, to imagine that we are separate from one another or the world around us. To understand this lack of separation, he says, is to let "confusion dawn as wisdom."

The room is warm from the number of people packed in so densely and from the late-day sun. I grow drowsy from the three-hour hike up from Boudha, and I fight to stay awake.

All that we need is within us, he assures us, "just as the flower is contained within the seed." Though we cannot see the flower's colors or smell its fragrance, we understand that by planting the seed and applying warmth, time, water, and sunlight, the seed will sprout tiny leaves and someday flower. Like the flower, the Buddha nature within each of us is unavoidable: if the right circumstances are applied, the enlightened mind will blossom of its own accord.

Suddenly Tulku Urgyen claps his hands. "Wake up! Hear this? Can a corpse hear this clap?" He laughs. "No, only present mind can hear this clap." The Tibetans include the awareness of death at every turn. We never know which will come first, tomorrow or the next life.

Tulku Urgyen's good cheer is infectious. There is a widespread feeling of lightheartedness in the room. His bottle-thick glasses magnify his mischievous warm, dark eyes. His face crinkles into a thousand tiny lines as he laughs with the relish of someone who knows that he may not have much longer to be with us.

The past is gone, the future is not here, he reminds us, only the present moment is available. When our attention begins to stray, just notice, don't push, allow.

The struggle falls away. Practice is hard because it's easy, unimaginably so, like the flower blooming. For moments I am free of disturbance, but only moments. My attention strays. So now I allow this. I notice, as Tulku Urgyen says, breathe, and let go.

What does it mean to be on a spiritual path? I came to Nepal planning only to go to Mother Teresa's to understand fierce compassion, to see the power of the bond between women in action. Sister Edwin and Sister Raissa have a clearly demarcated spiritual practice—daily mass and Communion, a day of reflection each Thursday—but Aruna, Agnes, and Olga do not. Meeting these women has complicated matters and helped bring to the surface an unconscious assumption that good works come most purely as an expression of a spiritual path.

Aruna told me that she meditates for five to ten minutes before her whirlwind days of family and work take off. She chants her mantras off and on as she can. Agnes runs in the forest when she's in Belgium, or when here, sits outside by herself when she can find quiet and simply breathes. Olga maintains that she has no spiritual practice, that she is not particularly inward looking, that she's an agnostic Jew. She is only doing what she loves, she says, what brings her joy—helping the orphans and street children build new lives.

"For the price of a good silk blouse at I. Magnin's, I can save a child's life," Olga told me; that was the turning point for her, when she found that out. It was so easy to help, meaningfully, not only by writing a check but by following through herself, giving fully of her own time and care.

All these women are passionately compassionate—another definition of fierce compassion—and in agreement on the role of action. I think of the New Testament, the surprising passage in James 1:27, "Pure, unspoilt religion, in the eyes of God . . . is this: coming to the help of orphans and widows in their hardships, and keeping oneself uncontaminated by the world." From this perspective, all these women are deeply religious.

I bring the focus back to my breath, sit up straighter, then drift, thinking of Khenpo Choga and his question, "Where is the anger?" The upset, the heat, the heart-racing that I felt are nowhere to be found now. The disturbance is gone, like a cloud moving across the sky, dissolved, the Buddhists say, into the vast emptiness of the space. Do not be attached to a cloud. Enter the endless sky.

My shoulders relax, my breath deepens. Don't push. Allow the cloud, the contradictions, in one breath, then allow their disappearance in another. Then be willing to start over again, a million times. This is the beginning of compassion. Recognize that the world is not as it seems. This is the beginning of the spiritual path.

The teachings draw to a close for the day. The young nuns make their way to the front of the room to sing for Tulku Urgyen as he prepares to leave. When they finish, we toss the marigold petals and rice pellets, then everyone stands in line, single file, to offer a ceremonial scarf, folded with a card and perhaps a donation inside. The autumn sun comes through the window and falls directly on Tulku Urgyen, setting his orange silks ablaze with evening fire. He leaves his throne slowly, with great effort, giving us an enormous smile, and makes his way out on the arm of Chökyi Nyima.

Now his seat is empty, the setting sun full on the white and cream ceremonial scarves that spill over the top. Empty. Gone, gone, gone, as he soon will be. I sense that we are witnessing a great passing, like the burning of one of the last great rain forests; not only is its sheer beauty and exuberant array of life lost, but with its loss, life's sustainability for all creatures is diminished. Soon only the story of Tibet will remain. Tulku Urgyen shuffles out slowly, slowly, nodding and smiling, leaning on the arm of his son. I cannot leave this room yet. I return to my seat and sit quietly.

I feel another pang of sorrow. Where are the old women teachers? What would it be like to honor the wise old women? What would it be like to stand and greet our grandmothers? What if we tossed flower petals and rice pellets in the air like this to honor them? What if a chorus of young men sang to them, if we offered them the ceremonial scarves, *khatas,* as signs of our deep respect, and envelopes with money tucked inside to assure their care? What if people spent hours walking, spent days, just to see them and hear them give teachings? Whom might we honor in this way, who are the women who are so learned, so wise, and so dedicated to the welfare of all beings that just to be in their presence is a cause for celebration? They may be present in ways we don't recognize, doing work that is little valued by society. Perhaps they would refuse to be singled out and would insist that all be honored. I don't know. I just know that I want to find women who have faced fully the terrors life can hold, who have known outrage, and who have been able to transform their anger into compassionate action rather than become embittered or violent or simply deny what has happened.

It's nearly twilight by the time I make my way back down the rutted path with Federica, Tsering, and a woman friend from Switzerland who was also at the teachings today. Walking, I realize how often I find myself with younger women and how much I enjoy them. I recently mentored an independent study course, "Women in the Wilderness," for a group of young women at Prescott College, in Arizona. They had sought me out because of my experiences running rivers, organizing women's trips or mixed trips led by women, putting on environmental forums.[1] Many young women today are vitally interested in the wilderness, both as a place to be and as a dimension of life that needs understanding, protection, and conservation. Federica, Tsering, Christina, my friend from Switzerland, all of them seasoned travelers, remind me of my friends in Women in the Wilderness.

Federica nearly trips on a pot-hole as we continue; it's time to get out our flashlights. We'll be walking in the dark now, we made such a late start from Tulku Urgyen's. This road takes us down to the nearest village for a taxi, a bus, or a *tempo,* but it will take close to two hours to get there walking in the dark like this. There's only one working flashlight among us and the batteries are weak, so we can flash it on only when the ruts get bad. Friendship with these women has developed quickly, deepened by the distances we've traveled to be here and the experience of taking these teachings together.

Tsering tells us about a recent translating job during which a teacher from another country has been making sexual overtures to her, a married man traveling with a retinue of women. She feels uncomfortable, she tells us, very uncomfortable, but she has said nothing, yet. I find myself telling her to pay attention to her body, how she's feeling, to honor her intuition, to express her discomfort, to draw a boundary. I didn't know how to do that at her age.

The contrast between where young women in their twenties are today and where I was at their age is hard to grasp. It didn't occur to me to talk to women friends as Tsering talks to us now, to ask for advice. When I was twenty I was married and pregnant with my daughter, Madelon. She was my second child, with her brother, Matthew, thirteen months ahead of her. I was uncomfortable about anything that had to do with sexuality, I kept quiet.

I remember going at age twenty for a routine checkup at a maternity clinic for student wives. The examination had not gone well. I had told myself that the examination was uncomfortable, painfully so, because I was upset, because visits to gynecologists were inevitably embarrassing and stressful. I was a very young twenty-year-old who had spent fifteen years in Catholic schools, ten of them with only girls.

I thought that I was nervous, that if I relaxed it wouldn't be so painful, but no matter what, it was excruciating. How can I describe it thirty years later? I remember only the burning, what felt like a cut. Still I did not make a sound, I did not complain. My father, an officer in the Army Air Corps, had drilled it into me: "Don't cry. You're the oldest. You have to set an example for your brothers." And I was my father's daughter. I didn't say a word.

While I was still on the examination table, legs splayed, feet up in stirrups, a second doctor strode in and introduced himself as though we were meeting for the first time at a dinner party. He walked over to my feet, leaned down, peered in, then did his own examination. "Oh, here's a problem," he said to the first doctor. "You've got a little piece of the labia screwed into the speculum." Then, to me, "I bet that's a little painful, isn't it, dear?" as he unscrewed the speculum.

I was relieved. It wasn't only that I was nervous. I was in pain. Someone else had confirmed it. It was real. A doctor had said it was true. But still I didn't cry out as I wanted to. I was a good girl. I was a polite girl, a girl taught not to cry. I mustered my best dinner-party manner as I let out my breath and said, "Yes. Thank you, but who are you, what's going on?"

The dinner-party doctor informed me that the man I thought was my doctor was actually only a medical student and I was his lesson for the day. Then he began to give me a second exam himself while a line of men came in to watch. He explained in his pass-the-butter-please tone that the others standing and looking were also medical students. Then he asked the first doctor, who wasn't really a doctor, "almost, but not yet," to do the exam over. I gritted my teeth.

I said nothing. As a good girl, a polite girl, a girl taught not to cry or show pain or feel pain, I hardly noticed that something inside of me died again. It was only a little death, a tiny one, one of those deaths that happened so often and in such small measures that it was hardly noticeable, until one day I woke up and found whole organs and limbs missing.

I ended up back in that same hospital within two months, hospitalized because of that kind of silence. The marriage was brutal, the periodic violence erupting more and more often until finally I was on the verge of losing that baby, my daughter. The doctors found a Catholic priest who told me that I wasn't expected to risk my life or my children's, and instructed me to leave, file for a divorce and an annulment simultaneously, and I did.

When I reflect back on that exam thirty years ago when I was pregnant with my daughter, I remember another woman being carried out of the clinic crying hysterically. I hadn't heard the warning in her scream. I found out later that they had done over a dozen pelvic exams on her. "Doctors have to learn on somebody," I was told. I know how I felt after three exams and how clearly this episode came back to me after thirty years. How had it been for her? Had I not learned to reject my own experience, to deny it even as it was happening, I would have been screaming too.

I now know that I could have gotten up off that table, but I was a child at twenty. I already had one child and had been humiliated as a pregnant woman by a doctor more than once. I thought protest in this situation was futile. I didn't know I had a choice.

Years later I would discover how common my story was. Like many women, I carefully constructed a life around what I had cut off and I anesthetized myself. Undoing my cultural upbringing and the choices that I've made and that only I am responsible for has been a motivating force in my life and undoubtedly part of my need to go into the wilderness, to run wild, to learn from other women, and now to find this fierce sacred feminine. I needed to know how to include the anger, the fierceness, everything that I was taught to leave out as I learned to live discreetly within the closed system of male dominance. How much do we as women, consciously or unconsciously, pass these lessons on to our daughters? How much do we ignore our experience and silently collude in breaking their spirits, if only to teach them to survive? This is to apportion no blame, assign no fault, but only to provide a point of reference, a starting point. Change begins inside, in one's self.

I did not have words for questions like this until I met Michel Henry and heard her say that the biggest problem is not between men and women, it's the wound between women that needs to be healed today.

Michel Henry was part Cree, part Ojibwa, and part Irish. Born on the Turtle Mountain Reservation on the North Dakota–Canada border in 1939, raised in cities, Michel returned to the reservation in her late forties to find the women's lineage, the Native women elders who still knew the plants for medicine and healing. She started the Grandmothers' Project in order to document Native women elders' teachings. She wanted to know how these women functioned in their societies and how their teachings were passed on. Her own teacher was a Potawatomi elder from Minnesota, a firekeeper. I met Michel in New Mexico, shortly before she died of cancer.[2] We sat outside in the sunshine, talking on the patio of the home she made with friends who helped take care of her as she was dying. She was refreshingly straightforward. She had beat her prognosis for two years running, "cheating death" as the Tibetans say. She knew it was coming, and she faced it with her eyes wide open.

Native elders honor the negative powers, Michel told me. Native people don't act as though they're not real, as if they're not here. Ten years earlier, Michel had a vision in which she was shown a tear in the shield around the planet. The message that accompanied the vision she received was that women would know how to repair this tear. Michel's task was to take part in this repair, of both her own cancer and this tear in the planet's shield.

"I cried and cried," she told me, "I knew I couldn't do this by myself. I saw the breaking of the link with the divine in this vision. It was the most painful thing I've ever experienced. In it was the breaking of the heart connections from woman to woman."

This was the task the Grandmothers gave her to work on, healing the wound between women. We have to learn the old ways from the Grandmothers, we have to bring in the young women, we have to mentor them, she said. The Grandmothers are waiting. How did the wound get there?

"The biggest betrayal has been women betraying women. Once the wound between women is healed, the wound between men and women can heal; once the wound between men and women heals, the family can heal; once the family heals, the community can heal; and once the community heals, the world can be healed. That's what the Grandmothers say. That's what they told me."

I thought about Michel's message when I heard the stories of child prostitution the other night. Though I resist notions of women bearing special responsibility for the fate of the world—the premise in the Book of Genesis that has been so destructive—the idea of women healing other women seems undeniably important. I've thought of Michel's vision when I've read stories of female genital mutilation in which girls are often held down by the older women. I've thought of it when I recalled American stories I've heard of young girls sent to their fathers' beds by their mothers to "save the marriage." There are ways in which we as women collude and participate in the very systems that ravage us. This is much harder to look at, our own collusion. I began to look at mine.

The phrase "the wound between women" led to fruitful discussions with my daughter, Madelon, as I struggled to articulate what the wound was that I felt I had passed down to her, what I had taught her about having a woman's body. Madelon and I are close now after the years of recovery, so at first she tried to assure me that whatever harm I had done had been healed. We talked further. The wound between women. Then she reminded me of the times that I had humiliated her as a teenager, rejecting displays of girlishness on her part, crudely telling her that she smelled like a whore when she tried out a girlfriend's perfume, another time embarrassing her with comments in front of friends about her experiments with eye makeup. She said that I had her convinced that high heels were part of a male plot to keep women off balance and vulnerable, less able to fend off attack. This she still half believes, and says that she continues to prefer flat or low-heeled shoes. She grew up with a condescending attitude toward young women who had full breasts and showed them, who wore short skirts, perfume, and makeup, who were considered "feminine." Her model was asexual.

For me to buy Madelon a dress was a major event, in part because of all the frills and lace. To have dressed her in the ways that advertising modeled would have been like training her to let me put a bit in her mouth, so that later she could be broken. I resisted—with little consciousness and less sensitivity. I had been heavily influenced in turn by a convent school upbringing and the Catholicism of my day: woman as temptress, Eve, originator of sin; the body as wicked, separate from the soul, dangerous, something to be curbed, switched, and fought—in short, the enemy. I grew up with Catholic stories of women saints who shaved their heads, or disfigured themselves if they were beautiful, or miraculously grew a beard in order not to attract men. My mother's contribution may have simply been her very honorable commitment to giving me the best Catholic education possible and sending me to the nuns—without question.

The wound between women is a large subject, its ramifications unending, the experience of it with women friends especially painful; perhaps that's why many of us at times may have focused more on issues between men and women—but this is limiting, Michel said, and I agree. We also have to look to ourselves, to each other. This is what we can change—our part—what we as women do to each other, the ways in which we can hold each other back or help each other forward. We can empower one another in ways that no one else can. I resolve to go back to the Kusali Devi and request an initiation into the family of Ajima, the protectress of children. Initiation is empowerment. I want empowerment from a woman, from this self-realized healer who has enough confidence to follow her own wisdom in helping others. Yes, the teachings and initiations from high lamas can be extraordinary, but there's something in me now that knows that indigenous traditions also need to be honored, and women's wisdom constitutes its own indigenous tradition of what it takes to make and sustain life. If we healed the wound between women, would mothers still sell their daughters, their sons, their children? Could we stop the earth's poisoning? There is no one answer, only fruitful directions. If women healed the wound between women, and men the wound between men, this indeed would be revolutionary. Healing the wounds creates the bonds, gives them power.

The wound between women is the water between us and the farther shore. I dreamed that my mother kept me from being swept out to sea. Kept me from swimming. Kept me from the farther shore. Boat woman. Never let me depart. Did not hold me when I cried, did not nurse me, as I did not nurse my own daughter, because I did not know what to do with her, as my mother had not known what to do with me.

My daughter cried tears I could not cry. I was a good girl, I thought it was rude to howl, to show pain. Now I can let the moon waters break, stop holding this in. I don't have to be brave anymore, at least not falsely so.

In this wound between women, the nakedness is the hard part. This stripping away. I have walked so many miles, I am older now. I've grown so much closer to my own mother, who was nineteen, only a teenager, when she had me, her first child, her only daughter. She, like me, is no longer the young mother who didn't know what to do with a girl child who kept crying, as my daughter Madelon did, as I did.

They said that Madelon was colicky. Maybe so. But I know now that it was also that I couldn't face her pain. I was lost in my own at twenty-one, a single mother, battered, my life threatened, my children's, a divorced Catholic, with two infants and no child support.

My mother at nineteen, a wartime bride, part of a generation of women who did not always nurse their children. It was during World War II. My father was a bomber pilot and flight instructor, a good man carried away by the war. He wanted me, his first child, to be tough and strong, for my own good. He told my mother not to pick me up when I cried, that it would spoil me, weaken me. She was to check to be sure that I wasn't bleeding from a diaper pin or in any real physical danger and then leave the room. His advice was innocent and well intentioned and I doubt always adhered to. How many of us when alone and away from home knew what to do with our first child?

I did something similar to my daughter, but there was no man between my daughter and me, no one telling me what to do, giving me orders, there was only this gaping wound that she touched and the fact that I couldn't cry. The wound between women.

So much has healed thirty years later that I rarely feel this wound between my mother, my daughter, and myself. My mother came to me when my own children were young, saw me pick them up when they cried, and then cried herself, said she was sorry. She regretted that she hadn't listened to herself. I was grateful for her apology and her candor. I know well how you can hurt a child innocently, believing that you're doing what's best. Part of my mother's legacy has been to show me how to heal things. She is a gracious, generous woman. She has great integrity. She taught me how to say to my own children, "I'm so sorry. I didn't know better. What can I do now that will help you?" My own mistakes have been many, and they continue.

I cannot touch the pain of that time in my twenties anymore, but I am still picking up the pieces of all that was broken, clearing out the debris, it was such a big storm, a war. It took decades to repair. And what did my mother and her sister, my aunt, learn from their own mother? My grandmother, fiercely proud, starched, and dignified, the family center. She could never have admitted there were problems in her family, never talked about them. It wasn't done. It was a matter of breeding, an issue of class. And with six children there was no time.

Mother, grandmother, aunt. These women loved me deeply. They cared for, fed, and clothed my children when I could not, carried them, carried me when I was broken, walking around in shock, putting myself through graduate school, working, teaching. We lived at first with my parents, then my grandparents, who still had the house that could hold six children. We lived near one another, supported one another as best we could, were a tight clan. Family saved us, my children and me, took us in. Only we could never talk about what happened. Even among the women.

The wound between women is that space between us, where we kept ourselves apart, where we didn't talk, where we couldn't hold each other and cry.

The waters between us. The farther shore.

CHAPTER 8

THE GANGES HOLDS
EVERYTHING

*Meetings at the River's Edge
Banaras, India*

B ells clang in the dark. Four-thirty in the morning. Voices. People making their way to the river. It's now the end of October. I've come to Banaras, India. I can't get back to sleep, so I rise and open the shuttered doors of my room onto the hotel veranda. Everyone is still asleep, including the houseboy, who lies on the smooth green stone floor with an olive-colored wool blanket pulled over his head. I take pillows from my bed, double them over into a cushion, and sit on the door sill of the veranda, the pale yellow shuttered doors on either side of me providing privacy, allowing me to be unseen but open to the river. The sounds of the day beginning flow and swirl around me like a current: a man hacking, a dog barking, bells ringing, and the soft sound of women singing at the edge of the water. Morning begins early on the Ganges, well before dawn. But the Ganges is not only one of the world's greatest rivers, she is also a goddess, Ganga, the one who purifies all sins. To dip in Ganga's waters, to wash in them, is to have all forgiven. She is the great cleanser, the great purifier.

The Goddess Ganga is so powerful, it was said, that if she descended to the earth, she would destroy it. When she came down from the Milky Way in the form of a river, Shiva let the river fall on his head and cascade through his curls to break the impact. Such is

MORNING ON THE GANGES RIVER, BANARAS, INDIA
(*Mary Ellen Mark*)

the power of the divine feminine, the *shakti,* the power of the cosmos. The Ganges is "liquid *shakti.*"

Banaras, also known as Varanasi, is one of the oldest continuously inhabited cities in the world. An antique map showing the pilgrim's route for circumambulating this city, sacred to Shiva, Lord of the Universe, hangs on the wall of the main room of this small hotel. It shows Banaras in the air, balanced on the points of Shiva's trident. If one dies in Kashi, the City of Light, as devout Hindus call it, it is said that Shiva himself will whisper a prayer, the Taraka mantra, in your ear and ferry you across the shores of birth and death to liberation. To die in Banaras *is* to achieve liberation.[1]

Though many come here to die, the city bustles with life and celebration. Commerce thrives in this holiest of Indian cities. I've come to Banaras on my way to Kali Puja, in Calcutta, to see Tara Doyle, my old friend, who is here awaiting the arrival of Chökyi Nyima and students from America for the Buddhist Studies Program of Antioch College.

Taking teachings together, traveling, sharing the twists and unexpected turns of the road has held my friendship with Tara Doyle together for years despite long separations and great distances. It was Tara Doyle who first took me to Pharping, who guided me through my first initiation into meditation practice on the Buddha Tara. It was Tara Doyle who first showed me a photograph of the Black Madonna at Einsiedeln, Switzerland, just outside of Zurich. And it was in Banaras, where I've come to see Tara again, that I first glimpsed a connection between East and West that has illumined my life. It was here during a visit to a Shiva temple that I was led into a small shrine room to see a striking coal-black statue that I was assured was the Goddess Kali.[2] She looked nothing like the fearsome warrior who sprang from Durga's forehead. Instead her peaceful, serene expression reminded me of both the Tibetan Buddhist Tara and the radiant Black Madonna of Switzerland that Tara had shown me. The Black Madonna gave me a way back, opened a door, let me go home and reclaim my own tradition, weave it back into this path.

At first light, Tara Doyle comes to take me to watch the sun rise. Music blares from a nearby radio and monkeys shriek from the parapets as we climb three flights of narrow stairs to the roof of Alice Boner's 250-year-old house, still a private home. Alice Boner, a Swiss painter and sculptor who moved to Banaras in the 1940s, between the two world wars, had visions of Kali and transformed them into large, powerful paintings. We step out onto the wide flat roof covered with hot pink bougainvillea in bloom and walk to the edge, leaning over the side to get a full view of the sweep of the river. Dawn on the Ganges is a raucous affair. The river, silvery and vast, turns pale pink under the rose of sky as the sun comes up. The birds in the pipal tree below are loud and insistent now. Women come to make their morning offerings beneath its generous branches.

Tara's dark hair is streaked with silver, as is mine. Many years have passed since we first met. She points to the pipal tree, beneath which women in colored saris light candles and sit in circles singing.

"This is a wonderful time to be in India," Tara says. "It's the lunar month of Karttika, the holy month for women. Many women vow to bathe in the river every day before sunrise, and on *chat,* the sixth day of the waxing moon, they fast. The *chat* ceremony can be performed only by women who have had children."

The Ganges is cold at four-thirty in the morning, when the women start to bathe and sing. Those who observe this fast eat no meat, no fish, no garlic, and no onions during Karttika, yet they continue their normal day's work, Tara explains. It is very hard to fast and to work.

At the river's edge a series of bamboo poles are stuck in the sand with small baskets suspended from them, some of them arching out over the river with candles burning inside. The candles are lit for the souls of the dead, a form of remembrance that dots the shore, every candle a prayer.

"Look, more are coming. The men support the women who observe Karttika, they're respected for keeping their fast. The other women, the children. See? Everyone supports them. Here they come," she says, pointing to the line of men and families carrying baskets of food on their head, passing below us now, with red hibiscus flowers on top of trays of saffron rice and fresh green sprigs. Some play music, all are singing as they file past Boner's house. More women gather under the pipal tree. The little candles in the baskets for the dead by the river can hardly be made out now, it grows so light, and still the women circle the great tree, chanting and singing, making their offerings, and dancing.

The Ganges gleams silver. A playful donkey rolls over on his back in the white riverbank sand. White donkey, white sand, he stands up and shakes, setting off fiery sparklers of light shooting out in the rising sun.

The sun warms my face as it rises, bathing Tara's face in the soft gold light that's now brightening. I marvel, watching her profile as she turns to the river to point out something to me again. Does this woman know how deeply she's affected my life, how rare our friendship is, strengthened over the years despite the distance, never diminished?

Later she takes me through the ancient streets and byways to a tiny perfumery, where we buy rose oil, jasmine, and ferouze. Banaras is famous for its silk saris—pinks edged in real gold, blues like midnight, muted moss greens—hanging in open-air stalls, next to minuscule shops, filled with ornaments of Kali, Durga, and Ganga, and bright-colored decorations for the coming festivals of Kali Puja and Dewali, the Festival of Lights. The streets are crowded with pedestrians, cows, and goats. Bone-thin dogs doze in the heat. On one street we walk past an enormous pile of garbage at least fifteen feet wide and four feet high, the heap sparkling with streamers of bright red, blue, gold, orange, and silver Mylar, and topped with three huge Brahma cows lying comfortably chewing their cuds.

We make our way down the street, a busy city thoroughfare, past a herd of water buffalo with black flat heads, curved horns, and wide bodies covered with thin hair swirled in large circles over their hides. In every street there are cows crossing, lying down, or lounging comfortably on traffic meridians. Buses, cars, *tempos*—motorized rickshaws—bicycles, taxis, and bullock carts weave their way around them in an ongoing cacophony of bells, horns, and shouts. I am grateful we're staying on the river, where there's more quiet.

The Ganges View Hotel is a small, tasteful hotel, formerly the women's house for the Raj of Banaras. Nineteenth-century blown-glass lamps hang from the ceiling. Prints and paintings of Krishna line the walls. A small statue of Kali, dressed in tiny clothes and jewels, sits on a table in the cool, high-ceilinged room.

By eleven at night, the air is still hot and full of the sound of crickets. The overhead fan churns the air in loud chops that drown out all noise but for occasional shouts from down by the river. A pale green grasshopper lands on my bed, a salamander scurries across the wall. I lie awake reading a copy of Alice Boner's *Diaries* that Tara took from the hotel desk for me after dinner. Boner says that we need to understand Kali, and though I agree with her instinctively, I know that I will never understand Kali by reading a book. This is why I'm going to Calcutta, for Kali Puja, the central feast of Kali for the year. For now it is enough to be in Banaras, by Ganga, the fierce Goddess for whom the River Ganges is named.

I go down to the river the next day in the morning darkness, the sand cold and wet on my feet. The women are again lighting candles and making prayers around the pipal tree. Some are still in the river, bathing and offering *arati*, waving the small five-flamed lamp over the water as I approach. I keep my distance so as not to disturb them. A young man appears and signals for me to climb into a boat. Yes. He gives me a hand in, then pushes the boat off as he stays on shore to find more customers. It is his father who is rowing, a strong, old man who wears a yellow-green shawl wrapped around his neck.

The devout and the pilgrims are at the riverside *ghats,* the broad steps into the water, the landings all along the river, praying, washing, and offering *arati*, their tiny flames waving from the shore in the half-light. *Dhobhi wallas*, the laundry washers, wring out clothes and swat them on the stone steps with a *thwap* that echoes across the river. A boat glides by, full of tourists armed with video cameras, and zoom lenses and fancy motor drives on their 35mm cameras. Whirr, click, pop: lights flash like small firecrackers going off in succession. Then they're gone and it's quiet again. I am happy to have brought no camera, no paper.

A large gray shape suddenly arcs up and out of the water, then disappears in a heartbeat, leaving my heart pounding. "Dolphin," the boatman says insistently. I shake my head. "Dolphin," he keeps repeating. No. Yes. He's right. It is a dolphin, a freshwater dolphin. The Ganges and the Amazon in Latin America are both home to this species. I take this dolphin as a blessing, a sign of the river's vitality despite the severe environmental crisis that it now faces.

Broad, flat leaves threaded together into tiny boats holding burning candles float by on the water, followed by the bloated corpse of a cow. The Ganges holds everything, purifies it, carries everything away—or so it was thought for thousands of years. Today pollution threatens the Ganges and consequently the 350 million people in this watershed who depend on her enormous body for life. The Ganges runs down from the Himalayas in the north, cutting across the plains to the Bay of Bengal at Calcutta. I think of Fran Peavey and Dr. Veer Bhadra Mishra, Mahant-ji, as his friends call him, as we row past the *ghats* and Mahant-ji's temple. Fran was in Banaras nearly fifteen years ago and met Mahant-ji, the head of the Sankat Mochan Temple, here on the river in Banaras. Mahant-ji is also a professor of hydraulic engineering at Banaras Hindu University. He told Fran of his concern for the river at that meeting, eventually asking her to join in his efforts as director of the Sankat Mochan Foundation to clean up the river. It is no easy task to clean up a river that 800 million people call holy. Even to say that the Ganges is polluted is to profane the river to a devout Hindu.

I think of Fran and smile to myself in the morning breeze, the growing light, with the sound of the oars creaking rhythmically in the oarlocks. Founder of Crabgrass, a nonprofit social-change organization with projects in both India and the former Yugoslavia as well as the San Francisco Bay Area, social philosopher, comedienne, activist, and author of *By Life's Grace* and *Heart Politics,* Fran

Peavey has differed with me about my use of the word "hope" for years. Some Buddhists reject it altogether.

"It's the wrong word," she insists. "Hope is not what you mean, China. It's grace, that's what you're talking about. It's inappropriate to expect hope. It's irrelevant. It's born out of denial. Hope doesn't walk you through the narrows."

"I do mean *hope*, Fran, not in a foolish sense. People need hope, they need inspiration. We have to believe that something is possible in order to take action. That's one of the most important things we can do for our children, give them hope. If people are hopeless they don't act."

"I still say it's not the word you want, China," she tells me. "I'm against hope," she says with a big laugh. "I still think the word is *grace*—or maybe *faith*. Grace and faith are much more of what we have, what's available. I think the Dalai Lama has given up hope. He's found grace. Hope is a burden."

Some years ago Fran and I had a heated interchange about space travel. We argued. At the time, she was for it, I was against it. I suspect that Fran and I might disagree on many matters, at least superficially. Nonetheless, I follow Fran's projects with interest. Whether she would approve or not, she gives me hope, points a direction.

Fran knows how to generate fierce compassion and plunge into what look like impossible situations. When war broke out in the former Yugoslavia, Fran and Tova Green decided to visit the women in the refugee camps and see what they could do to be helpful. They wrote a letter to eighty-five friends telling them of their upcoming trip, and offered to carry small gift packets to the women in the camps as expressions of goodwill. Fran and Tova suggested small items that one could not get during a war—lipstick, stockings, socks, hair ribbons, items for personal care, things that might remind them of the joy and dignity of being women. Their plan was to fill their allotted baggage quota with gifts and take their own few items of clothing in their carry-on luggage.

What happened was that the eighty-five friends were so moved by their offer and the idea of sending packets that they photocopied the letter, and by the time Fran and Tova were ready to leave, they had received eight thousand packages to take to the women in the refugee camps. Eight thousand carefully wrapped packages, with notes and letters attached. It was an outpouring of concern so large that at first they were overwhelmed. But in the end, they raised the money to ship all the packages and distribute them to the women of the former Yugoslavia. The people they visited there asked them to come back again and to bring artists to perform, so the next time they took a group of women performers and musicians, the Doves, with them. One trip precipitated another, and each time Fran and Tova returned, they knew what people needed—medical supplies, vitamins, embroidery thread and yarn to support women rebuilding an economy through crafts, training in elements of conflict resolution and learning to live with differences. This takes up one part of Fran's and Tova's prodigious energy for the year.[3]

Another part of Fran's time is spent on this project here in Banaras, helping Mahant-ji and his many colleagues in India clean up the Ganges.

Several years ago Fran decided that it would be hard to work for global change having rarely traveled outside of the United States. So she packed her bags, made herself a sign, and set out to travel. At key points on her journey she would find a central location in the city she was in, sit down, and put her sign on: "American Willing to Listen."

It was during this round-the-world journey that she first met Mahant-ji. Later he came to see her in the United States and told her that he was ready to expand his efforts for the Ganges. He wanted her to help.

"I was so scared," Fran told me, smiling at her initial apprehension. "I thought that meant he wanted me to move to India. I couldn't do that. But I always try to say yes, to find a way. So I said that I would come once a year for five years and help figure out a strategy. I didn't know anything about cleaning up rivers. I grew up along the Snake River in Idaho, and I never thought about cleaning it up. But I knew about social change—how to move a society from one reality to another. That's quite a project."

Fran came to Banaras for the next five years as she had promised, and developed what she calls "strategic questioning," a process to elicit information from people about how they would solve a problem. It was Fran's way of developing a strategy from the place itself rather than coming in with preconceived notions from the outside.

"The river Ganges, Ganga, made me develop that process," she told me, "in answer to her greatness. I just started asking people questions: 'What would you like to do to help the Ganges? How do you see the river?'"

At the end of five years, Fran told her Indian colleagues that she had fulfilled her commitment and she was going to stop coming to help them. They had a strategy, many strategies: there was an electric crematorium operating, three sewage treatment plants in various stages of development, a study on alternative sewage treatment systems (low-energy ponding) under way, and an international community of support for Mahant-ji and the work of the Sankat Mochan Foundation, the Friends of the Ganges.[4] It was time for her to move on. But her Indian friends couldn't understand why she would stop now. Because of what she had said five years earlier? Had she lost her mind? She had a relationship with them and with the river Ganges. They thought it was silly to stop because of some Western concept of work and professionalism and independence. Relationship was what was important. Finally they convinced her.

"I never thought I'd be cleaning up Ganga for the rest of my life, but that seems to be what I'm doing. I've made a commitment to come at least once a year from now on."

I think of the meanings of the word "fierce" that apply to Fran: valiant, ardent, zealous, passionate. She loves Ganga.

Fran taught herself about sewage treatment, water-borne disease, and water treatment, and organized a small NGO called Women for Water. With a group of women from Banaras called Jeevan Snayu Sanrakshan, which means "Nerve of Life," they co-sponsored a small international conference called "Women and Water," here on the river in Banaras. The first gathering followed up their work on "Women and Water" at the Fourth World Conference on Women in Beijing. Water is a woman's issue. Women and children around the world from India to Africa are spending increasing numbers of hours of the day finding and hauling water and wood/fuel for bare survival. Hours of the day must be devoted to these unpaid tasks for survival *before* work can be performed for wages. As more forests are destroyed, women have farther to walk to find fuel. With the trees gone the watersheds are drying out—meaning that women have to walk even farther to find water. Not only is hauling water time-consuming, it is exhausting. One gallon of water weighs eight pounds; carrying two gallons, sixteen pounds, of water, for even one mile is more than many of us can imagine. Often women have to walk two miles or more to find the day's water for their families. As chemicals and pesticides are used to stimulate crops, the waters are increasingly poisoned, both ground water and surface waters. Sewage treatment is poor or nonexistent. Women and children are the first to be affected. Seventy percent of the villages in India no longer have potable water. The bottled water I drink as I travel comes at a high price, easy enough for me to pay for, but the largest portion of India's population cannot afford such a luxury. The World Health Organization estimates that 80 percent of all diseases in developing countries are related to unsafe drinking water and inadequate hygiene.[5] Thousands upon thousands of infants and children under the age of five die of water-borne diseases.

As the boatman nears the cremation *ghats*, I understand why electric crematoria have been introduced. Small boats laden with trees extending far beyond their sides are slowly rowed to the ancient shore. The muddy banks with cremation fires roaring look like a scene out of Dante's *Purgatorio.* The temples here at Manikarnika *ghat* are blackened from thousands of years of funeral pyres. There are two burning this morning. A constant stream of wood is being laboriously hauled, one section of a tree trunk at a time, to a spot where men split the trunks into smaller pieces for the fires. Then the burning, the mourners in white, and the shrouded bodies golden in flames.

The last time I saw Fran was on a winter evening in a friend's home, to raise money for the Women and Water conference in India. We sat in front of a winter's blazing fire and went around the room telling stories of the bodies of water that had been important to us. We told stories of growing up by water, of the sweet waters of creeks and rivers, of salty ocean and bay waters, of the waters that we loved, or feared, of the waters in which we had almost drowned. We reflected on the exhilaration of a dip in icy snow-melt waters in mountain streams, of the bracing cold of the Pacific winter swell, and of the healing power of waters: hot springs, steamy sweats, our own perspiration—saltwater. But the most moving story of all that night was the story from Sarajevo of water as a telltale sign. Mircad, Fran and Tova's Bosnian friend, couldn't bring himself to tell his ninety-five-year-old deaf and blind grandmother that there was one more war in the former Yugoslavia. She had already survived four European wars in her lifetime.

Every morning he would bring her coffee and a bottle of water and her cigars, until one morning the most precious, most costly commodity—the bottled water that he had struggled each day to buy—was no longer available.

"Grandmother, there is no water," he finally had to tell her.

She shook her head. She knew then. "They have started another war."

I'm disappointing Tara by leaving so soon after my arrival. My sense of urgency about getting to Calcutta in time for Kali Puja, on November 2, has created tension between us, a strain, and I find myself with no way to convey my feelings to Tara, no words.

Many mornings I've recalled being with Tara back in Chökyi Nyima's room as he gave me my first meditation on Buddha Tara, a Green Tara initiation. I was in Nepal, in a sun-soaked room taking Refuge with a Buddhist teacher, learning meditation instead of plunging further into alcoholism, the direction in which I had been headed. I wept. Like the beggar in an old Hindu story who was chosen to be king despite innumerable others more qualified, I cannot account for my good fortune. Could I let myself give Tara Doyle a ceremonial scarf, a *khata*, as I would give a teacher, could I honor her for the spiritual treasures she's given me? There are no greater riches to be shared.

When we get back to the Ganges View Hotel, I ask Tara to take a moment and come to my room with me. Then I do something very daring—for me. I sit Tara down, turn to my suitcase and pull out the longest white silk scarf that I have, and turn back to her smiling, holding it up to offer to her, as I would to a respected teacher. She protests, but I insist. She accepts the scarf, taking it from my folded hands, tossing it over the back of my neck. We touch our foreheads together for a long moment, taking in this gesture, silently. Sweet sister.

Michel Henry's words from the Grandmothers come back to me, "The wound that needs to be healed is the wound between women. When that wound is healed, then the wound between men and women can be healed. When the wound between men and women is healed, the family will be healed. When the family is healed, the community is healed. When the community is healed, the world will be healed."

CHAPTER 9

LIFE REVERED IS
LIFE REVEALED

The Festival of Kali, Calcutta

Memsa'b, memsa'b," I hear a man's voice calling. I look around Calcutta's Howrah Station and see no one. Then I realize that the voice is coming from below, from a man on all fours who moves like a monkey, with a twisted body, unable to stand upright. He wears an aluminum begging bowl on his back and turns sideways so that his bowl is in front of me.

I give him what rupees I have, then remember the bag of apples and a package of biscuits left from the overnight train ride from Banaras in my pack. I pull the apples out and he nods approvingly. He follows me to the door of my taxi and hunches on all fours in the street by the car while I dig out the biscuits. The driver and the young man sent to fetch me are piling my luggage into the trunk when another taxi wants to back in next to us and begins honking angrily at the beggar as though he were a donkey in the road. I yell at the cabby to hold up. The beggar hops up on the curb, gives me another big smile from his open face, and begins to open the package of biscuits.

The level of pollution in Calcutta is especially difficult after I've already been choking on the fumes of Kathmandu and Banaras. Calcutta is larger. I pull out my greenscreen and put it on in the backseat of the taxi. Modern travel. We inch our way past enormous piles of rotting garbage, crumbling buildings, rusting poles, and traffic enclosures that have fallen off the traffic island into the street and are left to lie there. The traffic from the train station at Howrah

is in a gargantuan snarl. We wind our way down a major thoroughfare at ten to fifteen miles per hour. The taxi stopped next to us at a
long light is full of men weighed down with flowers. One has an
armload of red gladiolus, another has a lap piled high with garlands
of bright marigolds and red hibiscus, another holds an armful of
white tuberoses. It's sticky and humid at 10:00 A.M., the air stinking
with garbage and pollution, but the scent of tuberoses is so strong
and sweet that I can smell them through the open windows. Calcutta is Kali's city. It is sacred to her, and her celebration is in the air.

Dr. Aditi Sen, the Director of the American Institute for Indian
Studies, greets me at the door of the Institute, where I will stay, and
shows me to my room. She's a tall, graceful woman with lively, in-
telligent eyes, who wears a soft green sari. She has agreed to be my
guide in Calcutta.

Kali Puja is an annual celebration similar to Durga Puja, only it
takes place in November, the month after Durga's feast, and it is
shorter. In Calcutta, each neighborhood or district pools its resources to build a temporary shrine to Kali, a *pandal*. The first one I
see is small, not much larger than the statue itself, large enough for
only one person to step inside and leave some coins for an offering.
Others are more elaborate, larger, like the next one, three blocks up
the street from the Institute. Round, more like a yurt made out of
bamboo and canvas, nearly thirty feet in diameter, this *pandal* has
quite a bit of activity going on around it. Inside, a children's art con-
test to see who can draw the most imaginative picture of Kali has
been in progress. The drawings decorate the canvas walls: Kalis
with peace signs, a Kali with doves, and the winning Kali, an open,
inviting face with a big smile, drawn in crayon in the unsteady hand
of a child. To children growing up with Kali, she seems a loving
presence in whom they trust, not a fearsome figure. My eyes moisten
at the number of peace signs I see in the children's art, their yearning.

Other *pandals* are more elaborate and strung with lights. Some
look like extravaganzas out of movie sets. The city has the air of

Christmastime in the States, when people place Nativity scenes in their front yards, only here it's done on a neighborhood basis rather than by individual houses, and it's Kali who's being celebrated.

Though a smaller feast, five days as opposed to Durga's nine, Kali's celebration is lively, marked by the explosion of fireworks and marching bands at nights, especially bands of drums. At dinner that night our meal is interrupted by the insistent beat of drummers. We hurry to our third-floor balcony to watch the drummers passing, rounding the corner of our street below. Bands on foot follow a slow-driving flatbed truck with a statue of Kali on the truck bed, facing them, lit up from underneath. She is graceful and pretty, a pearl-gray color, not like the terrifying black hag of the *Devi-Mahatmya,* when she sprang full-blown from Durga's forehead armed and eager for battle.

Kali, like Durga, with whom she is also associated, defies easy categorization. Often misunderstood as being only the destroyer, Kali is also called the Creatrix and Preserver, the Origin of all things in the Tantra of Great Liberation. Called Kali because she devours Kala—time—she is also that force within the universe that cuts through misconceptions. It can be said that on one level she represents that which lives outside the boundaries of "normal" society. On another level she can be seen as a symbol of the fact that there is something larger going on in life that is not influenced by, nor does it yield to, the ways of humankind.

Kali reminds us of the fact that life is disorderly, wild, untamable, and unpredictable. At the same time, she is the Divine Mother to whom her children turn in times of suffering and disaster. Kali is full of contradiction. Even her appearance is shocking and unconventional. At times enormous, emaciated, with pendulous breasts and four arms, her long tongue hanging out; at times a beautiful, dark, dancing woman, glistening and gleaming. She has red forms, white forms, peaceful forms, and aniconic—nonrepresentational—forms too, though her best-known forms are dark and wild. I think of her as a way that Hinduism has found to affirm and include all that has been rejected.[1] She is a symbol not only of death but of life and victory over death. Fearlessness is the boon she grants. She is the fierce feminine personified, Queen of the Void, vast as space itself.

The boom of firecrackers in the street wakes me at 7:00 A.M. It's November 2, 1994, the beginning of Kali Puja, and still hot in India. Today we go to Kalighat, the main Kali Temple in the city and the center of Kali worship.

Our taxi pulls into a stall and stops amidst throngs of people coming and going around the temple complex. A *pujari,* a temple priest, is by my side the moment I step out. He speaks English well and tells me to buy garlands of red hibiscus and red bangles and sweets to feed Kali. My companions, two scholars of Hinduism, one Indian, one American, nod yes, yes. The red hibiscus is Kali's favorite flower. We join the stream of people going to the temple for Kali Puja.

Standing in line, waiting to go into the shrine, people chat amongst themselves, it's calm, but at the door to the shrine the way narrows. That's when the pushing starts, the energy gets wild. It's as though the air has changed and there's a storm inside, a storm of devotion, a hurricane of feelings as people call out to Kali, cry to her. Inside, people are reaching out to her statue, offering their red flowers, rice, money, the red bangles, to the priests, to the image, fighting to touch her, to get some of her power, to have their prayers granted. This Kali is an enormous piece of black stone, basalt, with orange *tika* on her head and a huge gold tongue, perhaps three feet long, hanging out of her mouth. She is wreathed in garlands of flowers. The energy is frantic with men yelling, with the heat, the pushing, cooking the crowds packed together, one moves as the crowd

KALI FESTIVAL AT NIMTALA GHAT, CALCUTTA, INDIA
(*Manuel Bauer*)

moves, alone you are powerless. *Pujaris* walk back and forth, chanting and shouting.

I'm jammed in the middle of the swell, the priests calling out Kali's mantra, bells clanging, the people pushing; suddenly I am pulled into the inner sanctum. A priest hands me orange *tika* powder to touch Kali herself on her *puja* day, the most auspicious day of the year. The *pujari* shouts in my ear, "Touch it! Touch the tongue of Kali!" I reach through the railing and touch what seems like an endless tongue. It's hot, smooth, and moist now, damp because everyone who touches it is dripping with the sweat of this frenzied throng, squeezed so small and tight, pushed, carried along in this energy that moves us all beyond our own doing. Then I touch her feet and in a moment I'm swept out into the surrounding courtyard.

This is the great tongue that Kali used to sweep the battlefield clean, to defeat Raktabija, the worst demon of all. This is the tongue she used to lick up all his blood so that no more demons could arise. Licked Raktabija clean, licked the ground around him, defeated him without a blow. With only her tongue. She surrounded him.

Kali's tongue is long because she's a purifier, there is nothing she's afraid to touch, even with her tongue. To have her approach you, her mouth open, her tongue hanging out, her terrible laugh, is horrifying, if you see her coming. But often you can't. You don't know she's there until your life is falling apart, being stripped away, and you're trying desperately to hold on but everything you touch falls away, down to the last tooth in your mouth.

First the darkness of her open maw—then comes her tongue, long, clean, licking everything off you, taking it away, cutting through and destroying your illusions. She will purify your life, free you, if you recognize her, with gratitude.

The *pujari* breaks my reverie, asking me if I want to watch the animal sacrifice. When I say yes, he pushes me toward some steps from which I can see the blocked-off area where several small black goats bleat, awaiting their death. There are bowls of money for offerings and two wooden staves that the goat's head fits neatly between. A *pujari* takes a young man's head in his hands and bangs it against one of the staves three times. My heart leaps for a moment, then the young man is thrust aside with great force. The small black goat he is offering is grabbed by the hind legs, bleating crazily, picked up expertly by all four legs at once, its head inserted between the dark, well-worn staves. Another man picks up a large, wide, curved knife. Everyone's eyes are on him. The *pujari* tells me that I can turn my eyes away if I want. I say nothing. I want to watch. I want to see this one small goat go through what millions of animals go through in American slaughterhouses, far away from any prayers or temples or blessings or thought that taking its life is a solemn ritual act.

Thwack! The knife comes down in one deft blow, leaving the small black head, eyes still open, between the staves. The body slumps toward the ground but is caught before it even touches. My stomach turns and I feel light-headed. In India what is so hidden in our culture—the killing it takes to feed it—is out in the open, visible.

Blood spurts out of the goat's neck. Another man removes the head from the staves, and, in one swift movement, the goat's body is gathered up and handed to another man to prepare for cooking. It goes immediately to the kitchen right outside the temple. There, food is cooked all day, and the poor are fed all the offerings. Nothing is wasted. Kali, I am told, is a vegetarian.

I return to my room at the Institute to prepare to go to the famous Kali Temple at Dakshineswar, in the northern part of the city, on the banks of the Ganges. Aditi, who will accompany me, warns that the dress I'm wearing from Banaras may be made of highly flammable synthetics, that people have died during this crowded celebration when their clothes caught fire from firecrackers or candles. I decide to change into cotton.

By evening when it's time to leave it's begun to drizzle. The road is pitted and full of holes. Because of the rain, many *pandals* are nearly empty, though strings of colored lights hang everywhere. Tomorrow, the day after Kali Puja, is Dewali, the Festival of Lights, celebrating the victory of good over evil.

We make our way slowly to the riverbanks. There the soaring curves of the temple at Dakshineswar loom softly white through the rain. This nineteenth-century temple was built by a woman devotee of Kali, the remarkable Rani Rasmani of whom Elizabeth U. Harding writes in her book *Kali: The Black Goddess of Dakshineswar*.[2] Born into a poor, low-caste family north of Calcutta, the Rani was devoted to Kali from the time of her childhood. She became an exceptionally beautiful woman. One day when she was bathing in the Ganges, a wealthy man from Calcutta saw her as he was being rowed down the river. He could not get the Rani out of his mind thereafter, and so returned to seek her out and ask her father to give her to him as his wife. When her father agreed, overnight the Rani became a wealthy woman and moved from a poor village north of the city to a mansion in a fashionable part of Calcutta. By the age of forty-four, she found herself a widow with four daughters and a vast estate to manage. The Rani handled it with great skill, success, and wit. It was said that her devotion to Kali made her fearless. She became an outspoken champion of civil rights who often bested the British. The Rani said Kali would protect her, and that if Kali didn't, then nothing in this world could save her. It was the Rani's profound devotion to Kali that brought the temple at Dakshineswar into being, and it is the effect of Kali on the Rani that draws and inspires my interest. Ardent, zealous, high-spirited, valiant, these several meanings of fierce apply to Rani Rasmani.

The Rani was preparing to make a pilgrimage to Kashi (Banaras) by boat in 1847, a six-month journey at that time. Provisions were made. It took twenty-four boats and months of preparation to accommodate the Rani, her daughters, and her entourage. Yet the night before she was to depart, Kali appeared to Rani in a dream and told her, "There is no need to go to Kashi. Install my image on a beautiful spot on the bank of the Ganga and arrange for my daily worship and food offering; I shall manifest myself in the image and accept your daily worship."[3]

The Rani halted her departure immediately, seeing to it the next day that all food and provisions were distributed to the poor, and that the money for travel was put aside for the purchase of land and the construction of a temple, which began that same year, 1847.

The Kali Temple is ornate, white, one hundred feet high, domed, with a walkway around the fifty-foot shrine where Aditi and I line up now to view this Bhavatarini Kali, this "Mother who is the Savior of the World," and take *darshan,* that is, see Kali and receive the blessing of her gaze. The temple itself sits in the center of a large cobblestone courtyard now full of people. It faces the Natmandir, Aditi explains, an open-air columned structure for singing and resting in view of the Goddess. The twenty-acre temple complex also includes twelve smaller Shiva temples to one side, a Vishnu temple, and a temple to Krishna and Radha, his wife, which we will view later, after we see Kali.

The temple was formally opened on May 31, 1855. Ramakrishna Paramahamsa (1836–86), the great nineteenth-century Hindu saint, came to the temple at the age of nineteen. Within a year he had become the chief priest, and he continued as such for thirty years.

Thus began the story of Dakshineswar, born out of the fierce devotion of a poor, low-caste woman who rose to great prominence. It was the Rani who found Ramakrishna, who became one of the most revered and best-known saints of India. It was the Rani who supported him and protected him for the rest of her life. Before she died she charged her son-in-law with the responsibility of caring for Ramakrishna, which he did faithfully until Ramakrishna's death. He then took over the care of Ramakrishna's widow, the beloved Sarada Devi, the emanation of the Divine Mother, whom Ramakrishna also worshipped and relied upon, as did his disciples after his death.

Ramakrishna's wisdom and visions have greatly informed my life, as they have untold thousands. His influence in the West has been profound.[4] He was renowned for his utter surrender to God. Though for him this took the form of devotion primarily to the Goddess Kali, Ramakrishna also studied Christianity and had visions of Christ and Mary. When he studied Islam, he had visions of Mohammed. Ramakrishna, like mystics throughout the ages, had not only grasped but experienced first-hand what many still struggle to understand today: that while God may be one, the faces and names of God are many.

It's nearly ten o'clock at night, the dark of the moon. We are early, so we wander down to the Ganges, making our way barefoot, as must all pilgrims, across the slick, wet cobblestone courtyard.

I want to stand in the water to be cleansed, I realize as Aditi and I walk down the *ghat,* the ancient steps into the river. Tomorrow is my birthday, the first half of my life is gone, I turn fifty-one at midnight. I want to be washed, freed, and healed by the Ganges. I stand barefoot on the lower steps, at the edge of the water, where the *ghat* is already wet from the river's ebb and flow, and step down into the water. Suddenly a man starts shouting. Others join him. Aditi is just behind me, about to follow me in. Why are they shouting? I can't understand what they're saying. I'm exhausted, excited; away from home for weeks, I want only the washing away of all unkindness and ambition, selfishness, pride—all hurt and anger at what is happening to the children, to the air, the water, to the earth, to all that is vulnerable. I want to be washed clean, purified.

The shouting grows louder. The crowd on the *ghat* turns like a flock of birds in flight suddenly changing direction with a flick of their wings; all the people around us are moving away from the water. They keep shouting, now at us. Is this part of the festival? I take another step, down further into the water lapping my feet. Aditi now joins the shouting. "Run!" she yells, grabbing my hand, pulling me back up the steps hard. "A tidal wave!" she shouts. Has she gone mad?

In that moment, I look up and see an immense wall of water stretching out across the entire width of the Ganges, bearing down swiftly, rising out of the darkness. It is a single wave, white-capped and arching, rising, I can't tell how high, only that it is enormous. From the time I look up and see the water under the bridge at what seemed like a distance, until the moment I realize what is happening, the wave is already here, breaking and sweeping over the *ghat*. Everyone, including me now, is running to escape its crash. There is a whoosh as it licks the *ghat* clean, and then it's gone, leaving the boats tied up nearby rocking wildly from side to side.

"A tidal bore!" Aditi explains. "Two years ago seven people drowned in one. They were standing in the water, like you. Nobody saw it coming. Suddenly it appeared, washed them all away, and was gone, like that. It happens every now and then at the dark of the moon."

My feet are wet, the wave licked them. Kali's tongue, her kiss.

Breathless, shaken by our near encounter with what could have been death, we make our way back into the main courtyard beneath the graceful temple complex to stand in the women's line for *darshan,* the viewing of the Goddess. I ask Aditi to buy extra flowers and incense in bowls made from fresh leaves filled with rice, marigolds, roses, and red hibiscus, Kali's favorite flower, to make offerings. I am grateful to still be among the thousands in the throng tonight. The wait gives me time to collect myself, the line moves along evenly until Aditi and I are inside and the temple doors close behind me. We are the last ones in.

Finally I am able to see this famous Kali in her room, framed by silver, standing on Shiva's white marble body, which lies on a large silver lotus. Ramakrishna was devoted to this particular statue of Kali. She sprang to life for him many times.

Brilliant lights bathe the shrine room. This statue of Kali looks larger than it is, only thirty-three inches tall. Standing erect on the chest of her consort Shiva, her right foot forward, this coal-black basalt Kali is dressed in a brilliant red, gold-edged Bengal sari tonight, covered with offerings of necklaces of white tuberoses, yellow and orange marigolds, and red hibiscus.

Ramakrishna sat before this image of Kali for years, tending her, living a life of devotion to her, for to Hindus, the *murti* is not only the image of the deity but is the deity itself, and it is treated as one would treat an honored guest. Food is offered, incense, flowers, music, chanting. The *murti* is clothed. She is said to need time to rest; the shrine is closed for her nap.

The Mahanirvana Tantra tells us Kali is black because everything disappears into her. "Just as all colors disappear in black, so all names and forms disappear in Kali."[5]

Ramakrishna explained her darkness as the result of distance. When we are far away from an object, it appears dark to us. "Go near and you will find her devoid of all color," he said. "The water of a lake appears black from a distance. Go near and take the water in your hand, and you will see that it has no color at all. Similarly, the sky looks blue from a distance. But look at the atmosphere near you; it has no color. The nearer you come to God, the more you will realize that [God] has neither name nor form."[6]

Finally we come to the wing of the complex where Ramakrishna lived. I stand before the closed door of his room and place my forehead on it, sensing that, even now, he is only on the other side, in another room.

Drums start up in the courtyard and lead the crowd, beginning to pour out of the temple courtyard, back to the river. We hurry to join them. The crowd is surging, people are shouting, louder and louder, the tension building long before we can see what's happening. The drums pound, the crowd grows larger. "Kali is coming, Kali is coming!" Aditi explains. The crowd shouts, "*Jai Ma! Jai Ma!* Victory to the Mother!"

The excitement mounts, thickening, taking on a physicality that is palpable, as though the heat of our bodies packed together, tightly pressed, suddenly has density, and sound has weight. On this holiest of nights, Kali's feast, devotees are pushing to see the dark of the moon, darkness to dark waters. I've lost track of time. Up and down the *ghat,* people are crowding, crushing us, I am at the front of the line, the police are holding us back. Behind me people are pushing, crowding; in front of me, the police push back, shouting, waving their billy clubs, threatening. The Indian police, smart in their olive-green berets over coal-black hair, their green uniforms, high boots shining black, red braid hung from an epaulet on the left shoulder, lithe and threatening, wave their hands for us to move, but there is no place for us to go. Kali is coming now.

Her entourage descends the steps, first the lesser priests, at least six of them, followed by the chief priest, who looks like a bride groom drawing his energy from another world. Aditi tells me that he is bringing the water pot out of the temple down to the water. Water to water. To recharge the waters, to freshen the waters, to make new the waters, to quicken new life. He is calm, intensely focused, his arms embracing the water pot, the vessel of his "liquid Mother" as tenderly as a bride. His dark, silver-streaked hair is pulled back smoothly into a knot, his full beard trimmed and clipped. His lips are full, his eyes black. He is trim, six feet tall, fresh from bathing, his skin glistening with a light oil. He wears an immaculate white *dhoti,* his chest is bare but for the long string worn diagonally across it by the Brahmins. He is oblivious to the crowd yet fully present and focused on his task, to recharge the waters of Kali. Down he goes with his retinue, sweeping past Aditi and me, down he steps into the waters on the *ghat* where the tidal bore licked it clean.

The drums keep time in complicated rhythm, the priests chant, the crowd is shouting. The chief priest pours out the vessel, empties her into the Ganga, then refills the vessel with living water, water that pours down from the Himalayas, water that explodes out of the glacier of blue ice at Hardwar, tumbles down the mountainsides, sweeps and scours the wide, flat plains of India for twenty-five hundred kilometers, joined by the Asi at Banaras, rolls down past Dakshineswar, through Calcutta, into the Bay of Bengal, and out into the open waters of the Indian Ocean. Kali is the vessel, the water, the priest pouring, the witnessing, the watching, the rhythm of the drums pounding, the heat, and the shouting, "*Jai Ma! Jai Ma!* Victory to the Mother!" It is not superstition or tradition or arbitrary, culturally bound beliefs that hold the waters, especially the waters of the Ganges, to be sacred, that hold the forests to be sacred, *Prakriti,* Nature Herself. It is a deep, abiding, ageless wisdom that has given us a way to remember what we know so deeply, so completely: Our bodies are made up largely of water. Without it, we perish. Water is by its very nature sacred. Water is made up of atoms of hydrogen and oxygen that lie against one another at an angle of 104.5 degrees. Always. This geometric angle is so unique that it has been called the angle of life, for without it, there would be no water.[7] When the waters are poisoned, we are poisoned. This great repository of the living tradition of the sacred feminine in India reminds us again to honor the waters, to praise the waters, to celebrate the waters, to protect the waters. We are born in water. Each and every one of us. Our mothers' waters break, then we are born. We live in the waters of amniotic fluid, float for three-quarters of a year, then we are born, carried on water to this human shore.

This is not a foreign, strange ceremony that I am watching. It is a ritual that shakes me, catches me off guard, takes me down to the water to see a deeper truth that the priest holds in the pot, in Kali.

Life revered is life revealed. It is not revealed until it is revered. Out of reverence comes the mystery, taking me deeper, down into the waters.

Now he is rising up, the chief priest is coming up the steps with Kali, charged, shimmering, ecstatic, he carries her, drums beating, hearts beating, the tension is released, no longer held apart we all fall into a column behind him and follow. We come together. The crowded lines follow Kali back to her temple, where she will reign mysteriously over life and death, over the waters, for another year.

Once again in the temple, Aditi and I are able to pass in front of the statue of Bhavatarini Kali, Saviouress of the World. Still I cannot "see" her. Her image is so strange, so foreign. I give silent thanks for this blessing and accept her impenetrability and my unknowing. We wander around the temple courtyard listening to the songs of devotion that people sit in groups singing. I take advantage of my foreignness and the politeness of the Indian people and join the edge of a group of *sadhus,* holy men, sitting in a circle singing on the portico. Blue and white candles burn and melt on the floor in the center of their circle, our only light. It is just past midnight on my birthday. I cross over to my fifty-first year singing with the *sadhus* on the porch of Kali's temple at Dakshineswar. It rains gently now. We are singing to Kali, to Tara, to Durga, to Ramakrishna and his wife, Sarada, the Mother in whom Kali also appeared to Ramakrishna. We sing of the divine love between Ramakrishna and Sarada, of the sacred marriage that happened between those two people. We celebrate their love and all it gave the world.

As I sing to them, I also sing to my own sweet husband, so far away. I see how far the love between two people can carry others. I sit in the shelter of the love of the Rani for Kali, of Ramakrishna for

Kali, and the love between Ramakrishna and Sarada Devi, grateful for my husband's love and how far it carries me.

One sees that death suddenly occurs unexpectedly,
with no specific order in terms of old, young, or middle-aged.
Betrayed by the evil of grasping the mind as permanent,
one pays no attention to these facts.
Bestow your blessings so that I may remain
*   from the depth of my heart*
mindful of impermanence and death.

—PRAYERS OF REQUEST TO THE LADY TARA
(*translated by Carol Savvas*)

I wake up thinking about the connection between the fierce feminine and facing death this morning. Today is the day I go to Mother Teresa's Home for the Dying, Nirmal Hriday (Pure Heart). I leave the Institute early, five o'clock in the morning, taking a banana from the still-dark kitchen, and meet the taxi below waiting to take me to Kalighat.

As we drive through sprawling Calcutta, I remember the words of the good Sister at Mother Teresa's in Nepal: "Just come and do." Though the face of the fierce feminine that Mother Teresa's Missionaries of Charity show is gentle, underneath is a steely commitment to the poor. Put aside talk and speculation. Do. Help someone else. Then the understanding will unfold, roll down like the water.

I want to arrive by 5:45, in time for the daily mass at Mother Teresa's, at the corner of the temple complex at Kalighat. The taxi driver lets me out at what I have trouble believing could be the right place. I know it is part of the temple complex, but I see nothing.

Then he points to the simple wooden sign over the double front doors: Mission of the Sisters of Charity. This is it.

I pay the driver and walk into the orderly hubbub of Mother Teresa's many Sisters and volunteers beginning their day. The room is full of dying men on clean, low wooden pallets that run in rows across the cool cement floor. The air is dim and gray, the light soft, darkened by the shutters in the corridors. I ask the first Sister I see, Sister Alcuin, where the chapel is, explaining that I've come to attend mass and help in whatever way I can.

"This way," she says softly, walking me up a flight of stone stairs to the roof and across a patio to a small, bare chapel with only a simple cross on the wall behind the altar. There are no chairs, only woven straw mats covering the floor. The shuttered windows above the street are thrown open, letting in the morning light and air. The doors to the chapel open to a courtyard, letting what small breezes there are circulate through. Just outside the chapel door is a bust of the Virgin Mary, Mother Teresa's inspiration, Sister Alcuin informs me. One candle burns in the chapel. Next to the simple cross on the chapel wall are the words, handpainted, "I Thirst."

"You're early," Sister Alcuin says. "Have you eaten? Let me get some food for you." I gladly accept her offer.

She leaves me alone, then returns and signals for me to follow her into a small room with a desk off the chapel, a room sometimes used by the priest who comes to say mass. There she has placed a tray with a piece of toast, two soft-boiled eggs, a piece of cheese, and blessedly, a cup of coffee. I came to volunteer, but the Sisters are serving me. I am embarrassed but hungry.

After mass, Sister Alcuin takes me back downstairs to meet the other volunteers, who have gathered in the dispensary. It's almost eight o'clock in the morning. The Sisters and the volunteers waste no time. Death doesn't wait. I am told where to lock up my bag, assigned the task of helping the other volunteers pass out the tin breakfast plates among the women, and then making the rounds of cleaning and bathing those who can still be moved. The men take care of the men, the women the women, in large separate rooms.

Not everyone here is dying. Some are merely very ill or crazy, but most are bedridden. Mother Teresa's is a catchall, a last stop, a moment of grace just off the streets of Calcutta. I am handed an apron and shown into the bustling kitchen full of large steaming vats of gruel. A woman stands in a large square cement vat on the floor across from the groaning stoves, washing laundry with her feet, like someone crushing grapes.

Sister Alcuin hands me a tray of plates with hot cereal, bread, and tiny clay pots of water, saying, "Take these to the volunteers at the beds." In moments I am busy too, bustling like the others, back and forth to the kitchen, back to the women's room, where volunteers feed the women in their beds.

"We need help here," I'm told on my third round with the trays. "Can you carry this woman to the bath?" a Sister asks me, pointing to a tiny old woman, maybe four feet tall, naked, teetering on the edge of her bed.

"I'll try," I say, going over to the old woman with clouded eyes. I lean over to pick her up in my arms and she wraps herself around me like a small child, her arms around my neck, her legs back behind mine. She is light, probably only seventy or eighty pounds, to my surprise, and she is easy to carry. Now comes the hard part, making my way down the crowded, narrow aisle of volunteers, nuns, and old women being helped to and from the bathroom as the beds are briskly stripped and changed, the floors mopped, the laundry taken out. Life is suddenly very simple.

But as I make my way down the aisle past the others, I realize that I'm taking this woman to the bathroom and that I may have to help her there. There is no toilet, only a trough to one side of the bathing area and a hose with water to rinse the waste off. My charge clambers down and manages to evacuate by herself. One of the Sisters takes over, begins to bathe her, and sends me back to help the

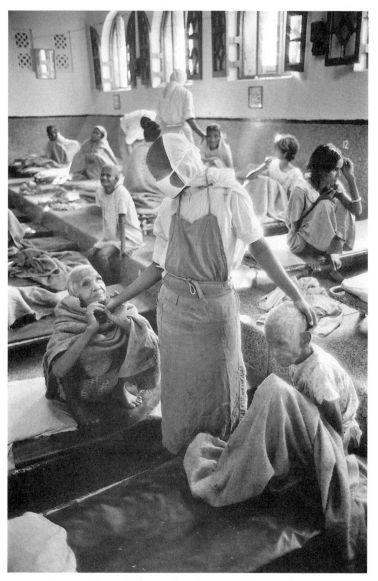

HOME FOR THE DYING, MOTHER TERESA'S MISSION OF CHARITY
IN CALCUTTA, INDIA (*Mary Ellen Mark*)

others. The Sisters are a hardy, cheery lot, showing me a different face of fierce compassion: a steady ardor, a quiet passion that does not waste time, that knows that every minute counts, that lives with death openly and freely.

I return to carrying trays. As I make my way back to the kitchen, I see a man on a pallet by the doorway who is struggling and coughing up blood. No one is tending him, so I stop. He's a young man in comparison to many who are here, in his early fifties at most, maybe younger. He motions for me to bring him some water, which I hurry to do, grabbing a towel while I'm at it. I sit down on the edge of his pallet. He's too weak to drink by himself, so I cradle his head and hold to his mouth the little pot of water, which he sips with relief. He has an IV drip in his arm. I don't know what's wrong with him, though the way he keeps coughing I suspect that it's tuberculosis, a growing problem here. His face is grave, his beautiful dark eyes are sad. He is alone and dying, and he wants more water.

When I return with water and a piece of bread in case he's hungry, his eyes begin to tear up. He doesn't let himself cry, but he whispers under his breath, *"Ma, Ma, Ma."* Mother. I can't communicate with him, only attend to him. He offers me a trace of a smile and a weak nod, when another volunteer comes by and asks me to return to the women's room. I'm needed there.

On my way back into the women's room, I take a moment to stop and look at another man who seemed to be alone and dying when I first walked in this morning. Indeed, he is dead. No breath. Still alone. I wanted to believe that people don't ever die by themselves at Mother Teresa's, but that's another foolish notion. It would be impossible with all that's going on here. A volunteer who has been here for weeks, a hospice worker from the States, walks with me to the women's room, criticizing the medical care and the way so many people, like the man I had just been with, are put on IV drips. I know nothing, only that I'm getting to see again how human institutions, whether Tibetan monasteries or Mother Teresa's, are not to be romanticized as divine solutions. Still, I tell her, at least the Sisters and the volunteers are trying. What would be better, to leave people on the street? There are no easy answers.

Back in the women's room, three of us struggle with an old madwoman, to get her bed changed, her clothes back on, and to entertain her. I give her my pen and paper, and she sits there writing what I thought might be a dialect, but am later told is complete gibberish. However, it keeps her quiet and busy, like a child, and despite the lack of meaning in the words, I feel the old woman is telling me something. It seems to be a letter that she's writing. To whom, there is no way of knowing, but I sit with her patiently as I hope that someone would with me.

Mary, one of the volunteers I work with, is a twenty-seven-year-old woman from Ireland who worked and saved her money for two years to come to Mother Teresa's as a volunteer. She will stay one year. She's now in her third month and very happy she's doing this.

Suddenly there's a stir, a woman on the bed across from the woman who has our attention is trying to stand up and walk. She's on an IV and has been nearly unconscious. One of our volunteers goes to help her and see what she wants, and she lies down, quiet. Our charge begins being difficult again, now trying to take off the clothes we put on her, so once more she has our attention. We convince her to leave her clothes on and I get her scribbling again on my notepad and for the moment she is happy.

Then I hear Mary say, "Oh, no!" under her breath from the bed of the woman who had just tried to walk. "She's dead!" Mary says. She died when she lay down, only a minute ago.

We all go to her bedside, leaving the other woman writing her letter. One of the volunteers checks the woman's pulse and her breathing. Nothing. She is gone. Another volunteer pulls the IV drip out of the dead woman's arm and begins to wrap the bedsheet around her like a shroud. It's all happening so fast that I'm dumbfounded. "But . . . but," I start to say, when Mary has the presence of mind to suggest that we stop and say a prayer for her departed soul, which we do. There is a moment of calm as we say a Hail Mary, and then it's over. The bustle resumes as a volunteer goes to get help carrying out the shrouded body. I'm alarmed at the speed with which this is happening. I can't help but believe from my own experience with people dying that the soul, consciousness, whatever one calls that principle of life, does not leave the body completely the moment the heart stops beating. Many traditions, Buddhist included, allow at least three days for the body to remain undisturbed while ceremonies are performed, prayers said, in the belief that consciousness seeps away slowly, like water. Now this woman is being carried out, down the hall. Who was she? I am powerless to do anything but follow the men who have grabbed either end of her sheet out of the women's room through the dispensary to a small screened-in room with long shelves, off the kitchen—the morgue. It's the only place to put the bodies until they are carted off at the end of the day. I stand on the far side of the kitchen watching, praying, as they place her sheet-wrapped body on a shelf and leave.

The cooks are busy getting lunch ready, making tea for the volunteers, washing more laundry. A row of old men sit against the wall to my left with their tin plates in their hands ready for food. The kitchen is hot. The smell of spices and food cooking mingles with the odor of laundry. The shrouded body lies alone on the gray cement shelf just beyond the kitchen, clearly visible. I stand in the doorway silently praying for the old woman, taking in the life and the death that is all a part of this one teeming room. The old woman had struggled to her feet, fought to stand before she died, fiercely. Only moments ago, only moments ago.

Though the main Kali Temple lies on the other side of these walls, Kali lives here too, dancing with death, cooking the food, serving it, to the dead, to the living, to her it makes no difference, we all are food.

HOLY GROUND

India's Sacred Geography

Tarapith

An ancient Hindu story tells us that Sati, the first wife of Shiva, the Lord of the Universe, immolated herself in a fire in a furious outburst of rage with her father. When Shiva discovered her body he went mad with grief. He picked it up out of the fire and began to turn faster and faster, whirling, circling, weeping so hard that finally the world itself was threatened by his grief, for his presence was essential to the balance of the universe. Finally Vishnu followed the grieving Shiva around and began to cut off pieces of Sati's body until nothing of her form remained. Shiva was so distraught he realized none of this until Sati's entire body was gone and his arms were empty. Then he came to his senses. Thus the world was saved again, this time by Vishnu.

Every place where a piece of Sati's body fell became sacred and is called a pitha, *which means "seat." The* pithas *are seats of the Goddess. The number of* pithas *in India varies according to the differing accounts of this ancient and often told story, ranging from four to one hundred ten sites.[1]*

This is a story of the sacred geography, the other map of India. Sati and the Mahadevi, the Great Goddess, of which Sati is a manifestation, unite all of India, for it is by the body of the Goddess that India is sanctified; indeed, India *is* her body. It is said that her toe fell to earth at Kalighat.

In another story it is said that Shiva tried to save the world by drinking up all of its poisons, but even he, the Lord of the Universe, could not withstand the pollution and began to die. Once again, the fate of the universe was dangerously out of balance. At the last moment, Tara came to him as he was dying and nursed him with the milk from her breasts. This is the Hindu Tara.

This Hindu Tara has a long tongue, like Kali. The lower half of her face is red. She is beautiful and smiling, like Durga. She is a fierce Tara. This is the image said to be in the rock at Tarapith, Tara nursing Shiva. Thus Shiva was saved by Tara, and thus the world was saved, one more time, this time by Tara.

Tarapith, in northwest Bengal, is the site most sacred to Tara in India. Though it is difficult to find what part of the Devi's body fell to the ground at Tarapith, one story holds that it was her wisdom eye, the third eye. At Tarapith, the Goddess is in the form of a stone and is covered by a silver mask. You cannot see the stone except at night, when the mask is removed, then the stone is revealed. It is said that on the stone one can find the shape of Tara nursing Shiva.

These ancient stories are parables, telling us that the world has been threatened many times, and saved, before. In this Tara story, as in Durga's, the fierce feminine takes on tasks that defeat even the gods. The sacred fierce feminine is indomitable. She transforms the world's poisons into a mother's milk, she turns tears of despair into resolve and help. She takes action.

Aditi Sen tells me that she's been able to find a car and driver to take us to Tarapith. Arya, Aditi's husband, will come with us. We can make the trip in one day if I want, a remarkably generous offer. Though it will not be an easy journey, I accept eagerly. The drive is eight hours each way. There is virtually no place to stay overnight. I tell myself that I want to go no matter what the difficulties because of my great confidence in Tara, the need to understand her strength, her ardor, and her relationship with the Hindu Kali.

As we pull out of Calcutta the next morning, we're quickly mired in traffic. There's a woman in the middle of the street, holding broken chunks of brick in her hands, walking between cars yelling and gesticulating. The woman is small, the size of a girl, but clearly at least in her thirties. She has on a red-and-white Bengali sari but no blouse underneath. She's barefoot; her black hair is loose, matted and wild.

"Probably a lunatic," Aditi explains, "an NCL, a noncriminal lunatic. The police will pick her up and she'll be kept in jail. It's pitiful." The woman chucks a brick at a nearby car, then walks in our direction. Though I look directly at her out of the rear window, she seems to be staring right through me. Is she one of the women I've read about who were sold into prostitution and who went mad? Is she a lunatic, or is she Kali? The traffic moves, and I quickly lose sight of her.

Aditi's black hair is pulled back smoothly, clasped with a barrette. It falls halfway down her back. Red powder is faintly visible in the part on the top of her head, indicating that she is a married woman. She wears a beautiful gray and-green raw silk sari.

"I wear this sari for *pujas,*" she explains, smiling at her husband, Arya, who is dressed in a simple white shirt and pants. Arya is a quietly elegant man. He is fifty-two, warm and open. He immediately puts me at ease and explains that Tarapith is a unique place for them, which is why he wanted to come with us. They had performed funeral rites for Arya's mother at Tarapith, and just after they were married he and Aditi went to Tarapith to celebrate and to pay their respects to Tara.

The eight-hour drive passes quickly in their company, full of stories from both Hindu mythology and their own rich histories of family in Bengal. Arya sings songs from Rabindranath Tagore, the

Bengali Nobel laureate, poet, and writer. We arrive at the shrine in late afternoon, just as the light turns gold on the deep salmon-pink temple.

A handful of priests in clear red robes stand by Tara's statue at this shrine, which is surrounded by brass railings. Her statue is not really a statue but a stone covered by a mask. This is the silver mask that is lifted at night to reveal the image of Tara nursing Shiva, an image barely discernible to the untrained eye.

With only one day to be here, I stand off to the side, taking in the small shrine, wondering why I have come so far. The mask is nondescript, the shrine like many others. We can stay two or three hours, then we have to turn around and make the wrenching drive back to Calcutta, only this time we'll be driving in the dark. I have no particular response to this image. Then the priest signals for me to kneel down and reach through the brass railing. He takes my hand, guides it underneath the dress the Goddess is wearing, underneath the silver mask, to touch the stone. As soon as my hand touches the stone I burst into tears. The room grows hushed, the priest, the pilgrims, Aditi and Arya, all are quiet. A great silence falls around us. Inside this silence I am held, I am heard, wordlessly. It is a deep silence. There is no end to this silence. Inside this silence there is all the time in the world.

This rock Tara is ancient, she is not the Tara I have known in Nepal, this Tara is older. This Tara's rock weighs me down, takes me under, outside of time, brings me into my own, lets me pour out the sorrows I do not speak of, absorbs them, takes them into the earth, swallows them, devours them like Kali. This is so unlike my experience of Kali at Dakshineswar—celebratory, communal. This Tara-Kali gives me back my grief. Then the moment passes and it is over.

I open my eyes. The priest is smiling. Aditi explains that he says I have received the full blessing of the Goddess. Then he picks up a pair of brass feet filled with water and flowers, the feet of Tara.

There are two pairs of brass feet on the altar, below the stone, in amidst the scattering of marigolds, red hibiscus, bright blue flowers, and old silver coins. He places Tara's brass feet on my head; he says prayers. He smooths the brass feet on my hair, on either side of my head. He wipes the Goddess's feet on my hair. The weight of her feet being placed on my head. The weight of Her. Then he picks up the larger pair of brass feet and holds them out to us. Aditi leads me and shows me how to place vermilion powder on them, an offering. Then I hold up the feet of the Goddess with both hands. Mother, carry me, Mother, keep me connected to your feet, ground me, let me stand under you, stand firmly planted on the earth. Now the priest goes back to the smaller, water-filled feet of the Goddess. Her feet are full of moisture. The powder from her feet is on my forehead and in my hair, the priest dips a marigold blossom into the leg of the Goddess, then drips the nectar into Arya's and Aditi's mouths as we kneel at the altar. Aditi whispers, "Don't open your mouth, the water is unsafe." The priest squeezes it onto my closed eyes instead. He "opens" my eyes. Returns my tears to me, moisture, water, wets my face with the nectar of the Goddess, tears of simply being moved, then still. The evening light is falling now, inside the narrow structure of this temple, across the black-and-white-tiled floor.

On a tree outside the temple the branches are bent, weighed down with stones that have been tied on, petitions and prayers to Tara. Tie them here and you can leave them, know they will be answered and taken care of, the fruit of a pilgrimage to Tarapith.

Driving up to Tarapith proved challenging, but the drive home, all ten hours of it, after driving up for eight hours, puts me over the top in terms of disorientation. The wonderful stillness of the shrine, the peace I felt, is gone once the sun sets and we drive in the dark with belching, growling trucks. Thick clouds of black exhaust smoke and fumes sour the air. I feel trapped by the enormous Tata trucks that take over the Grand Trunk Road, the main highway, and simply stop or park, and then might sit anywhere from five minutes to five hours. What side of the road we're on is immaterial. Trucks drive straight at us, swerving only at the last moment. Now the headlights of an oncoming truck create a tunnel of light around the dust-shrouded truck in the distance in front of us, a tunnel of light into which the truck's dark shape is always receding. We've descended into a hell realm with these behemoths belching poison. There are hundreds of trucks at choke points we come to in the road. Our Sikh driver, wearing a navy blue turban and white uniform, suddenly throws the car into gear and turns the steering wheel with his whole body just in time to miss going under the bed of a giant Tata truck by only inches, again. Seeing all these trucks knots my stomach. Aruna and Agnes told me that truck drivers are often the purveyors of the Nepali village girls sold into prostitution. They transport them. Dodging, darting, and weaving between these trucks I cannot help but wonder if there are Nepali girls inside them. I say nothing of this to Aditi and Arya. I am wordless and exhausted.

What happened at Tarapith has little to do with what I thought I was going for. I thought I was going to learn something about the the Hindu form of Tara, but in fact I was making a pilgrimage, brief and ragged as it turned out to be. What stays with me goes deeper than words. I feel it sinking in and returning me to the primacy of experience and to the wisdom that is the earth.

CHAPTER 10

THE LESSON
OF THE FOREST

We Will Not Violate
What We Hold Sacred
Gaya

he next night I take the overnight train from Calcutta to
Gaya. Sunrise, November 7. I raise the window shade by
my bunk at first light to see women in pale-colored saris
squatting around a bright fire in the dawn light, far out in the water,
on a river sandbar. A crumbling village looms in the early-morning
mists through the tinted railway glass, and beyond, an ancient temple towers into view. The train rocks from side to side, steadily
clicking beneath us as we roll across a bridge over shallow waters.
Sunrise. The countryside is swathed in mists. The landscape has
changed from the coastal environment of Bengal to the rolling hills
and ponds of the inland plains as we near Gaya, in the rural state of
Bihar. Then the temple, the women around the fire, the river, the
soft rounded hills and the ponds are gone. The mists take over.
When they part, they reveal a new landscape of broad, open fields.

We arrive at the station at Gaya. I'm relieved that my message
got through and that a driver is there to meet me. We pile my bags
into the back of his taxi, and I get in for the drive to Bodh Gaya, to
the Burmese Vihar, the temple compound run by Burmese Buddhist monks, where I will meet up with Tara Doyle, my teacher
from Nepal, Chökyi Nyima, and, I hope, Sister Jessie, a nun whose
work to bring about the unity of castes, creeds, and religions continues Gandhi's efforts and dream of people living in harmony. (Jessie

is the Anglicized version of her Indian name, Ma Jaishree Upad-haya.) Tara will be there to teach a semester-long course in Buddhist Studies for Antioch College. Chökyi Nyima has come to teach the Tibetan portion. Sister Jessie lives here.

But the car's battery is dead, it won't start. Three men quickly descend upon the taxi and open the hood. One begins banging an-grily on the battery, as though he could rouse it from a state of slum-ber. Now four more men rush over to help push the car so that we can jump-start it. The driver hops in just as we begin to roll back-ward into the parking lot full of rickshaws, chickens, people, open food stalls, cars, and cows. The taxi starts briefly, sputters, then dies. I can't watch. I stay calm in the backseat by following the movement of a cow as it grazes placidly through the apple stalls at the edge of the parking lot, then stops to urinate. Now one of the men hops in and tries the ignition, and it starts. He throws the gear into neutral and revs the engine, pumping the accelerator as the original driver slides into the driver's seat behind him. We're rolling again. The cow moves to another stall, upsetting a basket of apples, sending them rolling across the parking lot, the vendor running after them, shouting. Another man turns over a nearby rickshaw and shouts. I can't tell if my driver had anything to do with the fight that's brew-ing, but suddenly we're off, horn blaring, engine sputtering, coast-ing right into the crowd. I turn to find the cow setting off at a trot in the other direction. A sea of rickshaws parts hurriedly as our driver bears down on them, not yet fully in control of the taxi, holding down the clutch, gunning the engine, gears grinding and exhaust growling. We make it out of the parking lot without hitting anyone and we're off.

We set out through the dawn mists and the sparks of morning fires, past beggars and four-foot-high heaps of garbage being picked through by goats, past cream-colored donkeys, past people on their way to the river for their morning cleansing. The rising light turns golden.

Scrubbed girls in red-and-white uniforms hurry past on their way to school. Boys with crisp white shirts and red-and-white school ties make their way to school with them, on foot or on bicycles.

The sun rises across the fields in the distance as we drive down a road lined with enormous trees. I am so comforted to be in the countryside among trees that tears well up. The pollution of Calcutta was unremitting. Suddenly the driver pulls off the road onto a dirt track next to a flower field. I try to find out what's happening, asking questions in my broken pidgin Hindi, "Bodh Gaya?"

"Mechanic," he announces happily, one of his few words of English. I see only an overgrown field of tall pale pink flowers with deep pink centers, similar to hollyhocks. Unexpectedly, a serious-faced thirteen-year-old boy appears in a dirty gray torn shirt. He sticks his head in the car to look over the shoulder of the driver.

"Mechanic," the driver repeats emphatically, smiling as the young man confidently begins to unscrew the brake pedal. I turn my head, not wanting to speculate on whether or not we will have brakes again. A white cow, decorated for Dewali, the Festival of Lights, with circles of pink dye all over her, wanders past. There is nothing for me to do but to let go and take in the flowers, the trees, and the village women walking down the road. I know little about India, and yet one of its strengths seems to be the unusual forthrightness, strength, and sensibleness that Indian women are often able to summon up, no matter the difficulties of their circumstances. I watch the women here walking down the road carrying loads of hay on their heads, children trailing behind, and think of the remarkable stories of village women of the Chipko movement that started in the Garhwal Himal region of India north of here, vibrant examples of the power of women organizing for their families and for their forest environment. *Chipko* means "embrace." These women realized that destruction of their forests for cash crops was shortsighted, so they organized to halt logging by embracing the trees, putting their own lives at risk. Starting in the 1970s, they went on marches from village to village, organizing resistance, leading protests, standing in nonviolent, fierce, and creative defense of their forests. Many of the women leaders who marched were in their fifties.

I've been endeavoring to find a time and a place to sit down with Vandana Shiva, Ph.D., of Deradun, while I'm here in India. Vandana has written passionately about these women of the Chipko movement in her book *Staying Alive,* as well as having taken part in the movement herself.[1] Vandana speaks of feminism as a form of ecology, and ecology as the revival of Prakriti, the Goddess of Nature, another form of the Mahadevi, the Great Goddess, the source of all life in Hinduism. We will finally catch up with each other in person in the States when she comes to speak at the International Forum on Globalization. Vandana Shiva is a nuclear physicist and a human rights activist who left a rising career to place her formidable mind at the service of sustaining and restoring the world. Winner of the 1993 Right Livelihood Award, considered the alternative Nobel Prize, she speaks the language of science, as well as the language of Hindu cosmology, with authority and animation. She can speak of the Goddess of Nature, Prakriti, and gene patenting in the same breath.

I remember Durga's promise at the end of the *Devi-Mahatmya* to feed her followers with her body. Durga is more than a warrior, she is also Prakriti, Nature itself: she protects the world, she saves it from destruction, and she *is* the world. It is this sense of the world as infused with the sacred that comes through again and again in Vandana's thinking. Vandana Shiva could come only from India.

Vandana was raised in the Indian forests, she understands forests intimately. Her father was a forest conservator—a high-level manager—and her mother, Jagbir Kaur Shiva, was active in the Indian Independence movement, an educator who had become a farmer. Vandana's mother wrote several books about ecology and farming, and it is she who first stimulated Vandana's intellectual curiosity. It was Vandana's mother who encouraged her and supported her interest in science when Vandana announced that she was going on for her doctorate as a physicist. Her sister became a medical doctor. Her father was the nurturer, sewing all her clothes, as he does today for Vandana's son, whom he helps care for. Her father learned to cook and sew in the army and saw no reason to give up the independence it gave him. Her unusual parents' philosophy was framed by the idea that you live as you want others to live and let inspiration be the teacher.

"If people get inspired, they help a lot, but if you try to force them, you'll never get anywhere. It's like nurturing a tree, isn't it? You can't make a tree grow by pulling it harder, you make it grow by giving it water. That's how we were raised as children." It's become her philosophy of political action as a result, she tells me.

Family vacations were taken to the sacred sites of India. When Vandana learned to swim, it was in the Ganges, with her parents telling her the story of Ganga's fall from the heavens. Stories were woven into her experience of place. Vandana's mother constantly illustrated the relationships among nature, ecology, and the sacred, pointing out, for example, that camphor is a natural form of pest management. Camphor oil is used to offer *arati*, the five-light ceremony that I had seen so often in India and Nepal. When Vandana was in school, nylon dresses were in vogue and homespun Indian cotton was considered third-rate. Her mother would tell Vandana that she could have the nylon or the Indian homespun cotton. It was her choice, but her mother painted the consequences of her decision.

"'If you wear a frock of nylon, a millionaire gets his next limousine. If you wear homespun Indian cotton, four people get fed at the end of the day,' that's what she would say. It was always our choice, cotton or nylon. But she drew out the full implications of everyday acts for us."

Much of India's ancient civilization was modeled on the diversity, harmony, and self-sustaining nature of the forests. India worshipped its forests as the home of Aranyani, the Forest Goddess, a source of life and fertility. Indian culture has upheld forest life as the highest form of cultural evolution, Vandana notes, drawing on the work of the Bengali Indian Nobel Prize laureate, Rabindranath Tagore. Long ago, Tagore outlined the contrasts between modern Western life, which was urban, built on brick and wood, and Indian life, which was organized around the basic principle of the forest as a regenerative model. Tagore wrote of how the peace of the forest had helped develop the intellectual life of India and of how Indian thinkers traditionally withdrew to the forest, using the intimate relationship between human life and nature as their source of knowledge.

The Indian strategy for sustaining farms and water in arid and semiarid zones had been based on maintaining a mix of privately and commonly held stands of trees, planted in a variety of species such as the tamarind, the mango, the *honge*, the *jola*, the jackfruit, and bamboo, among others, which provided not only wood for small timber but also fuel, fodder, shade, pesticide, fertilizer, and food. Thus each rural home had a backyard nursery, each peasant woman was a silvaculturalist and held important, vital knowledge. In the indigenous system, forestry, agriculture, and water conservation all were tied together, and everyone in the village had a part. The forest system was invisible and decentralized; everyone helped protect and grow it.

Vandana uses a World Bank project in Karnataka to illustrate how the integrity of this system can be destroyed. The project was designed by planners with no regard for indigenous knowledge, who decided that the natural forests of the region should be replaced with a monoculture of fast-growing, high-yield eucalyptus trees—good only for pulping. This market strategy, driven by the paper and pulp industries and profits, separated forestry from agriculture and water conservation. Trees from the smallest farms became raw materials supplied to an industrial market, hundreds of miles from the local community. They ceased to be a source of supply to the local people.

Women's work, which connected trees and crops, was taken over by brokers and middlemen working on behalf of industry located somewhere else. The eucalyptus increased cash flow and was hailed as a "miracle tree" for development. But the women and peasants grew to despise it, Vandana says. It guzzled nutrients and water from the soil, produced no fodder for the animals, no food, and was exported for use outside the community. It had disastrous consequences on the local water table and soil conservation. Proponents of development had completely failed to take into account these very real costs of production.[2]

This rise of the monoculture constitutes a dangerous crisis, Vandana says. For example, India has grown thousands of indigenous varieties of rice, but by the end of the millennium, it is expected that this enormous diversity will have been reduced to fewer than fifty species. The trend toward uniformity of species—monoculture—leaves the global food supply increasingly vulnerable to disaster. Vandana is alarmed by the ways in which this trend is being supported by international law, creating a form of bio-imperialism.

"With the idea of intellectual property rights, what we have developed is a situation where a corporation or an individual or a scientist or a laboratory can walk into a Third World community, find out how the local women use plants, how the community uses them for health care and medicine, and come back home to the West, apply to a patent office, write up the same knowledge in English or in the language of chemistry or of molecular biology with nothing fundamentally new added, and treat it as a novelty, as an innovation—as a creation. Patents on life are an outrage against the intrinsic worth of all living diversity," she tells me. "They are also a very clever mechanism for theft and piracy of what still remains largely in the hands of women: the ability to create and sustain life. Agriculture and medicine still rely predominantly on women's expertise in the Third World.

"This 'creation' is then sold back to Third World people as the property of minds inhabiting white bodies who control large amounts of capital to 'develop' these markets."

Of equal concern to Vandana is the fact that not only is this freely given indigenous knowledge being privatized and sold as a commodity, but the capacity of women to look after the needs of their families and communities is being eroded by this monopolization of knowledge.

"In my book *Monocultures of the Mind*, I talk about how in Argentina, when the dominant political system faced dissent, it responded by making the dissidents disappear. The *desaparecidos* share the fate of local knowledge systems throughout the world, conquered through disappearance, not the politics of debate and dialogue."[3]

Water is inextricably tied to trees, crops and soil, and it is the one issue that is not treated seriously enough by ecologists, Vandana tells me. Yet a shortage of it constitutes one of the biggest threats to human existence.

More than 70 percent of the villages in India no longer have potable water, and the situation is worsening. Now that India has bottled water, those who can afford clean water are separated from those who can't. The poor can get jaundice, they can get diarrhea, dysentery, they can get cholera, while those who can drink water from bottles are safe, she notes.

Organizing to protect water is a complicated matter, "because water flows, it can't be locked into one place. There's no way of only organizing locally," Vandana says. "The solution to the water crisis requires major social change. No amount of local activism alone will take care of it. It requires change based first and foremost on the notion that water is sacred. And it is sacred because it is so essential to life. If we hold human life as sacred then we must hold water as sacred."

India's ancient system of reservoirs and holding ponds connected to Hindu temples astounded the engineers of the British East India Company. Because these waters were considered sacred, they were never contaminated. This ensured an ample, continuous supply of clean water across the entire country.

"As our concept of the sacred has become more diluted, pollution has become more aggravated. Purity of water can almost be measured in direct proportion to a society's understanding of the sacred," Vandana says. "The sacred is now a political necessity if we are to resist the colonization of nature that is destroying our forests, our water, and our air."[4]

Troubling as the global environmental crisis is, she feels that the colonization of nature, of women, and of the Third World can still be undone. "People must continue to resist," she says. "We must refuse to allow the disappearance of the sacred, refuse to allow the disappearance of diversity, refuse to allow the disappearance of decentralized living and organizing."

The women and men of Karnataka eventually revolted against the eucalyptus monoculture. They marched on a government eucalyptus nursery and pulled up millions of seedlings, and planted tamarind and mango seeds in place of the eucalyptus. The tamarind and mango trees are useful, providing food, shade, and fuel, not just money.

In her book *Staying Alive,* Vandana tells of a turning point for the Chipko movement in 1977, when the Indian government began to hire local contractors to fell the forests. The women continued to fight the exploitation of the forests, even though in some cases it might mean opposing members of their own village or family. One woman led a protest against her own husband, the local contractor.

When the forest officials arrived to break up the protest, they found the village women holding up burning lanterns in the middle of the day. The men couldn't understand what they were doing and asked their reasons. The women replied that they had come to teach the men forestry, they were coming to show them the light.

The men laughed, deriding the women for such foolishness, and for not understanding the monetary value of the number of feet of timber available to be cut. They were poor village women, struggling to make ends meet, surely they could see that modern forestry meant the valuable profits to be gained from the sales of resin and timber.

The women replied with a song that became a rallying cry for the Chipko movement, "What do the forests bear? Soil, water, and pure air. Soil, water, and pure air. Sustain the earth and all she bears."[5]

"I think to be outraged by violation and violence is a very necessary complement to being spiritual. To me this means that one has boundaries that say, 'This is sacred, it cannot be violated.' If the rage is directed to protecting the sacred, it can become a creative rage, it can be a compassionate rage.

"Compassionate rage does not kill anything or anyone. It does not harm. It is different from anger without compassion. Anger without compassion wants to kill the 'other.' But compassionate wrath, creative resistance, means being willing to put oneself on the line—put your own body in front of the trees, not point a gun at someone else. Creative resistance is not against a person but against a system."

As I sit here in the countryside watching the village women walking under the trees, it is easy to understand how Vandana's passion and sensibility are very much a creation of this landscape. The landscape, the sacred, and the story are infused with one another; they arise out of a profound intimacy with nature. It is the kind of intimacy that women understand and often share, hence the ability of the women in the Chipko movement to rally one another, to make long marches through the countryside, to go on campaigns to save the forests. The women understood that their bond extended beyond one another, beyond their families and their villages, to the forest and ultimately, to Nature, Prakriti, herself.

The thirteen-year-old mechanic slams down the hood of the taxi, jarring me out of my thoughts. He grins at my surprise and ambles off down the dusty road. The driver starts the car, and we proceed without further incident to Bodh Gaya.

CHAPTER 11

"I HAD TO DO SOMETHING"

The Literacy Movement, Bodh Gaya

God has chosen what the world regards as foolish to shame the wise,
and what the world regards as weak, God has chosen to shame
the strong, and what the world regards as low, contemptible,
mere nothing, God has chosen. . . .

—PAUL, FIRST LESSON, I CORINTHIANS 1:27–28

Voices drift through the open blue wooden shutters of the dimly lit meditation hall. It's 5:45 A.M. I am sitting with Tara Doyle and Chökyi Nyima Rinpoche and about thirty of Tara's students from universities all over the United States. They've come to India for five months to study Buddhism not only academically but experientially.[1] Their effort and willingness to expose themselves to other cultures and other beliefs inspire me.

The meditation hall slowly fills with light. My breath, back to the breath, I remind myself. Suddenly I realize how lonely I am for models of women who have stepped outside the traditional religions yet continue to draw on what underlies and unites them. My dear friend Tara, who sits next to me, has chosen to walk the Buddhist path, and though she supports me, she does not share my need to include the Christian. Not at this time. I don't fit in any one tradition, or even two, and I accept this. I walk a rich and nameless path, yet I need more sisters, models, mentors. I become determined to find Sister Jessie, this nun whom I started hearing about in Nepal, a woman making her own way, going beyond the traditional boundaries between religions and drawing on several as she lives out a life of dedication to the poor and the transformation of poverty.

Outside, the day takes off with the startling blast of a bus horn. Someone switches on a radio nearby and turns Hindi music to full volume. Can I give up my need for quiet, my attachment to silence? In this moment it feels more possible. Just as I settle into a deeper meditation, the bell rings signaling the end of the period. Time to go.

At breakfast Tara tells me that I'm in luck. Sister Jessie often stays here at the Burmese Vihar in the row of rooms for pilgrims, just behind the meditation hall, but I should hurry. She leaves early for the villages.

Rounding the corner behind the meditation hall, on the narrow path to the row of pilgrims' rooms, I come face to face with a full-grown deer with large, warm eyes, whose coat was covered with circles of pink dye for the festival of Dewali. Just behind her, standing in the doorway laughing, is a dark woman wearing the orange-and-yellow robes of a *sanyasin,* one who has renounced the world. Her black hair is pulled back into a knot on the nape of her neck. She can only be Sister Jessie. She motions me to the doorway of her room and office, maybe eight feet by ten.

"I would invite you in, but as you can see, there's no room," she says, laughing again, as I stand looking in her doorway. She's utilized her small space as efficiently as a sailor on a round-the-world journey in a twenty-four-foot vessel. Not an inch is wasted. She offers tea as if she'd been expecting my visit. I introduce myself and tell her that I've heard that she found life as a nun in a Catholic convent in India too luxurious. I ask her if this is true.

"Yes, life in the convent was too comfortable. Everything was taken care of, our food, our shelter, our clothing. We had a large, beautiful home, life was very easy. But I had an inner call to leave and put on the robes of a *sanyasin*.

"A *sanyasin* belongs to everyone and everyone belongs to her. *Sanyasin* means 'mother to all.' A *sanyasin* has no one of their own, yet everybody is their very own. A *sanyasin* has no religion. Every

SISTER JESSIE OF THE CAMPAIGN FOR AWAKENING WISDOM
LITERACY PROGRAM WITH HER PET DEER, BODH GAYA, INDIA
(*China Galland*)

religion is her religion. My religion is a blending of Christianity, Hinduism, Buddhism, and Gandhi's philosophy of nonviolent action. I don't believe in labels anymore—Christian, Catholic, Hindu, Buddhist. Religion causes so many problems, so much division. From Hinduism I draw on the ideal of selfless service; from Gandhi the principles of truthfulness, *satya*, not doing harm, *ahimsa*, and nonviolence; from the Buddha, compassion; and from Jesus, the primacy of love. Jesus is my guru, I hold on to him by his little finger."

147

Jessie's decision to leave organized religion behind, to follow her own path with the poor, to put aside the labels and divisions, is tremendously heartening to me. She's gone straight to the core of the traditions that she draws from. She tells me what set her on this nameless way.

Dom Bede, Father Bede Griffiths, a Catholic priest who lived in an ashram in India and was one of the pioneers of interreligious dialogue, was a profound influence on Jessie's life. Staying with him for the two years before his death, and being with him when he died, led her into making a silent retreat for two years after his death. It could easily have been for longer, she said, but she received another call, this time to activism.

"I could have stayed in that silence forever, I was so happy," she tells me, but one day when she was walking to the market she overheard a man in a bullock cart arguing with two women over the price of wheat they had to sell him.

"They asked for five rupees and he refused. They begged him. Still he refused. 'Two rupees or nothing!' he shouted at them."

Each bundle represented hours of hard labor in the fields, then the long hot labor of carrying the load on their heads from the fields to town. These were women with families to feed, with hungry children. Two rupees wouldn't buy them one half-kilo of flour for *chapatis,* and it was late in the day, Jessie explained. They would have to take what he offered or return home empty-handed. They took the two rupees.

"I kept walking, but I was so upset by this conversation that I couldn't sleep that night or the next night. I had never had trouble sleeping before in my life, never. I wanted to stay in silent retreat, but after that incident I couldn't, not any longer. I had to do something to help."

Though she didn't know these women, she felt profoundly connected to them, and that connection gave rise to her solution: to start her Campaign for Awakening Wisdom, a literacy campaign to educate people.[2] Bihar is one of the poorest states, if not the poorest, in India. The villages around Bodh Gaya are home to some of India's poorest, the Musahers, people whose work historically was to hunt rats for food. Low-caste, untouchables, Harijan, Gandhi called them—Children of God. Rather than try to feed them, Jessie said that she wanted to "give them a hook and show them how to fish, not give them the fish itself." Education is what they need, that's the hook they can use, but education is extraordinarily difficult to give them because after centuries of acculturation to their role, they have little or no self-esteem and think that they deserve nothing—the result of the caste system, Jessie assures me, even though it's outlawed—they think it is their fate in this life to be badly treated and to suffer.

"So we begin work with the children," she tells me. "If the child is happy, the mother is happy, if the child is sad, the mother is sad. We start with the little ones and teach them nursery rhymes. Once they learn the nursery rhymes and begin to know their letters, they start to get excited by the experience of learning and they begin to teach the mothers. Then the mothers are happy and supportive and more open to our project. They become interested and some of them even have begun to learn to read.

"Excuse me, I have to eat something too," Jessie said, handing me a copy of a flyer on her literacy campaign. "We never know if we will be offered food when we go to the villages. Sometimes the people are so poor that they have nothing to give us. Would you like a *chapati*?" she asks with a warm smile, turning over the half-cooked batter on the griddle of her propane stove.

No, I've eaten, thanks, I tell her, relishing the scant amount of time I have with this woman. Jessie explains quickly that it takes less than two dollars of U.S. money a month to pay the salary of a village teacher. Three thousand children are now in the literacy campaign program, learning to read. The children also are given a rudimentary environmental education, being taught to save trees and to replant them. Jessie tries out various means of helping village women become self-sufficient, one year distributing enough money for each family to buy a piglet. The small fund I've brought from a supporter of hers in Nepal will go a long way.

Jessie shows me another face of the fierce feminine, fiercely committed to her own inner calling that has led her out of organized religion onto the path of the *sanyasin*. She practices "contemplation through action," *karma-yoga*, and "action without reward," *nishkarma*, living virtually without possessions, relying on donations such as the one the woman in Nepal gave me for her. Out of the comforts of the convent into the lives of the poor, she took that feeling of "I can't stand this" and turned it into a path of action. Following Gandhi's example of service for the poor, Jessie sees God in the poor, or, as the Hindu expression translates, one sees "poor-God."

Sister Jessie's attitude toward the poor calls to mind a quintessentially Indian story. Shankara was one of the great Hindu philosopher-saints of the ninth century C.E. As Linda Johnsen tells the story in *Daughters of the Goddess,* one day Shankara entered a Shiva temple and found himself blocked by a low-caste Hindu woman weeping hysterically over the corpse of her husband. He ordered her aside brusquely.[3] Not only was she a woman, she was low-caste. The woman exploded, demanding to know if he wasn't the famous teacher who said that everything is Brahman, everything is God, there is no impurity anywhere?

"If I am not impure, why should I get out of your way? If I am the all-pervading reality, how *can* I get out of your way?" she demanded to know of him.

Shankara was too shocked to reply, but the woman was not yet through with him.

"Your mighty Brahmin is no more than this," she shouted, pointing to the corpse of her dead husband.

In that moment the great thinker's mind burst open. He remembered the image of Kali dancing on Shiva, who would be a corpse but for her. Shankara realized that in neglecting the Goddess he had missed the very essence of life. Kali was manifesting herself to remind him of her glory.

In the midst of this realization and to the horror of his disciples, Shankara got down on his knees and clasped the woman's feet, thanking her for the lesson.

"No, you are not impure," he said. "It was my mind that was impure. I have never met a greater teacher than you."

Shankara stopped writing philosophy and spent the last years of his life devoted to the Goddess. He acknowledged the primacy of first-hand experience. What he had rejected, what he had cast out, was what saved him, and it came to him in the form of the fierce divine feminine. She cut through his illusions, she woke him up, she shocked him. He was wise enough to recognize her, to say yes.

Stories of Indian women like the widow in Shankara's story continue to surprise me. I think of the report I read of the women in the state of Manipur, India, who finally organized themselves against increasing numbers of rapes.

Tired of living in a state of siege and being at the mercy of the soldiers imported to their region to quell a guerrilla war, the women of Manipur decided to defend themselves rather than turn to the police or army. Too often the police or army themselves were the offenders. Though the authorities denied that there was any problem, they did not oppose the movement.

What the women did was simple—they agreed upon a signal. If a woman felt threatened when she spotted a soldier in her area at night, she took out a rod that she carried with her and banged it on the nearest lamppost. Throngs of women would come to her aid carrying flaming bamboo torches. They did nothing but surround the soldier and look at him. That was enough to put an end to any possible thoughts of harm. No one was hurt.

Called Meira Paibis, the Torchbearers, the women became known for their crusades against human rights abuses.[4] I think of the divine fires out of which Durga rose up blazing when she returned to save the world. I think of these women bringing light to dispel the darkness, responding to each other's calls, not leaving each other isolated and alone to contend with danger but coming to each other's aid with a firm, clear form of nonviolent resistance— their steady gaze, their unmovable presence, the light they carried.

The day has passed. Yesterday's rains have filled the fields, the roadside ditches, and the pot-holes, leaving the rutted road full of warm gold pools in the fading light. As I watch the arc of the sky over the fields I see that night doesn't fall, darkness does not descend—it rises. I watch it come up out of the earth, inky, and fill the sky. Tonight I say good-bye to Tara Doyle and Chökyi Nyima, for I leave India and start the long way home in the morning.

Drums start up in faraway fields, and I hear the distant voices of women singing. It's still Karttika, the lunar month, one of the holy months for women. Tonight after the moon goes down, women keeping the ritual fast will take no more food or water until sundown tomorrow; then they will gather at the river and, the following morning, begin the dancing.

PART TWO

BRAZIL AND ARGENTINA (*Rand McNally*)

The Handless Maiden

$\mathcal{O}$nce there was a young woman who lost her mother at an early age.[1] Her father gave her to a farm family to be raised. He told the family that if he did not return for her within ten years, the girl would be theirs to have as their daughter. The family was enchanted with this small child, and she grew up as one of their own many children.

Ten years passed, and her father had still not returned. Finally it was safe to call her their own. Everyone celebrated her formal entry into the family. Now she truly belonged to them. No one could take her away.

One day, when she was eighteen, a strange man entered their farmyard. The geese the maiden was tending honked and hissed at the stranger, but he would not go away. The young woman did not recognize the man, but her parents did. It was her father. He announced that he had come to take back his daughter. How could he do this? the young woman and her family protested. More than ten years had passed. He had promised. She was their daughter now. The case was taken before the village elders. The elders were sympathetic, but they ruled that there was nothing they could do, the girl belonged to her father.

When the day came for the young woman's departure, her adoptive mother gave her a book of prayers to the Blessed Mother to console herself with when she grew lonely. She stuffed the book into her belongings, climbed into her father's wagon, and left the farmyard weeping, looking back at every turn in the road while her father sat silently urging the horses on.

Two days later, they arrived at the village where her father had established himself as a prosperous merchant. He showed her to her room, gave her a maidservant to attend to her needs, and went about his business of buying and selling, having no mind for how heartbroken the young woman was.

One day he came upon her reading the book of prayers that her adoptive mother had given her. He was furious! He snatched the book out of her hands and told her that she was never to read it again. But her longing for the solace that the book provided was unbearable. One day when her father was out, she searched the house, deciding finally that the book must be locked in the chest at the foot of his bed. She found the key to the chest under his pillow and opened it. On top was a small painting of a young woman who looked so much like her that she knew that it must be her dead mother. She burst into tears at the sight of what she realized was her mother's face. Underneath the small oil portrait was a beautiful satin gown that had belonged to her mother, and underneath the heavy folds of satin was her book of prayers to the Blessed Mother.

She pulled out the book, turned quickly to her favorite prayer, and began to read. Immediately, she felt consoled. Suddenly she heard her father's horse gallop into the courtyard. She hurriedly jammed the book back under the dress, locked the chest, placed the key back under his pillow, and dashed from his room down the hall to hers. She closed her door just in time to remain undiscovered.

From that day on, whenever her father left the village, she would steal into his room, unlock his chest, pull out her book, and begin her prayers. But one day her father's horse went lame and he walked home, catching her unaware in her secret reveries. He was furious. He beat her, threatening to cut off her hands if she ever read that book again.

The next day he bought another horse and told her that he would be gone on a week's journey. She waited for the sound of his horse's gallop to die away and then stole back into his room to pray. But this time he came home two days early on foot to surprise her. He caught her in his room reading the book of prayers, with the portrait of his dead wife nearby; his grief and anger ignited, and he exploded in rage.

This time he grabbed her by the wrists, dragged her outside against her pleas, tied her wrists together, held them down on a block, and chopped off both her hands in one cruel blow. He railed against her disobedience, spun her around, and shoved her off alone into the forest nearby.

The young woman walked and walked, on through the night, frightened, wounded, and weeping. Dawn came. Birdsong rose to greet her, but she was so exhausted, hungry, tired, and thirsty that she couldn't hear them. Suddenly she found herself in a clearing surrounded by wild roses and honeysuckle vines. She was in a flower garden, and in the center of the garden was a carefully tended orchard of pear trees. The trees were heavy with fruit; their branches hung so low that, handless, she was able to eat the pears. She returned daily to feast from then on.

The garden belonged to the king. When his gardener reported that some creature was eating all his pears, the king ordered him to catch it. When he found out that it was not an animal that was eating his pears but a beautiful handless maiden, he went to see for himself. He was smitten immediately by her beauty and her plight. He took her back to his castle and ordered that her every need be provided for.

The king's mother was dismayed by the turn of events. As her son fell more in love with the handless maiden, the mother grew that much more jealous. She claimed that a handless maiden was not a suitable bride for a king, but the king refused to listen. He married the handless maiden and crowned her queen of the realm to celebrate their wedding day. The king's mother feigned acceptance and withdrew to bide her time.

Life went well for the young queen, despite her lack of hands. Her husband loved her deeply and gave her servants to wait upon her smallest wish, so that she had no need for hands. In time she became pregnant and there was much happiness and celebration throughout the realm. Even the king's mother seemed happy.

When the time came for the young queen's labor and delivery, her mother-in-law insisted on being present to direct the midwives and servants. At the last moment, she sent away the midwives and the queen's most trusted maidservants and delivered the pair of twins herself. She let *the young queen bask in the birth and allowed her to rest for a while. Then, with her own courtiers in tow, the king's mother turned on the handless maiden with a dagger, and had her dragged down a secret castle passageway, a babe under each arm, to a place outside the castle walls.*

At dawn the king's mother told her son that his wife and baby had died in childbirth, the child so deformed that she had had the bodies taken out and burned. The king went wild with grief, tearing at his clothes and hair. The next day he renounced his throne and went into mourning and seclusion.

The handless maiden was once again banished to the forest, only now she had a newborn infant under each arm. Exhausted from her ordeal, hungry, faint from thirst, the young woman stumbled on, coming to a pond where an old woman sat washing her clothes.

"Oh, good woman," she cried out, "please help me. Squeeze some water into my mouth and into my babies' mouths. We're about to die of thirst."

"No," said the old woman firmly, "get some water yourself."

"I can't!" said the younger woman. "Are you blind? I have no hands. I have to hold my babies. Oh, please help."

The old woman was unmoved. "Get it yourself," she said.

The young woman was frantic. Her head was spinning. Not knowing what else to do, she knelt down at the water's edge and leaned over to sip from the pond. As she did, her babies slipped out of her arms and went under.

"My babies! My babies! They'll drown, help, help, oh please help! Can't you see?!"

The old woman replied, "Fish them out."

"I can't," said the handless maiden, "I can't! I have no hands!"

"Plunge in your stumps," the old woman said. "Plunge in your stumps."

In frustration, and despairing of help from any other source, the young woman plunged her stumps into the water, frantically groping for her babies. Suddenly, her hands began to grow back. As she plunged deeper and deeper in the dark waters, she felt her hands growing and stretching. Then she could feel her fingers and she grabbed her babies, pulling them out of the water just before they would have drowned. She fell back from the water's edge and lay on the grassy earth, by turns laughing, crying, and cooing to comfort the infants now at each breast.

After a while she sat up and looked at the old woman, who was now done with her laundry. She was an old peasant woman, dark from the sun. She sat on a rock, patiently waiting for the young woman. There seemed to be a glow of light radiating from her. She stood to speak.

"Now you have your hands back and you can do for yourself," said the old woman. Her voice was strong and sure. It rolled like thunder over the young woman.

"Now go. Go back to your husband. He was heartbroken at the news of your death. Take matters into your own hands. You have them. You grew them yourself. Your life is your own now. It's in no one's hands but yours, and no one will ever be able to take it away again." Her words fell like rain, washing the young woman, refreshing her.

"Go," said the old woman, and disappeared. A bolt of fiery lightning cracked the sky, then it was whole again and the world was quiet. A flowering pear tree stood in the old woman's place, glowing.

CHAPTER 12

LEARNING TO ROAR

An Initiation
San Francisco Bay Area, California

. . . I
Have a self to recover, a queen.
Is she dead, is she sleeping?
Where has she been,
With her lion-red body. . . .

—SYLVIA PLATH, "STING"

A t home from Nepal and India, going through my slides from the trip late one December night, I find a photograph of Kali that troubles me. It's a statue, a lovely one, softer and less fierce than many versions of Kali. But I can't shake the feeling that the eyes that look out from the statue are not a statue's eyes, but human. I keep looking at the slide, then putting it aside and coming back to it. Each time I have the same eerie experience.

I went to Asia to understand more about fierce compassion in cultures where the Goddess is still worshipped, but I came away with more questions, not fewer.

I begin to transcribe the tapes of my interviews with Agnes and Aruna and further research the problem of child prostitution. I read the Human Rights Watch *Global Report on Women's Human Rights* to find that many laws that would protect women and children exist, but they are simply ignored or not enforced.

I thought I was writing a book, but I am cutting blocks out of stone. Every time this subject of violation and rape comes up, I want to put it aside. I find that it has different faces and a slew of names now, many of which disguise the real subject—"enforced labor," "child labor," "debt bondage," "the new slave trade"—like the different forms the Buffalo Demon takes in Durga's story. I learn quickly that one can't look at the problem just in Nepal. The Nepalese trade in women and children is tied to India, and increasingly to China, to international tourism and to trade, to drugs, alcohol, and international development policies including those supported by the United States. Nepal's problems are part of what's happened to an estimated thirty million women in Southeast Asia since the 1970s, and the problem is hardly confined to Southeast Asia. It's become global.[1] Child prostitution is one of the threads woven into the fabric of the globalization of the world economy. Literally.

I want to forget that this is going on in the world, I want to forget what went on in my life, but I can't. I see my hands on the keys as I'm typing. It's as if I see them from a great distance. My lower back seizes up. A spasm shoots up my spine and within seconds I can no longer turn my head. I am rigid with pain. The spasms last three weeks, confining me to bed much of the time, with alternating treatments of ice and heat. My doctor tells me that my sacrum has gone out, that low part of the back that connects with the pelvis. The Latin root of the word *sacrum* is *sacer,* sacred. No wonder my back went out after listening to stories of violation and reading the reports I have. I stop reading, try only to listen, only to take in the tapes of Aruna and Agnes, there are not that many.

Gradually I improve, but as I return to transcribing the tapes, my back goes out again. I am in a battle with myself. I can sit only for fifteen minutes at a time, and I've become terrified of listening.

The rainy Northern California winter sets in. I discover that Tsultrim Allione, an American teacher of Tibetan Buddhism, is in town, staying nearby. I've known her for a long time, and call to arrange to see her. Tsultrim is known for working with the energy of the fierce sacred feminine deities. She is a longtime Tibetan Buddhist practitioner, a Western woman who has emerged as a respected teacher in her own right, with a growing Buddhist retreat center called Tara Mandala on five hundred acres of wilderness outside Pagosa Springs, Colorado. One of the meditations she teaches is on a fierce female deity: Simhamukha, the lion-headed dakini, female enlightened being, known as the Queen of the Wisdom Dakinis, a female form of the Buddha.

I find her at a friend's house, near San Francisco Zen Center's Green Gulch Farm. Tsultrim sits on a window couch with her legs tucked up underneath her, her prematurely silver shock of hair and creamy skin set off by the black velvet shirt she wears. Framed by the bare December trees outside the window, a red shawl across her lap, her face is calm and beautiful, reassuring. Outside it's drizzling, blanketing the day in a cover of soft gray. We take a moment to sip hot tea. It's chilly. I cradle my cup in both hands for warmth.[2]

Tsultrim lived in Nepal and was one of the handful of Western women who became Tibetan Buddhist nuns more than twenty years ago. Though no longer a nun, she continued her practice and now in her teaching is bringing her hard-won effort to fruition.

I had known Tsultrim for more than a decade and liked her, but I kept my distance because I didn't know what to make of her, I saw her as so unconventional. More than anything, I was unsure if she was acceptable as a teacher. I was still in the thrall of male authority figures, and I didn't know if Tsultrim had their respect, whoever "they" were.

Tsultrim tells the story of going to India and Nepal when she was nineteen, in her groundbreaking book *Women of Wisdom*. She returned when she was twenty-two and became a Tibetan Buddhist nun. With the permission of her teacher she gave back her robes and her vows after three years. Over the ensuing years, she married twice, and bore four children, one of whom died in infancy.

Through all these difficulties, including those of being a single mother, she continued to study and practice Tibetan Buddhism as a student of Namkhai Norbu Rinpoche, a Dzogchen master and expert on the Bon religion—the indigenous tradition of Tibet prior to Buddhism. Not only did her life have similarities to my own that were apparently not acceptable to me in a teacher—the struggles of a single mother seemed the height of raw practicality, not spirituality—she is a contemporary of mine, and so physically beautiful that I found it hard to take her seriously. What that says about my own preconceptions of beauty, I continue to sort through.

Further, Tsultrim's elevation to her role as a teacher seemed in large part the result of adhering to the challenging path of single-minded devotion, practice, and study under Norbu Rinpoche's guidance, a particularly difficult concept for me. I don't fit within one tradition, much less under one teacher.

During our visit, she invites me to attend a retreat she will be giving on the fierce Goddess Simhamukha, and in accepting, I see that Tsultrim mirrors parts of my life with which I have not yet made peace. Why can't a woman be beautiful, sincere, devout, and coming into her own spiritual maturity? What would it cost me to let myself see Tsultrim that way? It would cost me only the misconceptions I've held on to that were part of the wound between myself and other women.

In April 1995, I arrive at a rustic retreat center on a river in Northern California for the three-day meditation retreat and the Simhamukha initiation, joining twenty-five other women and one man.

Before dinner on the evening of my arrival, I take the time to go to the meditation room where we'll gather after supper. The large, airy room is empty. On the wall behind what must be Tsultrim's seat is a dynamic blue-black painting of Simhamukha, the lion-headed dakini, dancing on a sun disc, a corpse beneath her feet, the symbol of the ego. She stands with her right knee bent and raised, her left bent slightly as though she's dancing on one foot, and the painter has caught her mid-motion. Her right hand is raised, holding a knife to cut through illusion, and her left hand holds a skull cup. In the crook of her left arm is a staff topped with a trident, symbolizing the inner masculine.[3] The dancing dakini shows us an image of the feminine that has integrated the masculine energy within and can use it skillfully. Her staff can be either a weapon or a support, depending on the occasion. The mantle of lion skin that Simhamukha wears and her skirt of tiger skin symbolize her fearlessness. She dances ecstatically against a backdrop of gold clouds and flames. I stand before this *tangka* and gaze at her for a long time.

The group gathers in the meditation room after dinner for our first meeting with Tsultrim. We sit on cushions on the carpeted floor in a circle, facing each other with Tsultrim as part of the circle, not separate from it or above it. Her relaxed teaching style puts me at ease. As we go around the room, introducing ourselves, I discover that several of the others have already taken this initiation and have come to have a chance to practice with Tsultrim. For the rest of us, it's our first time either with Tsultrim as a teacher, or with this deity, the fierce Simhamukha.

Tsultrim gives us a context for the meditation she will be teaching, explaining that this is a tantric initiation we will be receiving and that we can think of the word *tantra* as meaning "continuity."[4] And what is it that is continuous? The awakened state that arises when we let go of self-clinging.

Tantra is a spiritual path that includes the world of the body, the senses, sexuality, and the emotions, rather than turning away from them. It's a tradition that has been deeply influenced by the goddess-worshipping tradition within Hinduism, Shaktism, in which all women are considered emanations of female divinity. All that arises is seen to have come from the space of the self-generating matrix, the primordial feminine. Out of this matrix, out of this womb of enlightenment, arise compassion and luminosity. The world is born, not made.

Tsultrim explains that in Tantric Buddhism, what might ordinarily be described as positive and negative are seen not as separate energies in opposition to one another but as one continuous stream. The negative contains within itself the seeds of its own transformation. Our worst qualities contain the seeds of our greatest wisdom. There is hope for my anger that rose up in Nepal, seeds of wisdom in it, from this perspective. The challenge is not to act on it, or from it, but to persevere in its transformation, to burn through it. To reject it, disown it or ignore it, that's the poison.

Wisdom will arise, Tsultrim assures us, when we relax and let go of self-clinging. The purpose of practice is to transform our misapprehension of reality, our dualistic tendency to constantly create a split between "self" and "other." In Tantra, energy itself is believed to have wisdom, a "luminous continuity," Tsultrim calls it.

We have a brief concluding meditation period and then rise, stretch, unwind, say good night. I make my way down an unfamiliar path back to my cabin by the light of the moon through the thick, wet spring grass.

Tsultrim's long silver hair is pulled up into a knot when she comes into the meditation room the next morning looking radiant. She sits in front of the Simhamukha *tangka* at a small table covered with red silk and lays a black shawl across her lap. A cup of tea sits on the table in front of her, its steam drifting across a shaft of early-morning sunlight. The day outside this sun-drenched room is clear and bright. Vases of blood-red carnations sit on the window sill.

We begin by creating an altar in the center of the circle we make. Tall votive candles flicker in blue, red, yellow, white, and green glass holders, around the altar. Incense burns in the air. Tsultrim's teaching style is unpretentious and informal. The older students, who have done the Simhamukha practice for some time, pull out their Tibetan bells and *damarus*—ritual drums—and begin the rhythmic chanting of Tibetan Buddhism that always stirs me.

I find myself staring at the *tangka*. A woman's body with a lion's head looks strange. At first she seems extraordinarily foreign, then I recall the Egyptian goddess with a lion's head, Sekhmet, and the Madonna in the Christian tradition. There are Marys in medieval religious art who sit on lion thrones. Mary is flanked by lions as she rises out of a mountain of amethyst in one medieval painting. Mary carries this powerful association with lions too, as does Durga in Hinduism and the Great Mother in many traditions. Artemis in the Greek pantheon, goddess of the hunt, was accompanied by a lion. Hera, the queen of the Greek gods and goddesses, is seated on a lion throne. The Anatolian goddess Cybele rides a chariot drawn by lions. In the Mesopotamian world, when Ishtar goes forth as a goddess of war, she rides the lion. One of Inanna's names is Labbatu, which means "lioness."[5] I've heard of the indigenous deity María Lionza in Venezuela, who rides naked on a lion holding a pelvic bone up over her head. The lion is one of the most potent images of the power of the Goddess cross-culturally—her strength, her ability to protect, and her fierceness.

My mind has wandered. I bring myself back into the room with Tsultrim and the others comfortably spread out on this brown carpeted floor listening, some taking notes like me.

"In Buddhism, it is believed that we can discover the cause of suffering and that we can find the path to the end of suffering. Vows and meditation practice are about ending the cycle of suffering that we go through," Tsultrim tells us, smiling.

We review the traditional five Buddhist precepts: not to kill, not to steal, not to lie, not to commit adultery—disturb an existing relationship—and not to use intoxicants. Keeping the moral precepts simplifies our life so that we cease to cause harm to ourselves or others.

Tsultrim sees female Wisdom beings—dakinis—such as Simhamukha as transporters of Buddha's teachings, appearing at critical moments of transition in the lives of great teachers. A dakini may appear as a human being, as a goddess—either peaceful or wrathful—or she may be perceived as the general play of energy in the phenomenal world.[6] Simhamukha is not only the Queen of the Dakinis but also a fierce female Buddha.[7]

Dakinis speak their own language, indecipherable to ordinary humans.[8] Some teachings are passed down in whispers known as "the dakini's breath" or are given in a "twilight language," in essence, they are an alternative way of knowing, of perceiving reality. Yeshe Tsogyal, the eighth-century consort of Padmasambhava and emanation of Tara, the one famous for the *terma* tradition, was said to put whole teachings into dakini language, a language so condensed that one syllable can encapsulate an entire teaching.[9] Deposited in the earth, in diamonds, water, or in "unchanging boxes," the *termas,* those teachings given in ages past, lie hidden until the appropriate time.

A *terma* is a time-specific teaching, revealed only at the appropriate moment in history. Until then, it remains hidden, in a mountain, in a lake, in the sky, in the mind, guarded by the dakinis until the right person finds it and makes it known.[10] Unlike the Bible, the Koran, or the Torah, texts that lay claim to ultimate truths for all time, *termas* are also context specific. Time activates the teachings, setting them off like chemical reactions when the moment is ripe, at the time when that specific teaching is needed, though it may have been hidden away centuries before. *Termas* continue to be found, freshening the stream of revelation and guidance.

Tsultrim explains that the practice she gives is a mind treasure of

A-Yu Khadro, a great woman practitioner, who transmitted it directly to Namkhai Norbu Rinpoche, Tsultrim's teacher, who then transmitted it to her.[11]

A great dakini herself, A-Yu Khadro was born in 1839 in Tibet and lived until the age of 115. Norbu Rinpoche met Khadro when she was 113 and he was fourteen and studying at a monastic college in Tibet in 1951. A-Yu Khadro's hair had grown down to her knees, and though white at the roots it was still black on the ends.

He had been sent to A-Yu Khadro by his master at the monastic college. His mother and his sister went with him. At first she refused to speak with them and said, "I am just a simple old woman. How can I give you teachings?" But the next day she sent for the young man. Her teacher had appeared to her in a dream and advised her to give Norbu Rinpoche certain teachings. She would begin the next day. It was during this time that she also told him her story.

A-Yu Khadro began practicing when she was seven years old with her aunt Dronkyi, who was also a great practitioner and lived in a cave. A-Yu Khadro stayed with Dronkyi until she was eighteen years old, bringing her water and firewood. During this time, A-Yu Khadro learned to read and write in Tibetan and received meditation instructions. When she was nineteen, over her protests and those of her aunt, her parents forced her to marry a man with whom it seemed she would be happy. Her husband was very kind and generous, nonetheless, after three years of married life, A-Yu Khadro became increasingly ill. For two years she weakened until she was finally close to death. No one had been able to diagnose or relieve her illness. Finally a great yogi, a meditation practitioner, who lived in a cave near A-Yu Khadro's aunt was called in. Both he and her aunt insisted that the worldly life she was being forced to lead was not what she deeply wanted and she should be released.

"My husband was a very kind man," she told Norbu, "and agreed that if married life was endangering my life, it must be stopped." He loved A-Yu Khadro and was willing to help her, taking her to the caves of her aunt and the yogi, acting as her patron, bringing her food and supplies during the year it took her to recover. From then on, they remained close friends, like a spiritual brother and sister.

After A-Yu Khadro was well, she traveled all over Tibet, taking teachings from great lamas wherever she went. When she was thirty, she met a nun named Pema Yangkyi, who became her close friend and traveling companion for many years.

Eventually they met a lama who instructed them in meditation and told them to practice in cemeteries and sacred places in order to "overcome hope and fear."

The lama gave A-Yu Khadro and Pema Yangkyi each a drum, she told Norbu, "and after further advice and encouragement we saw no reason to delay and set off like two beggar girls. Our only possessions were our drum and a stick." They spent three years traveling around Mount Kailash alone, staying in caves and sacred places. When A-Yu Khadro was forty-two, she decided to return to the area of Tibet she was from and set out to find the caves of her now deceased aunt and the yogi, the two people who had helped save her life and set her on this path.

When she found the caves they were in ruins. Saddened, she stayed the night there and practiced meditation, going down the mountain the next day to a cemetery to meditate as well. The next morning, during her meditation, she had a vision of an egg-shaped rock in Dzongsta that she could reach through a cave. She told Norbu Rinpoche about this cave that she saw in her vision.

"When I got inside the cave there was a very intense darkness which suddenly was illuminated by multicolored light streaming out of it. This illuminated the cave and pierced the walls so that I could see through to the outside."

For A-Yu Khadro the vision was a portent. She immediately set out for Dzongsta, having heard of such a place, and found the rock that she had seen in her vision, but it was on the other side of a river from where she was. There was no way to cross by herself, the water was so high. She would have to wait for help or until the river went down. She began doing intensive meditation practice, and on the third night, when she fell asleep, she dreamed that a long white bridge appeared that reached from her side of the river across, almost to the rock itself. In the dream she thought it was good that now she could cross the river and so she did. But remarkably, when she woke up, she was indeed on the other side. She had crossed over, "but I did not know how," she told Norbu Rinpoche.

By the time she was fifty-four, she had decided to stay in retreat the rest of her life. When she was 115, she told her attendants to begin preparations for her funeral.

"With no sign of illness, we found that she had left her body one day at the time she would normally be finishing her meditation session. She remained in meditation posture for two weeks...her body had become very small...many people came to witness it." She was cremated not long thereafter. It was said that at the time of her death that "there was a sudden thaw and everything burst into bloom. It was the middle of winter."

To Namkhai Norbu Rinpoche, A-Yu Khadro left, among other things, "a volume of the Simhamukha Gongter and her writings and advice and spiritual songs." This is the lineage of the practice Tsultrim is teaching us.

That night, the night before we are to receive the formal initiation into the Simhamukha practice, I am asleep in the cabin I'm sharing with three other retreatants when I waken out of a dream.

In the dream I am roaring like a lion and Tsultrim is roaring with me. We are roaring to scare away the men who are coming to steal the children. From deep in the bowels of my being, from inside my own body, comes a primeval roar. Over and over in my dream I am roaring, and in my sleep it comes out, a full-throated growling howl of a roar.

My roaring wakes up the three women sleeping in the next room, and finally it wakes me up too. I sit bolt upright, catching myself in the middle of a guttural growl, when I suddenly realize that I am dreaming.

"Are you all right? What's going on?" come the voices through my closed door. I am in a room by myself at the end of the cabin. I get up to get a drink of water and to reassure my cabinmates—and myself—that it was only a dream.

I have never made a sound like this before. I try to roar again now that I'm awake, but I can't begin to get my voice that low again. The sound came up out of the sacrum, the part of my body that had been rigid with spasms, frozen in pain. Though I have only seen her image, heard about her, not yet had the initiation, Simhamukha is coming to life in me.

Bright sun pours through the many windows of the meditation room the next morning, warming us. We sit, alternately chanting and praying, then listening to detailed instructions as to how we are to visualize the deities and do the meditation on Simhamukha.

We are opening ourselves to be helped by the wisdom of the deity, the wisdom of the body, the wisdom of the earth, and our own senses. The world is the matrix of enlightenment, and we are learning to move through it like magicians. We see through it, recognize it as a continuum of opportunities for transformation and redemption.

The sacred circle, the mandala we hold in our minds, creates a perimeter, a boundary, around which layers of fierce guardian deities form a ring of protection, a place from which to send forth streams of compassion for all.

Inside the sacred circle, we imagine an enormous dark blue dakini, an enlightened female being with the head of a lion, dancing on the sun in the center of this vast, clear, open, circular space.

Simhamukha. Along with Simhamukha, four enormous, dancing, lion-headed dakinis represent the transformation of anger, ignorance, pride, passion, and jealousy into different forms of wisdom. The dakini of the East is white, of the South, yellow, of the West, red, while the North's dakini is a brilliant green. A retinue of sixteen powerful dakinis dance wildly in the fiery courtyard, just inside the perimeter of the mandala. Then we imagine these same figures above us, a mirror image emerging out of the crystal light of pure space, hovering. Tibetan bells are ringing, their sound vibrating. The room is warm, my eyes are closed, the sound of chanting carries me, steadily rocking me back and forth. Cutting through it all is the sound of Tsultrim's voice giving us instructions. The moment of initiation is coming. Click, she snaps her fingers, the mandala above and the mandala in my mind become one. Energy pours in, sparks fly—the mandala is ignited, the courtyard spins, the dancers whirl faster and faster, flames shoot out, sparks fly to all corners of the universe. May the world catch fire with loving-kindness and compassion!

A red string of sacred syllables, the mantra of Simhamukha, circles inside my heart. I can hardly remain seated, chanting, I am so filled with energy, buzzing, as the dakinis in my mind's eye whirl, the dancers turn. Inside each cell of the body there are worlds of mandalas with deities dancing and spinning—galaxies—and in each one Wisdom is dancing, spinning out worlds upon worlds of buddhas and bodhisattvas. And inside each cell of each buddha and Wisdom being and bodhisattva is another entire universe of buddhas and bodhisattvas dancing and whirling. We are enormous.

An ocean wave washes over my heart. In a twinkling I can see inside the wave, only "I" disappear and there is only an ocean of compassion. For a moment there is the movement of waves, silver, blue-gray, and glistening, a cloudless horizon, then it is gone.

CHAPTER 13

STONECUTTING

The Foundation of Compassion

. . . that you too, may be living stones making a spiritual house . . .

—1 PETER 2:5

I am getting ready to leave for Latin America. Fall has arrived in California. I knew from the moment I began this journey that I would have to go to Laura Bonaparte in Buenos Aires and meet the Mothers of the Disappeared. I met Laura nearly twenty years ago when she was traveling in the States, speaking out against the dictatorship that had taken over Argentina.

The clarity of Laura's speech, the moral conscience she brought to bear, and the luminosity of her presence was electrifying. I never forgot Laura Bonaparte and her commitment to nonviolence despite her own terrible circumstances—the worst a mother could bear—the disappearance of her own children. Though the fate of several members of her own family was unknown, she spoke out on behalf of all who disappeared in Argentina. She refused to be intimidated by the military. I had never met anyone with so much courage, so much valor.

Fierce compassion. When I thought of it, Laura Bonaparte came to mind. I contacted her and was stunned to discover that despite Argentina's return to democratic government in 1983, Laura and the Mothers of the Disappeared still did not know the fate of their children. These women continue to demonstrate weekly in the center of downtown Buenos Aires, in the Plaza de Mayo, as they have since 1976, when the military took over. The bond between the

Mothers of the Disappeared is fierce. Though differences have arisen over two decades of demonstrations, their spirit remains unbroken in the Línea Fundadora, the Founders Line, of the Mothers of Plaza de Mayo. For many, the Mothers have become the conscience of Argentina.

I knew that to go to Argentina was to descend into the underworld. If I was going to the land of the Disappeared, as I came to think of Argentina, I would begin by making a pilgrimage to Aparecida, "the one who appeared," the Patron of Brazil, the Black Madonna, the Mother of the Excluded, whose feast, like Durga's in India, takes place for nine days each October. There, in a retreat house with the Canisian Sisters, I would gather the reserves I needed to go to Buenos Aires.

From Argentina, I would return to Brazil to meet Yvonne Bezerra de Mello, whose work with street children gained international notice when several street children were gunned down and killed in their sleep on the steps of a cathedral in Rio. This woman, too, had to be fierce, fierce and compassionate to fight for the street children. I knew a little of what those children faced after my education in Nepal by Aruna, Agnes, and Olga.

Now as I begin the preparation for Latin America, I realize that it has taken nearly four months for my back to heal. Having completed the retreat with Tsultrim I sense why: I couldn't heal until I began to have a different way to be with the stories of child prostitution. The image of the lion-headed Simhamukha no longer seemed so foreign, so strange. A lion-headed woman dancing on the sun was energizing, it made sense psychologically, it helped me face the work in front of me. The meditation on Simhamukha gave me a vast, clear space to sit in, inside the mandala, an ancient symbol of wholeness. The mandala contained symbols and reflections of the soul's own vast capacity for creativity, health, and healing. It gave me a psychic boundary, a border, and a shield of prayers to put on before I sat down to listen to the stories from Aruna and Agnes again. It gave me a different place from which to send kindness and compassion to all beings, without exception.

Tibetan Buddhism challenges me to an expanded view, shows me that compassion, even when depicted in an image as fierce as Simhamukha, is always about loving-kindness, about treating others, even one's enemies, as oneself, and about the transformation of negativity. I think of Khenpo Choga's story of demons who instead of being destroyed were transformed to be of benefit to all.

I'm standing at my desk looking for my passport when the phone rings with an unexpected request.

The call is from a priest who has been asked to go to a hospital to administer last rites to Jim, now a dying man, a man this priest found so full of rage and hatred that he was frightened. He had never seen anyone in such a state. Jim, the man who raped me when I was four years old, the man whom I confronted directly several years ago. The priest is calling to ask me if I would please help him with his deathbed task by searching my heart and reconsidering whether or not this episode really happened. Jim has never forgiven me for confronting him. The priest is concerned for the state of Jim's soul, afraid to see him die with so much rage.

This is hard enough to hear, but before I can say anything, he goes further: Would I consider asking Jim's forgiveness for upsetting him and causing him so much suffering? From Jim's perspective, I am responsible for the rage and hatred he feels on his deathbed.

It doesn't seem to have occurred to this priest that if there was no truth in what I said, Jim might not be in such a state on his deathbed. I had spoken of this episode to hardly anyone, and the handful in whom I had confided had sworn they would keep my confidence. I had not sued him, though I had considered it. I had not made this public, though I had considered it. I worked it out over the years as best I could, privately, discreetly. I want to roar into the phone, not talk.

I look down at my desk, the telephone in my hand looking as though it's at the bottom of a cliff. The priest is still on the other end of the line, waiting for my response to his questions. The demons are back in full force, waiting to be transformed. I can see Khenpo Choga in his room in Nepal, asking me if I could have compassion for the man selling the child as well as for the child: "Are you compassionate enough to do that?" Choga's question becomes a refrain, stopping me from reacting. I take a breath, and for the moment, I say nothing. I think. I breathe again.

Am I compassionate enough to remember that Jim is dying and apparently terrified—trapped in his own rage and hatred—and that this priest, whom I know to be kind, well-meaning, and sincere, is also untrained for this situation? I take another breath. I tell the priest that I had searched my heart for years before I confronted Jim. I tell him that I had written Jim right after that visit, making it clear that I had forgiven him for any harm and reminding him of my offer to speak with him with a third party.

"Jim chose never to speak to me again. I don't know what more I can do but continue to pray for him as I have for years," I tell the priest with all the equanimity I can hold on to.

The fact that I do not explode has nothing to do with my limited powers of forbearance. It is a profound testament to that fact that there is a much greater benevolence in the universe than what I am able to summon up on my own.

Late that night I wake up in a sweat. What is not healed keeps reappearing. I sit, I pray, I meditate. A picture from a film I've recently seen comes back to me. It is a grainy black-and-white image of a Tibetan Buddhist nun being tortured in a Chinese prison.[1] The nun's arms are crossed and pulled up tight behind her with rope, her arms tied up so high they nearly reach her shoulders. She sits on the floor in silence. The film was shot from behind, I cannot see her face. She is being beaten by Chinese prison guards. In a voice-over narration, one of the nuns who had been tortured and released speaks in a steady, calm voice of having compassion for her torturer. She knew he was harming himself by being so cruel to her, and she was concerned for him.

If I could see this nun, she would show me another face of the fierce feminine—a fierce commitment to compassion, a zealousness beyond what I've believed possible or appropriate. She challenges me, makes me remember Adhi Rinpoche, who after twenty-one years of imprisonment was able to speak of seeing our enemies standing with us before the Tree of Refuge, and to tell us to remember that they too want happiness, they too want to be released from suffering. This is the depth at which compassion must be practiced, must become part of us. I am being given another chance. I had only cut off the demon's head in my confrontation with Jim, I did not pierce the heart, mine or his, as Durga did the Buffalo Demon's. Could I do that now? I don't know. Finally I pull out pen and paper and begin to write to Jim.

I try to put myself in his situation: on the verge of death, in pain, and frightened. I acknowledge how painful his position might be, to be told of doing something terrible that he does not remember and can't imagine doing. I assure him that I believe that he was telling the truth as he understood it. I reiterate that I forgave him, long ago. I tell him how one afternoon, long before I confronted him, I was walking along a deer path through the tall dry summer grasses on the flank of a mountain. The light was soft and fading. I was praying. Suddenly I felt a presence on my right, that's the best way I know how to describe it, a very gentle, kind presence. It seemed to be him, Jim, as a young man, walking beside me. He had come to tell me that he was sorry for all the pain he had caused and to ask me to forgive him. He said that something terrible had happened to him as a young child too, something that had twisted and marred him, though he did not say what it was. He too had been deeply wounded, and his wounds had crippled him in such a way that he could not help harming me, and he now understood that. This presence was so gentle, so kind, sincere, and remorseful that it was easy to say, "Yes, I forgive you." Then he, this presence, disappeared and I was alone again, walking on the hillside.

Who that presence on the hillside was, what it was, whether or not it was "real," what "real" is, these were all questions that I could have explored at length but chose not to. Instead I went back to the biblical notion "By their fruits you shall know them," and decided that no matter who or what that presence was, whether it came from an interior or exterior event, it was beneficent. Something in my heart shifted because of that interchange, and I experienced compassion for someone who had been only loathsome beforehand. A deeper level of healing. Grace was at work.

In sum, I tell him that I'm praying for him at this critical time. I wish him peace of heart and mind. I assure him that I have put that episode behind me and gone on.

It is a hard, awkward letter to write, one of the hardest I've written in my life. A test. It takes nearly two days, but finally I have a document that is as kind, honest, and compassionate as I can make it. It is a relief to discover that no matter how awkwardly I put it, I want no harm, I genuinely want only peace for this man. This is further testimony to the kindness of my teachers, the healing power that comes through the community of recovery, and the goodness that simply is.

I send the letter to the priest to deliver.

I dream that I am walking back through the life of Mary, the Mother of Christ. I have to cut up big blocks of stone to rebuild

Mary's house. That is my task. A voice in the dream tells me to notice the difference between the physical experience of walking back
through her life and the experience of stonecutting, the labor necessary to rebuild the house. When I walk back through Mary's life, I
feel sad. But when I am hard at work, cutting up the blocks of stone,
I am no longer sad but absorbed and satisfied.

It's raining. I pull on a rain parka and set off for a hike on the
mountain. I hike hard and fast, taking a steep, difficult shortcut up
to the ridge. I head straight uphill for half an hour to reach the place
I want. I stand in the rain, jotting notes on a scrap of paper that was
in my pocket, the letters blurring as I write. My heart is pounding.
It's gray, wet, and windy, with a heavy fog. The mountain billows
and breathes as I look down into the canyon below and across.
Everything is in motion, even the mountain moves, turned to fluid
by this strange fog light. It's dizzying to look across the canyon as
the fog moves up the mountainside, the light constantly shifting its
play on the dark trees—what is shadowed becomes light, what is
light shadowed, in a liquid moment, faster than an eye can blink.
The rain comes down harder, and the wind picks up a steady beat.
Perspiration rolls down my back as I stand here peering into the fog.
I'm looking for the spot where we are building what I call "the spirit
house," a tiny circular stone structure that always seems to be in the
process of being built up or torn down.

I don't know who began building the spirit house. I found it one
day alongside the trail. No one person is building it, it is an anonymous communal effort. Many stop to add a stone or a stick to the
tiny structure that grows slowly, stone by stone, across the days. We
are all building it. I have never seen another person working on it,
yet each day something has been changed, added or taken away.

I finally find the spirit house in the fog. A few days ago it was
knocked down. A friend and I laid out the stones for a new foundation. Now I finish filling in the circle and begin a second layer, each
stone a prayer, especially for Jim and the priest. Forgiveness. To

cease to cherish displeasure. How long does this process take? The great teaching is that, like love, I have to keep choosing it. This is the hardest lesson for me, I want it to be over and done with, finished, but here it is again. I have to make the choice. Stone upon stone, the cornerstone. What I had cast out is becoming the new foundation.

THE STORY OF INANNA

Inanna, beloved Queen of Heaven and Earth whose cult lasted over four thousand years, giver of the me, the laws of justice and civilization, passed through seven gates to reach her sister Erishkegal, who ruled the underworld. Inanna had to go down, to descend, to unveil, to disrobe at every gate, handing over first her crown, then her scepter, her earrings, her necklace, her breastplate, then her girdle, finally the very cloth that covered her. When she arrived in the Great Below, she was naked. Erishkegal fixed the eye of death upon Inanna, hung her like a corpse on a peg. She hung for three days in the Great Below. She did not return. In the Great Above nothing would grow. Ninshibur, her servant, secured divine intervention, sent helpers to the Great Below, saved Inanna's life. Inanna ascended.

Inanna returned to the Great Above radiant and glowing, regally adorned, fully robed, bringing the return of all life with her; only then Erishkegal fixed the eye of death on Inanna's husband, Dimmuzi, the shepherd. Now Dimmuzi would have to descend to Erishkegal for half of the year, Dimmuzi's sister, the other half of the year.[1] Reciprocity is necessary. The return was not without sacrifice. The word sacrifice comes from sacer, "sacred," "holy," and facere, "to make," "to do." Sacrifice makes something holy. Redemption is costly.

CHAPTER 14

"RAISE UP
THOSE HELD DOWN"

A Pilgrimage to the Black Madonna,
Mother of the Excluded, Aparecida, Brazil

. . . as black
as the black Madonna,
who answers all prayers from the heart . . .

—KATHLEEN NORRIS,
Little Girls in Church

According to legend, in October 1717, a poor fisherman, João Alves, and two companions had been unable to catch any fish in the Paraíba River of Brazil. On the last cast of the day, the fishermen pulled up a net empty but for the broken body of a statue of a Black Virgin Mary. They cast again, and pulled up her head.[1] They named the statue Aparecida, which means "Appeared." They rejoiced in finding the Virgin and resolved to keep her, and thereafter their nets were filled with fish. This was the first "miracle" attributed to this Madonna.

This small statue of the Virgin, little more than two feet high, was passed from house to house in procession after this event. More miracles were reported, especially among the poor, and the fame of this Black Virgin began to spread. The devotion to her became so strong that she was declared the Patron of all Brazil.

How a statue of Our Lady of the Immaculate Conception came to be at the bottom of the Paraíba River is the subject of many stories. One of the best-known legends is that she was thrown there to chase away a water serpent who was terrorizing the people. The serpent fled, the Virgin protected her people.

Ivone Gebara, the indomitable Brazilian feminist theologian of liberation who writes of this story, notes that the Virgin whom the people threw into the river was white, like the Portuguese colonizers who brought her. Legend holds that the river turned the Virgin black. In the river she lay broken, on the bottom, like the people whom the Portuguese enslaved and colonized, until the fishermen found her and made her their own.[2]

Aparecida became beloved by those shackled by poverty and slavery for the miracles she performed for them. An eighteenth-century story credited with helping spread her devotion in Brazil follows:

One day a slave was traveling with his master near the small shrine that had been constructed for Aparecida. The man entreated his master to stop the wagons and let him pray at the door of the shrine. As soon as he knelt down in the doorway, the heavy chains he wore fell off his hands and feet, and the wide iron collar around his neck broke apart. His master declared him free: the Virgin herself seemed to command it. Word of this event spread rapidly. Though it did little to end slavery, the telling and retelling of the story gained this Virgin an even stronger following as a symbol of liberation among the disenfranchised and the poor.[3]

In the twentieth century, Aparecida became the patron of the black intellectual movement in Brazil. Bishop-poet Pedro Casaldáliga and composer-musician Milton Nascimento sing of the struggle of black Brazilians in their "Praise to Mariama" in the Mass of the Quilombos, the settlements formed by runaway and freed slaves in Brazil. Gebara points out that ama *to black Brazilians means "wet nurse." Thus "Mariama" is the black woman who nurses and cares for not only her own children but also the whites, she is mother to all. She does not discriminate. It is to Mariama that Brazilians sing this song from Mary's Magnificat in the Gospel of Luke from the New Testament, when they say,*

Sing on the mountaintop your prophecy
That overthrows the rich and powerful, O Mary,

Raise up those held down, mark the renegades,
Dance the samba in the joy of many feet.

. . . .

Give strength to our shouts,
Raise our sights,
Gather the slaves in the new Palmares,
Come down once more to the nets of life
of your black people, black Aparecida.[4]

The whir of hundreds of doves taking flight echoes in the cavernous basilica of Aparecida, Brazil's national shrine. It is a basilica reportedly larger than St. Peter's in Rome, larger even than the Cathedral of St. John the Divine in New York. Handbells ring out from the altar while the thick smoke of incense rises in the air. There is a great stir. Seventy thousand people rise to their feet, waving tiny green Brazilian flags and shouting, *"Viva Aparecida! Viva Aparecida! Viva Aparecida!"* The refrain rolls through the basilica like thunder, filling the air. A priest lifts the small black statue of Our Lady of Aparecida high in the air, turning from side to side for all to see.

It is October 12, the Feast of Aparecida, Brazil's Patron. Today is the culmination of nine days of prayer, rosaries, and masses in honor of Aparecida. Hundreds of buses from all over Brazil sit in the oversize parking lots outside. For many, the open baggage compartments of the buses provide their only shelter. For some, this is a pilgrimage made every year; for others, like myself, it is the first time. I meet no other North American in the crowds over the days I spend here at the Canisian Sisters' Retreat House near the shrine. I think of Durga's nine-day October feast going on in Nepal and India. The Great Mothers.

An enormous white banner hangs across one of the four naves that open onto the main octagonal altar. The Portuguese words emblazoned high in the air across the western nave in bold black letters are *Aparecida Mãe dos Excluidos do Brasil*, "Aparecida Mother of the

Excluded of Brazil." Archbishop Dom Aloysius Lorscheider tells me that all who have been marginalized by conventional society are upheld and revered in the figure of this Virgin—the poor, the broken, and the dark. She is their champion. She is black because she is the Mother of All.

This Dark One who champions all that is left out also symbolizes what must be included now. Standing in this basilica amidst the shouts for Aparecida, I think of the statue in Banaras that I was told was Kali, that set me off on the path to find the Black Madonna. I find the Dark Mother in culture after culture. She weaves a bond that reaches beyond cultures, across time, that gives us back our history with one another. She provides a way across cultures, a bridge. She gives us back not only the connection between the sacred and world of nature, the body, but she gives us the ground of being, the world body in which we live with all creatures. She gives us earth, water, air, and fire. Creation. Then goes beyond. Helps us cross over. Is the other side, the river and the shore.

Whoever this Dark One is, whether she appears as Virgin, Mother, Crone, or Queen, she is found underlying tradition after tradition: the Aztec Goddess Tonantsin, at whose site Our Lady of Guadalupe, the Patron of All the Americas, appeared in Mexico; La Pachamama, the source of all life, beloved by the people of the Andes; María Lionza, the mountain goddess of Venezuela; the Egyptian-African Goddess Isis, whose worship spread throughout Europe up until the second and third centuries C.E.; the Hindu Kali, carried from India by the Gypsies on their migrations; the Orishás, brought from Africa to Brazil—she is the ground, she is both the earth itself and the root below. She gives us our depth, the darkness we need to grow. The taller the tree, the deeper the root system. She is also the Tree of Life, this little dark one, *la morenita,* our mother. I too, a white woman, can claim her, the ancient Earth Mother of Old Europe, the indigenous black Caucasian goddess of regeneration and fertility of whom I was told, the Earth Mother

CELEBRATION OF THE FEAST OF APARECIDA, THE MOTHER OF THE
EXCLUDED, THE BLACK MADONNA AND PATRON OF BRAZIL,
APARECIDA, BRAZIL (*China Galland*)

who was worshipped in pre-Indo-European Europe when the color
black symbolized life and white meant death. We need only examine our own tradition, look beneath, she has been there all along,
right under our feet.[5]

Venerated for centuries in great cathedrals around the globe, the
Black Madonnas have long been proclaimed to be especially powerful miracle workers and healers. Yet few have commented on the
darkness of her face. Some say it was because she survived fires that
destroyed all but her, that she was darkened by candlesmoke. Could
it not be, as I have written before, that she is dark because she enters
lives on fire, because she has absorbed so much suffering?

Some say that she is black for no reason, that her darkness means nothing. Others say she is a symbol, an archetype, psyche's shadow. I say she is all these things and also that she is a black woman, a woman of color, a brown woman, a red woman, and more. She is not white. She is more, she includes all colors. She is dark because we come in so many colors, hues, and shades, and none is to be left out.

Like a river, her darkness comes from numerous sources, a multiplicity of streams. She surfaces in European and Near Eastern sites where black meteorite stones fell out of the sky and were then venerated. She rises by healing waters, streams, rivers, and deltas. In some places she is associated with storms, lightning, and thunder. Her waters are fed by streams of a tradition in which black symbolized Wisdom. The Womb of God. The world of medieval mystics. The Womb of Enlightenment from the East. From Africa. The Root. Wisdom herself. She is rising to remind us that what we call darkness is invisible light. That ninety percent of what is, is invisible. That darkness matters, is to be valued, treasured.[6]

The image of the Black Madonna, the Dark Mother, is arising in the human psyche now because we need her. Images of the sacred are vessels, containers. They function as portals, doorways, porous membranes through which the unseen world can pour. What we need now is an awareness of the indivisibility of our relationship with each other—peoples of all races, nationalities, ethnicities, and classes—and with the earth and all her creatures. We suckle and feed upon her, this planet we share. We are completely dependent upon our relationships. We are dying because we leave out our relatedness—with the earth and with one another.

The shouts for Aparecida reach a new crescendo. The priest is taking her from the altar and elevating her again for the crowd to see, this little Dark One, this Black Mary. Suddenly I remember Gabriel and his answer to Mary when she asked him how she could conceive a child: "The Holy Spirit will come upon you, and the power of the Most High will cover you with its shadow. And so the child will be holy and will be called Son of God," he told her (Luke 1:35).

The Black Madonna is also Mary at the moment of conception, impregnation, when she was shadowed by God. It was God's shadow that made the child holy, His darkness. This is what it looks like to be covered by God.

The crowd goes wild as the priest holds Aparecida aloft, turning slowly in all four directions, then finally plunges down the red-carpeted steps for the long walk to the end of the eastern nave of the basilica. The priest slowly makes his way down the long aisle with the Virgin, holding her up for people to see and touch. The glare of television lights is blinding; he makes his way patiently, pale and perspiring.

The faithful strain against heavy velvet ropes, their hands outstretched to touch the statue as it passes by if they are lucky. If not, they seem equally happy to receive her graces from a distance. People hold up babies, rosaries, little statues of Aparecida, bottles of holy water, slips of paper with thanks or requests for miracles. Whatever they have brought, they wave high in the air for Aparecida to bless. The priest turns when he reaches the end of the red carpet and slowly makes his way back up the aisle to return her to the altar.

Is there an upstart in the crowd? A young woman in cream-colored pants and top with a pale purple scarf around her neck follows the priest to the altar, takes the microphone, and begins to walk around, speaking passionately to the enormous crowds on all four sides of the altar. She speaks with her whole body, pacing back and forth across the altar, of the "Excluded" to whom Aparecida is the Mother. And as she speaks, an old dark woman wearing a gray skirt, black slippers, and a scarf over her head begins the long walk down the aisle to join her on the altar. Just behind the old woman, thirty feet or so, is a slender, attractive, well-made-up woman in skin-tight black pants, with a bright red sequined body-hugging top and black spiky high heels. Behind her is a tall young woman in a blue jumper at least eight months pregnant, holding her stomach. I don't know why they are doing this. Next in this surprising procession is a man in the striped suit of a convict, followed by a man in a hospital gown, holding up a bottle of IV fluid for the tube that runs into his arm. As they walk slowly single-file down the nave of the basilica to the altar, they stop every few steps to hold up their hands and cross their wrists as though they are in chains.

Once they reach the altar, they climb up the steps and turn away from one another, each finding a place to stand alone with their backs to one another on the octagonal altar, creating a vivid tableau of the Excluded, the forgotten and the rejected. The convict comes forward as the woman in the purple scarf narrates. She tells us that he is a man trying to start his life over, that he is unable to find work, that no one will give him a chance. The woman in red now steps forward. She represents the women and girls who are forced into prostitution to merely survive. Next the hospital patient, who represents the people ravaged by AIDS whom no one will touch or acknowledge. All the members of the tableau move away from him with gestures of fear of contagion. The young pregnant woman represents the young mothers with babies, left to fend for themselves, abandoned by society. The old woman stands for the elderly who are left out and ignored, discarded. I am spellbound. This is a service such as I've never seen. The entire basilica of seventy thousand people is hushed, the truth of what is being depicted on the altar so fully recognized.

A young man in a white robe, representing Christ, then approaches and embraces each person in a simple liturgical dance. He draws the Excluded around him into a circle and gives the old woman the statue of Aparecida. The mood of the tableau shifts dramatically. The sorrow of the Excluded is suddenly transformed. The old woman holding the Madonna becomes the center of the circle. She turns and turns, radiant and laughing, on the altar, holding the Black Madonna high in the air as Christ and the circle of the Excluded move counterclockwise, dancing, around her. The congregation explodes in applause.

It is fitting that it is the old woman who holds the Madonna aloft. The wisdom of her devotion shines in her face as she dances before thousands and thousands of people. She is a sister to Indramaya, the old woman who danced at the Devi's in Kathmandu last October. My heart leaps now, as it did when Indramaya danced, leaps at the sight of this old woman, encircled by a love that excludes no one. She turns and dips, and waves the Virgin. *"Viva Aparecida!"* we all shout, rising to our feet, hands in the air, flags waving, shouting louder and louder, *"Viva Aparecida! Viva AparecíiiiiiiiiidAAA!"*

I think of the women I've seen in churches around the world, praying before the altar of the Madonna. Many times there might be no one in the church but the old women. They care for the altar, bring the fresh flowers, trim the candles, embroider the vestments and the altar cloth. As I watch this old woman dancing, it occurs to me that these women have been doing something important for everyone. Through their prayers and devotion, through their practice of the Rosary—telling the story of Mary's life with Jesus, over and over—they have been keeping Mary alive, they have been honoring her. Wisdom itself. They have been upholding the feminine face of God.

Yet before the day's celebration comes to an end outside with singing and dancing, the priests are exhorting people to "be more like Mary . . . be obedient, reasonable, serene." Above all obedient. Once again I see how the devotion to Mary can be full of ambiguity and used by the Church to control people, especially women.

Does anyone praise Mary for her fierce side? It exists. Consider the Mary who praised God for bringing down the mighty, the Mary of liberation, the Mary who agreed to bear a child under circumstances which she could not explain, for which she could have been stoned or ostracized, the Mary who was a refugee, who rose in the night, took up her child to flee to Egypt with only Joseph and his dream. Consider the Mary who entered the bastion of the temple, the one who spoke publicly, who chided her son, held him accountable. The Mary who raised a rabble-rouser. The Mary who watched her son be beaten, humiliated, nailed to the cross; who watched him die and who kept standing; who bore witness, powerful witness; who withstood the pain and then kept going. The Mary who went on, some say, to lead the Apostles. This is a woman of towering strength. Mary as the Black Madonna, the Dark One, carries this earthy, fiery energy.

Now I feel ready to go to Argentina, to Laura Bonaparte and the Mothers of the Disappeared, to the Madres de la Plaza de Mayo Línea Fundadora. Seeing the old woman dancing touches something in me, taps an energy. Now I'm more eager than ever to be with women who embody this energy in the world.

The old woman dancing on the center of the altar, holding up the Black Madonna, is prophetic and victorious.

CHAPTER 15

"A HIROSHIMA INSIDE HER"

The Mothers of the Disappeared
Buenos Aires, Argentina

A nahi was a Guaraní warrior woman, a hero from two centuries ago. The Guaraní were one of the indigenous tribes of Argentina. Anahi led a resistance movement to protect her people from the colonists. She was captured but managed to escape and then was captured again.

The next time she was captured, they dragged her to the center of town, built a pyre of wood, and lashed her to a stake and set it on fire. But her spirit was so strong and her resistance so powerful that even as they were burning her, the sparks from her fire exploded into a million carmine red flowers, and her body melded into the wood of the stake like a tree in its flowering. The tree became the ceiba tree, the national tree of Argentina.

The narrow French doors to a small balcony stand ajar. I can step outside, almost into the blossoming tree that flourishes there. It's a sunny, clear afternoon in Laura Bonaparte's flat. Although it is still October, fall for me, it is spring in Buenos Aires, and the air is balmy. On such a beautiful day it is hard to remember that nearly thirty thousand people disappeared during the military dictatorship here, from 1976 to 1983. Today we know that they were kidnapped, tortured, and brutally murdered. Then, however, it was said only that they disappeared, as though they might one day reappear.

Laura lost seven members of her family to that regime of terror. She is a member of the Madres de la Plaza de Mayo, the organization of the Mothers of the Disappeared that began in 1977. From April of 1977 up until today, these women have marched in the plaza, demanding to know what happened to their children, asking for justice and remembrance. In the earlier part of this century, Argentina, with its extraordinarily rich natural resources, vast agricultural lands, and educated population, was predicted to become one of the world's most prosperous nations. Instead it was plagued with military coups and dictatorships that prevented it from achieving the necessary political stability to become a world power. Until now. Now, as Argentina seeks to strengthen its democracy, its success may well depend upon how it handles the demands of those whose loved ones "disappeared."

Starting in the 1930s, the armed forces have unconstitutionally overthrown and taken over five elected governments. In the chaotic aftermath of Juan Perón's death, in July 1974, when his third wife, Isabel, took over his presidency—with inflation soaring to 700 percent—extremist groups operating on both the right and the left killed government officials, police, each other, and civilians. The military took over again with hardly a protest on March 24, 1976.[1]

The initial rationale for the military takeover—re-establishing order in the chaos of Isabelita Perón's rule—evaporated quickly as the original insurgents were destroyed, and the insanity that accompanies state-sponsored torture and murder quickly took over.

Many of the military were fascists. Thoughtful Argentineans soon began to feel trapped in a nightmare that again would destroy all possibility of constitutional government. Congress was dismissed; judges and members of the Supreme Court were replaced by military appointees. People, especially young people, began to disappear. Barbarism became the rule. The military kidnapped whomever they wanted: for suspicion of being a guerrilla, for suspicion of knowing a guerrilla, of harboring subversive thoughts, for being listed in an address book of a dentist who was under suspicion of having had subversive thoughts. The reasons became further and further removed from reality, and soon there was no reality left.[2]

The military's power was broken finally by its own ineptitude, which culminated in the Falklands War with the British, in 1983. The Argentine military suffered a crushing defeat and could no longer retain power. Democratic elections were held, and Raúl Alfonsín, one of the few politicians who had been critical of the military, ran on a human rights platform, promising to investigate the disappearances and prosecute the wrongdoers, and won handily. He promptly appointed a distinguished panel of citizens to investigate the kidnappings, abductions, and disappearances—the Sábato Commission, the National Commission on the Disappeared.

What is remarkable about Argentina's case is that unlike Germany after World War II, unlike the former Yugoslavia and Rwanda of today, no outside international body came in to prosecute the criminals. Argentina decided to investigate and prosecute its own military. This was both its genius and its failing. Compared to the atrocities committed, little has come of what began as a courageous attempt to bring its own military to justice. Further military uprisings, pardons, amnesty, and limits on the length of time for prosecution helped cripple Alfonsín's enterprise.

Of the nearly thirty thousand people widely believed to be missing in Argentina, at least ten thousand disappearances were confirmed by the government's own investigation and its official report, *Nunca Más,* published in 1986.[3] People were abducted at gunpoint and never returned.

Ever since democracy was established, in 1983, the government has continued to maintain that the records of the Disappeared can't be found, or that they were destroyed, or that the military had never arrested or detained the person in question—myriad excuses to avoid the fact that these people are gone, leaving their families and friends in the prolonged, agonizing suspense of not knowing what happened, with no information about the unrecovered bodies, no way to heal the pain, no way to put an end to their grief.

I am the incomprehensible silence
and the memory that will not be forgotten.

—THUNDER, PERFECT MIND
second to fourth century,
Gnostic Gospel, Nag Hammadi Library

Laura calls me in to tea. I quickly pile my duffel bags along a wall of bookshelves that run from the floor to just below the thirteen-foot ceiling of her study.

We sit down at a circular dining room table at the end of a broad hallway. The floor is covered with black-and-white diamond-patterned linoleum squares. The room is bright with a bank of open windows facing east. There is a bowl of fruit in the middle of the table, a plate of cheese and crackers. Our translator, Diana Zermoglio, sits next to me. She is a well-dressed woman in her forties, with short, dark, curly hair and a slow, luxurious smile. Diana has a sister among the Disappeared.

Laura comes in with a pot of tea. She wears a navy blue turtle-neck shirt, faded blue jeans, and well-worn black tennis shoes. She wears no makeup or jewelry except for a watch and the Hebrew let-ter *chai*, which means "life," around her neck on a silver chain. Laura would look elegant no matter what her attire. At seventy, she is still an extraordinarily handsome woman: tall, strong-bodied, with large brown eyes, high cheekbones, and a widow's peak.

On the pale yellow wall behind her are photographs of her speaking at human rights conferences in Washington, D.C., New York, Spain, and Italy. There are snapshots of two of her grandchil-dren as small toddlers hugging each other in a shower—wet and shining and laughing. There is a profile of her oldest son, Luis, in his thirties, with thick, dark hair, an open, handsome face, and pensive eyes. There are photographs of her as a young mother under a spreading tree on a lawn with her four young children sprawled about her smiling and laughing, her arms around them, photos that any happy, proud mother would have. All those children, but for Luis, "disappeared" during the dictatorship.

What I've come here for suddenly seems impossible: to understand how Laura could lose seven family members—three of her children, an unborn grandchild, her children's spouses, and her children's father—to kidnapping, torture, and murder, and not become embittered, broken, consumed with rage, or driven mad with grief and a desire for vengeance. I want to know how this vibrant, glorious, profoundly sane woman survived, how she continues to transform this tragedy, to be effective, to take action, as she does, on behalf of the Disappeared.

"No one disappears," Laura begins. "People are born, they live, they die. They don't disappear. I searched for the missing members of my family. I needed proof. If my children were alive, I was going to be able to find them. If they were dead, I should be the one to bury them. This is not the natural thing to do, for the mother to bury her children. The natural thing is that mothers should die before the children. But nothing that happened here in Argentina is natural."

The sound of Laura's Spanish echoes in the high-ceilinged room, followed by the staccato of Diana's sentence-by-sentence English translation. As Laura begins to speak of her daughter Noni, her deep voice drops to a whisper. A great quiet comes into the room, a quiet so palpable that it becomes a presence in itself. It surrounds us. Laura speaks inside this quiet—calmly, deliberately, and with great dignity.

"Noni was killed December 24, 1975. She was twenty-four years old. She was nursing her baby when they came and took her and her husband. They were living in the *favela,* the slum. Noni was a teacher. She was teaching children to read and write. That was her 'crime.'

"Noni's husband, Adrian Saidón, was shot on March 24, 1976, the day of the coup, the day the military took over. Their baby, Hugo, was taken in by Irenita, my other daughter, and her husband, Mario Ginzberg. Irenita was a sculptor. They had two small children, then three with Hugo. That is, until they came for Irenita and Mario. Irenita and Mario disappeared on May 11, 1977. Irenita was twenty-one.

"Then they took Victor, the younger of my two sons, and Victor's fiancée, Jacinta Levi. He was twenty-four. They were kidnapped on May 19, 1977. That was the year the Mothers of the Disappeared started, by now so many were disappearing.

"Luis, my older son, was in Mexico. He's the only one still alive. Luis saved my life. I stayed with him in Mexico until 1985. With Luis and Hugo, Noni's baby. I was able to save Hugo and get him out of Argentina. He lives with me now, he's twenty-one. He is *fantastico!* What Hugo and I have been through together is beyond grandmother and grandchild. Hugo is like a brother to me."

Laura was visiting her son Luis in Mexico when she received the news of her daughter Noni's disappearance. She came back to Argentina to try to find her. In the first days of January 1976, authorities told Laura that Noni was dead. She looks straight at me, and says quietly:

"They wanted to give me the cut-off hands of my daughter in a glass jar, but I refused. I said I had to be given the whole body of my daughter, not just her hands. They refused."

My head begins to throb. We sit quietly for a long time, licked clean by the tongue of a great silence.

"So then I began a legal proceeding with Noni's father, Santiago

Bruchstein, from whom I was divorced. We sued the military so that we could find the whereabouts of Noni's body and get her remains, to bury them.

"They said we couldn't have the information about her body. They said that Noni's body was a military secret. Then they came for Santiago because we had given his address on the legal papers. That was June 11, 1976. He was sixty years old, bedridden with emphysema. He was recovering from a heart attack. A nurse was with him. They dragged him out of bed, calling him a 'dirty Jew, a filthy dog' for having the nerve to sue the military. Then they killed him.

"I know now the way Noni got killed, but I don't want to speak about it."

She pushes her chair away from the table, stands up, and says, "I will be back in a moment," then walks slowly down the long hall to her office.

"She is going to get the photographs," Diana explains.

Laura returns with a large envelope filled with photographs. Sunlight pours through the high windows onto the packet and the table where we sit.

"Look," she says, pulling out and unfolding a large color photograph made into a poster and spreading it on the table before us as Diana and I quickly push aside the teacups.

In the photograph, Laura is standing in front of a mass grave, freshly opened, revealing only a jumble of bones of different body parts. My throat tightens, I can feel my eyes sting and moisten. I don't want Laura to have to comfort me, but there are so many bodies it makes me dizzy to look.

In the photograph, Laura stands in a dark blue Mexican dress with beautiful embroidered panels of blue birds and flowers of all colors across her shoulders and around her neck. There are a handful of others in the photograph. They are all looking down into the large pit of jumbled human bones. Laura's eyes are downcast. Her head remains high, her carriage erect. Her hands are by her sides, her right hand pointing into the pit in front of her. She looks composed and contained, yet at the same time vulnerable and crushed.[4]

"This is where they buried Noni," she explains. "Someone had told me that I would find her in one piece. That's what I believed. When others said that the remains were mixed, I could not hear what they said. I thought, No, she will be alone, in a wooden coffin. But when I went that day for the grave to be opened, all I found were pieces of bodies in the ground, everywhere. There were only pieces of bodies, many bodies, different bodies, different parts of bodies. It was a common grave, a mass grave. I could not identify the remains of my own daughter. Everything was shattered. It was very terrible. *Muy terrible.* I could not think. I could not imagine," she says, pausing quietly for a moment before pulling out the next photograph.

"This is Noni," Laura says of the ravishingly beautiful young woman with short dark hair and a warm smile like her own. Laura smiles proudly as she tells me, "Noni was a mezzosoprano, and a first voice in a choir, with a very well-known choir conductor. She played the piano very well.

"Here is my daughter Irenita with her husband, Mario, and their daughter. Irenita was very tall. She was younger than Noni. Irenita played the harp. We were a musical family. Irenita was the baby of the family. This is Irenita too," Laura says, smoothing out a well-worn photocopy of a photograph of a laughing young girl with medium-length blond hair looking off to the side. Another beauty.

"And this is Mario, her husband," she says wistfully, pulling out a picture of a striking young man with short wiry hair standing outside a house with a thick flowering vine climbing up its sides. "He was a sculptor too, Mario Ginzberg. And this is their daughter, Victoria, as a baby, my granddaughter. She is still alive.

"Here is my son Victor," she says fondly, handing me another striking image, this one of a tall young man, thin, with a shock of thick hair and a face pretty enough to be a girl's.

Then she takes out a grainy 8½-by-11 black-and-white photograph of a man's upper body, badly burned, charred and crisp, only the head recognizable as human remains. I catch my breath as she explains, "This was Noni's father, Santiago. I had been divorced from him, but together we made the lawsuit to find Noni. I know the fact that he was Jewish made it worse for him. The military was very anti-Semitic. It is still. I know. I am not Jewish but I was married to a Jew, as were my daughters.

"Santiago was shot. His body was left on the ground that night. It was winter, below freezing. The side of his face that was on the frozen ground was preserved. I could make out his ear and his mustache, that's why I was able to identify him. I recognized the mustache, the way he shaved it, on that side."

She looks in silence for a moment at the photograph. Diana sits across the table from me, next to Laura. I stare at the photograph too, my headache suddenly intensifying.

I am drifting in the face of all this horror. It is a beautiful day in Buenos Aires. Spring. The sun is shining. It is Monday. I have to remember something—what is it that I have to remember? Yes, the Buddhist precept I took: *Do not turn away from suffering.*

My attention returns to Laura. Almost whispering, looking at me gently, her eyes completely open, Laura says, "They also showed me this picture." She is pulling out a photocopy of a photo of a perfectly normal-looking baby on top of a pile of bodies. A line of some sort seems to run from the baby and then disappears outside the frame. I don't understand what I am looking at.

"A group of six people were abducted that night with Santiago," Laura explains. "In that group there was also a young girl, twenty years old, very pregnant. After they killed them, they set the bodies on fire. The pregnant girl was burning, and with the fire, the womb burst open and the child sprang out."

"My God," I groan. Laura whispers, "*¡Muy fuerte! ¡Muy terrible!*"

I see it now: The "line" in the photograph is a taut umbilical cord running from the baby to its mother. When the amniotic sac began to boil from the heat of the flames, the girl's body exploded and the baby sprang out, the umbilical cord intact and stretched, keeping the baby and its mother connected even as they were burning in the fire.

In that moment, I lose whatever innocence I had left, some vestigial fantasy that there was such a thing as a safe place in this world. Even the womb can boil you alive. A motorcycle roars by on the street below. Now I weep openly, and so does Diana. I take a sip of tea, trying to collect myself.

Laura stops and waits quietly for us as we struggle to regain our composure. One by one, we fall into the stories of Laura's family. Laura tells them in a sea of calm, dry-eyed. They are so familiar to her.

"My emotions are different now. In the first moment, I only wanted to find my children alive. I remember the moment I found out they were dead. That moment was a scream that would split the earth. Every Mother of the Disappeared has a Hiroshima inside her.

"After that came fantasies of revenge. I invented as many ways as I could to kill the assassins. I thought I would hide a bomb in my dress, then go and stand at a parade, waiting, and with this bomb I could take personal vengeance, but then I realized that these fantasies were damaging me even more. I could not get so dirty, so low as to want that. I would be transformed into what I never wanted to be. That would make me an assassin, a criminal. I am not them. That is when we decided to go to the legal system, that we must find justice there.[5] Justice defines democracy.

"What remains in the end is a deep longing for justice. Part of justice is that it is legally settled; there is a kind of public justice, related to history, to identity. Then there is another kind of justice, a private justice, mine with each of my children, related to that wish to find their remains. But it is very hard."

Silence falls between us. Reality has been altered. We move

slowly, as if underwater, shifted by invisible tides. My words become elongated and travel slowly, full of moisture. I struggle to speak.

"What you do, Laura, you are doing for all the mothers, for all the people—men and women—who are losing their children, their loved ones, to wars and oppression. Your voice is a voice for all the people who have disappeared."

Laura sits quietly while Diana translates, looking at her hands in her lap for a moment, her expression peaceful, her mouth hinting at a smile, her eyes dark and open, moist, but not in tears; then she looks up saying, "It has taken a long time. Eleven years it has taken. Eleven years since we found and opened their common grave. It has been covered with grass, four meters by three meters. We are going to have a ceremony. We will keep the wall that the military built. They didn't want the people to see what was happening inside. I will plant a tree there.

"On the wall we put the names of everyone who was killed there that we could find. On one side of the wall, there is the cemetery, and on the other side, there are slums. Very poor people live there. The city agreed not to destroy the wall. I think that our children have the right to exist, even though they are not alive anymore. Even though I cannot hold them in my arms.

"Their existence is memory. As long as I live, I will be my daughter's memory. When I die, my daughter's memory, the memory of her will live."

After some moments Laura asks us to walk with her in the park. I jump up too eagerly, saying, "Yes," fairly shouting, surprising us all with the amount of conviction in my voice, so much so that we all burst out laughing and repeat with a shout together, "Yes!"

Laura's large brass key clicks and turns in the upper lock of the heavy wooden front door, then in the lower, then we step out into the hallway and we are gone!—the three of us nearly running down the worn marble stairs, Laura leading, singing softly, no one thinking of waiting for the turn-of-the-century elevator-in-a-cage to come. No, we dash down the three flights of stairs, fairly skipping, to get out, to get away from the stories, from the horror, out into the sweet air, onto the avenues with the trees.

We are walking fast, so fast to get away, then riding a bus, getting off to change to another bus. Then walking more streets. The air is cooler now, late in the day. The wind is up. We walk even faster to stay warm, my sweater is too thin. The stories of the Disappeared have disoriented me. What are the names of the trees? It no longer matters, nothing matters, only that I am among the trees.

"I am taking you to the park with the most beautiful tree in all of Buenos Aires," Laura announces with pride. "I will show you. Many times, my husband and I would go there just so we could have dinner under the branches of this extraordinary tree. It is enormous."

Palermo Park is in the center of Buenos Aires, forming an oasis of relief and beauty in the center of this large, elegant, European-style city. The tree Laura is taking me to is quickly apparent with its limb span of more than a hundred feet and exposed roots growing as tall as a person. The limbs are so long that supports have been built under them to help bear the weight. Its leaves are large, broad, and smooth.

"Very old. *Ficus elastica* is the Latin name. It's a fig tree," Laura says as we walk around the tree. I circumambulate the tree like the stupa at Boudhanath in Kathmandu, Nepal, like the Bodhi tree the Buddha sat under in Bodh Gaya, India. It is a venerable tree. We wander past stalls of vendors along the sidewalk, out into the center of the park, onto the open lawns, where people sit and lie, sunning, chatting, playing music, rocking babies, and join them. We lie down on the warm, soft grass. I treasure the length of ground under me, every hard, uneven bit of it.

We grow hungry and make our way back through the park to the restaurant under the tree. We stop to watch a clown jumping through a hoop, turning somersaults, running and jumping through the hoop again. I am thrilled by the nonsense, the play, the children's laughter, reassured. The world is in motion and I am part of it; children shriek with laughter at the clown.

Suddenly he changes character. The clown becomes Romeo calling for Juliet, rushing back and forth within the circled crowd, children fleeing gleefully with screeches as he runs up to them with his big red nose, looks disappointed, and then dashes off again, crying, "Juliet, Juliet!" To my delight, Laura enters into the play, running out into the circle to meet him, laughing, calling, "Romeo, Romeo," her arms outstretched as he rushes toward her with his arms outstretched, looking just over her shoulder, as though he is running to someone else, and runs right past her. We all burst out laughing, Laura laughing the hardest of all.

We sit for hours underneath the branches of the giant fig tree, having our evening meal and talking. We stay outside until well after dark. After dinner, the talk turns again to Laura's story where we had stopped when we left her apartment. We can resume now. It is safe. We have the tree above us, the bushes flowering, and the sweetness of the spring night air to hold us. A blessing.

"I remember Claudia Lapaco," says Laura, "the daughter of my friend Carmen Lapaco, who loved her daughter so much that when the police came to take Claudia away, Carmen took her daughter in her arms and held her fast. She would not let her go. And so the soldiers took both of them. Carmen was tortured with her daughter.

"Once Carmen and Claudia were held in the same room. Their hands were tied behind their backs. The soldiers were coming to take Claudia, the daughter, to torture her more, and Claudia said, 'Mother, I cannot, I cannot bear it anymore. I will not stand one more session of this.'

"At this Carmen crept across the floor, her hands still tied behind her, until she reached her daughter. All she could do was put her head on the knees of her daughter. Then a soldier—someone—came and tore them apart.

"Carmen lived and Claudia disappeared. She is dead, surely. But we don't know. We don't know anything of what happened to her. Carmen keeps on for justice—fighting, fighting—going through the judicial process."

Laura continues. "The memory that Carmen had been able to touch Claudia, to let her know how much she loved her—that memory keeps Carmen alive. It keeps her happy and well. Carmen suffered with Claudia. And though the soldiers tore them apart physically, they could never touch them really, the love between them was so strong. They couldn't kill that."

I sit up late with Laura, going through book after book of clippings, letters, and articles by her, about her, about the Madres, posters, notices of talks from around the world. One of the few stories in English is a *Los Angeles Times* article about a navy officer who recently came forward and confessed to throwing people out of airplanes over the South Atlantic ocean. Adolfo Francisco Scilingo, a former lieutenant commander in the Argentinean navy, is the first military man to acknowledge what the Mothers and many people know were routine murders.[6]

Haunted by the image of bodies on the floor of the cargo plane, Scilingo came forward to describe openly what happened. A group of prisoners at the Navy Mechanics School, a notorious center for detention and torture, were told that they had to be vaccinated for transport to a prison in the south. The first sedative rendered them zombie-like, many having to be carried to the plane and helped into the transport, whereupon a second injection that put them to sleep was administered. Once they had passed out, the crew undressed them. Sedating them assured no resistance, and rendered them faceless, with no eyes to look back or express terror and pain.

Once, as they finished undressing the victims, a young crew member began to weep at the sight of these naked, unconscious people, many his own age. Scilingo comforted him and tried to explain why these people had to be thrown into the ocean. For a moment, he said, he grasped the enormity of the crime in which he was participating. He searched and struggled vainly for justifications. Finally he muttered, ". . . for the Fatherland." Scilingo said that the scene reminded him of photographs of the Nazi death camps. But as the chief of the extermination crew for that flight, he put aside his realization and helped drag their victims to the door and throw them out himself, one by one, finally slipping as he struggled with an unconscious body and almost falling out himself.

Officers were rotated and assigned to every flight so that no one would tell. Everyone was compromised and guilty. The men were told that the Catholic clergy sanctioned this form of death as "Christian." When Scilingo himself became distraught over the experience and went to confession, the priest absolved him and told him that "the killings had to be done to separate the wheat from the chaff."

I find a copy of a speech Laura delivered. Once again, I'm struck by how Laura has transformed her own loss into a fierce hunger for global justice.

The laws that limit prosecution of crimes against humanity . . . and pardons, are an attempt to erase history. No one can plead ignorance, because we presented testimony to all international organizations, including the Vatican. They maintained silence or they believed those who committed the crimes. There has never been a meeting to declare the disappearance of people to be a crime against humanity.

There is no country in the world powerful enough to resist this disease if there is no justice within the country that initiated it. It corrupts absolutely. Perhaps the recent events in the former Yugoslavia could have been resolved differently if there had been a universal law that classifies crimes against humanity, such as the disappearance of people.

Impunity, allowing those who commit these atrocities to go free, to bear no consequence, carries the germs of violence and corruption in it and spreads out of control.

President Menem's pardons have given the impression that Argentina is a country with justice, but to the contrary, the impunity has had devastating effects. The corruption in the government is uncontainable. Justice has been killed.

Justice, as well as our children, has disappeared.

In Argentina, and in many Latin American countries, none of the thirty thousand Disappeared were tried in a court of law. We want to know the whereabouts of their remains, and for the perpetrators of the crimes in Argentina and in all Latin American countries to be tried and condemned. We want the United Nations to recognize once and for all that forced disappearances are a crime against humanity.

We will never ask for capital punishment for the murderers of our children. There will be no mercy for them, nor will there be revenge. Mercy and revenge are not the business of human beings. Nevertheless, we ask for a trial before all humanity, for the sake of our children, for the sake of justice. We want to be part of the international civilized community, that is, one in which nations can live together with each other's differences, in a community that can shelter variety in its bosom, that can allow diversity of beliefs, that is able to respect people's differences and uphold them. These crimes against humanity must be stopped.

CHAPTER 16

ISIS IN ARGENTINA

Can the Body Be Re-membered?

The choice: memory or oppression.

—MILAN KUNDERA

It is three-thirty in the afternoon on Thursday. The Mothers of the Plaza de Mayo are demonstrating, and today I am with them. They have been demonstrating here, in the Plaza de Mayo, every week since 1977. Every one of these women has lost at least one child or member of her immediate family. Many, like Laura, have lost multiple family members. I join the promenade in the circle around the monument. Some people are quiet, solemn looking, but many are chatting and laughing. Several people, myself included, take photographs of the women and the various people who join them on their walk. One man places himself and his video camera at the edge of the circle so that he photographs us all as we walk toward him and then past. Is he a tourist? Off to one side, two sad-looking women stand at a table and sell books on the Mothers and the Disappearances.

In addition to their weekly demonstrations, once a year the Mothers are joined by the Grandmothers of the Disappeared and the organization of the children of the Disappeared, HIJOS, as well as members of human rights organizations, politicians, union workers, children, and many others. Together they make the rounds of the plaza for twenty-four hours without stopping: La Marcha de la Resistencia.[1]

Each Mother wears a fragment of history on her head, the white scarf worn only by the Mothers of the Disappeared. Each scarf is cross-stitched or embroidered in blue thread with the words *Las Madres de la Plaza de Mayo*. Some scarves give the name of the Disappeared person or persons whom their wearers are grieving, some give dates, some also say *Argentina,* and *Desaparecida,* and *Línea Fundadora.*

The Mothers began to march in 1977, out of desperation. Laura has told me how she wrote to the archbishop, begging him to use his good offices to help, only to have him reply that she should commend herself to the Virgin Mary and resign herself to her loss. Out of more than eighty bishops, only a handful were known for denouncing the actions of the military. The voices of the number of courageous priests, nuns, and bishops who opposed the military were drowned out by a great and weighty silence. But it was not only the institutional Church that often failed to help the Mothers. The United States has its own part in Argentina's tormented history. A number of the elite cadre of officers and torturers throughout the Latin American military regimes were trained by U.S. forces at the infamous School of the Americas, in Georgia.[2]

With no one to help them, their children lost, fourteen grief-stricken, furious mothers turned to themselves, forming the Association de Madres de la Plaza de Mayo. In defiance of the military, and putting their own lives at risk, they began demonstrating in the plaza. Shortly thereafter, nine of those who had joined them, including a French nun, were taken away by plainclothesmen after a meeting and never heard of again. They too "disappeared." The Mothers returned to the plaza on the following Thursday. They refused to be cowed, intimidated, or bullied. Called *las locas* at first, "crazy" for such open defiance of the military, the Mothers have become international heroines. Some call them the conscience of Argentina.

Two of the original fourteen have since died, and two others left to form their own group. In 1986 the ten remaining founders added the words Línea Fundadora, "Founders Line," to their name, and the movement is now called Madres de la Plaza de Mayo Línea Fundadora. This is the group that Laura is a part of. This is the group that I join today. They operate by consensus, without president or director. All members participate in decision making.

I am amazed that this disparate group of women—from different classes, different religious backgrounds, and with different beliefs and values—has retained such solidarity for almost two decades. I ask Laura what has kept them together. "We are all mothers of the *desaparecidos—detenidos y desaparecidos,* the many people who have been taken and disappeared," Laura replies. "This is what unites us, it is sometimes the only thing we have in common." Motherhood seals the bond between them.

A small, elegant, silver-haired Mother, wearing a black-and-white dress, gold-and-pearl clip earrings, and a beige cardigan sweater, greets Laura with a kiss. Laura introduces her as María Adela Gard de Antokoletz, who at eighty-four is now the oldest of the original fourteen Mothers.[3]

"I want you to meet my friend China," Laura explains. "She is having trouble trying to understand *los desaparecidos.*" María Adela's face breaks into a warm smile as she looks at me, amused, offering her hand.

"Of course she doesn't understand," she says almost laughing. "How can she? We can't either!"

The life of Buenos Aires goes on around the demonstration. People sit on the grassy lawns that border the circle, eating, chatting, just as in any park, others sit on benches, watching. Two businessmen in fastidious gray and blue suits, carrying polished leather briefcases, chatter as they stride briskly through the circle of people, cutting across the circle to cross the plaza, oblivious to the demonstration. Mothers and children play. Students, government employees, all manner of people continue to mill through the plaza as the hundred or so Mothers and their supporters continue to make their rounds.

After an hour, the demonstration ends as quietly as it began. People stand chatting, taking leave of one another, gathering in clusters. Some of us will go, as Laura, María Adela, and a dozen others do every Thursday, to a nearby café for tea and sodas.

Laura takes off her scarf as we walk through the park and cross the street. There is a large gray-green police tank parked on the other side of the street next to two large police buses. I'm taken aback at the appearance of so much police power. For what reason? The buses are empty but for several uniformed policemen standing inside them. In front of the two buses are police jeeps. On the next corner is a cluster of motorcycle policemen all standing, watching us, their arms crossed. I look around thinking that something must be going on, they must be expecting some kind of trouble around the presidential palace or the Congress building nearby, but there is nothing obvious, only people walking to and fro as in any major business center around the world.

As we pass the tank, Laura and I decide that I will photograph her standing on the sidewalk next to the tank. It is the government and the military that refuse to give the Mothers the information they have so long asked for. Is this their response—arms at the ready against a hundred unarmed people, mostly women, peacefully demonstrating?

"Put your scarf back on, Laura," I instruct her, ignoring the looks of the nearby police. "Now turn your face toward the light." As I stand taking pictures, I become increasingly aware of a tall, large man in his fifties who is stopped next to me and is watching us. He wears very dark glasses, a crisp black suit, and a white dress shirt. His hair is smoothed back and has a faint sheen of pomade. At first I pay no attention, though I'm aware of his presence. Then he moves closer, close enough to make me uncomfortable. I keep shooting. He pulls a cellular phone out of his breast pocket, quickly punches in numbers, and starts speaking in rapid-fire Spanish. He seems to be looking right at us, but I don't stop. Finally his presence becomes impossible to ignore. He isn't going to just walk off. To break the tension, I turn and say, "*¿Que pasa, Señor, que pasa?*"

"I am only watching this tableau you are constructing, this collage, this fiction you are making up," he says, his voice edged with disdain.

Mira, a European woman who has lived in Argentina for many years, is our translator this afternoon.[4] She shoots back, "I think it's rather perfect, the Mothers of the Disappeared and the police, don't you? Think of it. Who has the information about the people who disappeared? The police, of course. It's a perfect photograph," she says vehemently.

"Nothing happened in Argentina, nobody disappeared," he says now, turning directly to Laura. "You're making this up, this is a fiction."

"This is a fiction?" Laura replies, raising her voice, tapping her finger on each of the wide metal buttons pinned on her coat lapel, the photographs of her disappeared family members. "These are no fiction! Where were you in 1982?"

"I was here in Buenos Aires," he says. "Nobody disappeared," he repeats. "Nothing happened. You're making this up," he says, waving his arms vehemently. Laura's eyes are flashing; Mira's voice is louder and more insistent, her face is flushed. I can't understand what they're saying. The man is white with anger. I take another picture of Laura.

"Let's go," Laura says abruptly, turning on her heel, and walking away briskly from the man in the black suit. I hurry to catch up, as does Mira. I don't want to turn around, but I wonder: Will he follow us? Laura and Mira both assure me that nothing will happen, even if the man was a member of the secret police as they suspect. "In this regard, we do have a democracy now."

The man's denial helps me understand the incredible struggle of the Mothers to keep memory alive, to tell the truth, to see justice done. "This is *tierra de nadie*, the land of nobody," Laura had said earlier, shaking her head sadly. "Nobody's responsible. That means you can do whatever you want if you can get away with it."

Still, I find myself wondering aloud, trying to grasp how this could have happened, how people could disappear from sight in an instant, how their disappearance could be denied to this day. Mira tells me a story that chills me to the bone.

"How did it happen? People were picked off one or two at a time," she begins quietly. "You simply looked the other way as a man walking down the street was suddenly hurried into a police car, or a couple was taken from the table next to you at a restaurant by four plainclothesmen. How could you know why they were being taken? And you didn't want to think about it—the waiter was bringing out your dinner, you went on with your conversation.

"As the ten P.M. curfew tightened and more roadblocks were put up, you got off the bus you had taken to the restaurant sooner, you walked home further after dinner. Your world became smaller and smaller. Finally you stopped going out.

"Friends wrote to me from Europe. They wanted me to leave, to get out. They said, 'Can't you see what's happening? It's like Germany. You see the smoke from the smokestack, you smell it, you know that something is terribly wrong, but you ignore it.' My best friend disappeared. I didn't cry about it until last year, seventeen years after he disappeared."

We join the others in the café. Two tables are pulled together in the middle of a crowded room where a dozen of the other Mothers are sitting laughing, drinking coffees and sodas, and eating ice cream. It's all so normal looking, a gathering of friends, a mix of older women and a handful of younger ones and one man. I understand little of the conversation, but I am so relieved to be sitting down, with an order for tea and ice cream coming, that I don't care.

"Now you must meet more of the Mothers," Laura says, turning to a woman at the table on her right.

"This is Dionisia López Amado," Laura says, introducing me to a woman with short blond hair and blue eyes, wearing a white sweater over an orange blouse. Dionisia López Amado shakes her head back and forth every third sentence when she speaks, as though she is always fighting back tears that I cannot see but only feel.

"My son was Antonio Adolfo Díaz López. He was twenty-four years old when they took him. His wife, Estela Maris Riganti, disappeared the same day, May 15, 1977.

"I am struggling for nineteen years now and I will go on as long as I live," she assures me, shaking her head back and forth again, then bringing her fist down onto the table firmly, with a bang. "We are strong! We go on. Nobody crosses the Mothers."

The strength these women summon up in themselves is inspiring, all the more so because we both know that the truth is that if no one crossed the Mothers, they would have long ago been able to find out the whereabouts of their children. I shake my head in agreement; of course no one crosses them. I can easily imagine that I might need to feel the same way too—true or not—to be able to go on, to continue.

"Inés Adriana Cobo," Laura says now, turning to an ample woman with blue eye shadow, fanning herself with a wooden fan, on my left.

"My daughter, Carmen, was twenty-two when they took her. September 1, 1976. She studied psychology. She worked with young people at a community center. She was seen by someone who had been freed from the Navy Mechanics School. This is the last I know of her.

"Her boyfriend, Rubén Alberto Stockdale, was studying to be a doctor. He disappeared on September 3, 1977. He was never seen again.

"We cannot be silent. If you are silent, you cooperate with the people who killed your children. You become an accomplice."

Laura turns to the animated younger woman sitting next to Inés.

"This is Nora Anchart. She was a friend of Carmen's, Inés's daughter. She is making an exhibit of the detained and Disappeared, the political prisoners." Nora is forty-two, with long dark hair that falls halfway down her back.

"My friends and I belong to the same generation as the Disappeared," Nora tells me. "Those thirty thousand people were our companions; their children are our children. I am a mother too. I have a son, fifteen years old. How do I tell him what happened? The only way this history can be real for my son is for him to meet the Disappeared as real people rather than the empty outlines they have been for so long."

Nora is planning a traveling exhibit that can be taken all over Argentina. Anyone who knows someone who disappeared will be asked to share their remembrance of that person.

"I am taking whatever people give me—photographs, report cards, letters, a note passed in school, anything—and making a panel for each person who is Disappeared."

For years the Disappeared have been represented only by outlines of figures. They have had no faces, no names. Nora is filling in the blanks, giving them back their names, their faces, their stories, bringing them back to life, in a way, by telling how they lived.

"They say that our generation wanted to die, that we are morbid. It is crazy talk. The Disappeared in our generation died because they loved life so much! That's what the exhibit will show. Their aliveness! This is why I am here with the Mothers."

Laura asks about the book I wrote on Tara and the Black Madonna. I show her a photograph of the Black Madonna in Switzerland, at Einsiedeln.

"In Switzerland? Why is she black?" she asks, as does everyone.

"No one knows for sure, but this particular Madonna in Switzer-

BLACK MADONNA AT EINSIEDELN, SWITZERLAND,
"OUR LADY OF THE DARK FOREST" (*O. Baur*)

land may have something to do with Isis, the Egyptian goddess. At least Carl Jung thought so. Isis was worshipped all over the Roman Empire during the third and second centuries C.E., and later, as far north as Switzerland and Germany, maybe farther. We know that Isis came from Egyptian Africa, her main temple was at Philae, in southern Egypt. She had several forms, some that were black—"

216

"Isis?" Laura leans closer across the table toward me, as though it takes her a moment to hear me. "The Black Madonna? Isis?! *La apasionada*..." She is suddenly overcome with feeling. Her eyes shine. I don't know what's going on.

"I became obsessed with Isis," she explains, "I was passionate about the ability of Isis to reconstruct the body of her husband." The intensity with which Laura speaks of Isis is physical: her hands dance in the air, her head moves, she is full of graceful excitement, her eyes are bright. She is in motion. The words pour out. She is filled with the story.

"Isis becomes a great winged bird, then an old woman, a healer, then a goddess. Her story is a story of transformation. Isis searches, Isis investigates—she finds all the places where the pieces of the body of Osiris are hidden. He has been betrayed and murdered by his brother, cut into pieces, his body scattered up and down the Nile. She collects the pieces of the body. She puts the body of Osiris back together.

"For me the story of Isis is symbolic. It contains the meaning of the reconstruction of human history. Isis tells us that we cannot go forward with only one step, we have to keep going back and finding more pieces."

To re-member is literally to collect the members, the pieces, the parts—to put them back together again. Is this not re-membering? I tell Laura. "Remember" is related to "record," from the Latin root *recordari*, Eduardo Galeano says, which means literally "to pass again through the heart." Laura's identification with Isis is complete.

"When Noni was kidnapped, I was hopeless. I knew I wouldn't find her alive. But in spite of everything, I didn't stop looking. I didn't give up. Isis came to me, many times, and she stayed with me as a sign of hope. More than God. More than God, she gave me hope. She helped me.

"The mythic face of Isis is hope. She goes such a long way to find

LAURA BONAPARTE, ONE OF THE MOTHERS OF THE DISAPPEARED,
WEARING BUTTONS SHOWING HER MISSING CHILDREN
AND THEIR SPOUSES (*Alan Pogue*)

the body of her husband, Osiris. It is not over in just three days. I know very little of the Bible and religion but for what I know from my good friends. Except for the resurrection of Christ. That is a different thing. Christ rose from the dead in three days. *Sí.* His mother suffered, but only for three days. But there is nothing like this work of Isis that goes on and on, reconstructing, re-creating.

"The search of Isis does not take place inside of time. It is timeless, outside of time. We are always rebuilding, reconstructing. *¿Cuanto tiempo, cuanto tiempo?* How long does it take? Isis's search for Osiris goes on so long we cannot even count the days. There is no limit to the time it took for her to re-member Osiris; then Seth found him and killed him again. She had to start over. There is no limit for the work of Isis. Isis's work is not made in time." She pauses, her words reverberating.

"The difference is that Isis could bring Osiris back to life, whereas we can't. Our reality is limited. We have to accept the difference between myth and reality. It means accepting the limitations of being human and knowing that you are not God. This makes you lose your arrogance.

"Until the last moment of my life, I will want to know what happened to my children and where they are. I want a full memory of my children, to remember them whole, integrated. There are different ways to compose a body and give it life, to reconstruct a body. Mine is to remember."

ISIS AND OSIRIS

n the time before time, Isis and Osiris were. Born of the Goddess Nut, the Sky, and the god Geb, the Earth, Isis and Osiris loved each other from the time they swam together in their mother's womb. Osiris became the first king of Egypt, civilizing and teaching his subjects the art of cultivation: growing of wheat and barley, cultivation of the vine, and how to honor the gods. He established justice. Isis, his beloved and devoted wife, also ruled wisely, and taught the arts of weaving and healing.

But their brother, Seth, jealous of Osiris's fame and good works, envious of his marriage to Isis, plotted to steal the throne of Osiris. One evening, in the midst of a great feast, Seth brought in a jeweled chest and offered it to whoever could fit inside. Seemingly in jest, he challenged Osiris to lie down in it. Osiris accepted his challenge and climbed into the chest. Seventy two conspirators leapt forward, slammed down the lid, nailed it shut, and sealed it with molten lead. Then they carried it out and threw it in the Nile.

Isis was distraught. She cut off her hair, tore her clothes, dressed in mourning, searched up and down the Nile for Osiris's coffin, but it had floated out to sea.

Eventually, the chest washed ashore in Byblos, in Phoenicia, and lodged itself in a tree. Over the years the trunk of the tree grew around the coffin, hiding it inside. The tree became known for its great beauty and sweet fragrance, and one day the king and queen had it cut down and made into a pillar to hold up the roof of the palace.

In her grief and fury, Isis spent many years searching for Osiris. When she learned of the coffin's entombment in the pillar, she made haste to Byblos. There she disguised herself, veiling her true identity, and sat in mourning by the well, patiently waiting until some of the queen's hand-maidens came for water. She greeted them so kindly, braiding their hair and surrounding them with such a remarkable perfume, that the queen herself, Astarte, sent for Isis and made her the nursemaid for her child.

At night Isis would lay the child in a fire, burning away all that was mortal in him so that he would become a god. Then, changing herself into a swallow, Isis would fly around the pillar that held up the roof of the palace—the pillar that enclosed Osiris's coffin—and cry.

One night the queen came into the nursery to find her child surrounded by flames. In horror, she let out a terrible scream. At that, Isis changed back into herself in all her majesty as the Goddess and gave Queen Astarte her child. She told Astarte that her child had just lost the only chance he would ever have to become a god. She demanded that the queen give her the pillar that held up the roof. The queen did as she was asked, and when Isis received the pillar and cut into it, there lay the coffin of Osiris inside. Isis let out such a cry when she found it that one of the queen's children died.

Isis took the coffin and departed from Byblos by boat. Alone, she opened the coffin, weeping at the sight of Osiris's dead face and showering it with kisses. Then, taking the form of a bird, she hovered over the corpse with such great love, beating her wings and breathing so closely, so deeply, that she breathed life back into Osiris and conceived his child, Horus. Horus, conceived through the enormous love of Isis for Osiris, would one day take back the throne that united Egypt, the throne that Seth had stolen from his father. But that is another story.

In the meantime, Seth discovered that Isis had found the body of Osiris, had conceived and borne his child, and was keeping Osiris's body hidden. Seth's hatred for his brother knew no limit. He found the body of Osiris alone and unattended, and attacked a second time, this time cutting Osiris's body into fourteen pieces and tossing them into the Nile. When Isis returned and found Osiris lost to her again, her grief was *boundless. But she would not let Osiris be scattered and forgotten. Her grief became her strength, a towering strength that would make the name of Osiris known forever upon the earth.[1] In a papyrus boat, accompanied by her sister Nepthys, the wife of Seth, and Nepthys's son, Anubis, she set sail down the Nile to retrieve Osiris's body now, piece by piece. Thoth, the god of wisdom and the moon, helped. Each time they found a piece of the body, they mourned and celebrated their find. At each spot, Isis built a temple and taught the people sacred rites to honor Osiris. Together they found all the pieces of Osiris's body except one: his phallus, which had been swallowed by a fish.*

But Isis would not have Osiris's body be less than whole. She fashioned a phallus to replace his, and blessed it, re-membering Osiris. She became a great bird again, fanning the great, re-membered body before her with her enormous wings, reviving Osiris once more with the power of a love that defied all bounds. From that moment on, Osiris took his place as ruler of the underworld, where he now sits in the Hall of Two Truths, the Ruler of Eternity, weighing the hearts of the dead against the feather of Maat, the goddess of justice. If a heart is heavier than the feather, it falls into the mouth of the crocodile and the soul cannot enter eternity.

Isis did not die with the demise of ancient Egypt. She became part of the Greek world after Alexander the Great conquered Egypt in 332 B.C.E. There, Isis became linked with the cult of Demeter, who searched for Persephone as Isis searched for Osiris. A Greek hymn to Isis illuminates the fierce side of Isis:

> *I made an end to murders. . . .*
> *I made the right to be stronger than gold and silver.*
> *I ordained that the true should be thought good. . . .*

I have delivered the plotter of evil against other men into the
hands of the one he plotted against.
I established penalties for those who practice injustice. . . .
With me the right prevails.
I am the Queen of rivers and winds and sea. . . .
I am the Queen of war.
I am the Queen of the thunderbolt.
I stir up the sea and I calm it.
I am the rays of the sun. . . . I set free those in bonds. . . .
I am called the Lawgiver. . . .
I am the Lord of rainstorms.
I overcome fate.
Fate hearkens to me.
Hail, O Egypt, that nourished me![2]

CHAPTER 17

"HELP, THEY
ARE KILLING US"

Yvonne Bezerra de Mello and the Street Children
Rio de Janeiro, Brazil

I
n late October, it feels like summer in Rio de Janeiro, and at
nine o'clock in the morning it's dripping hot. I'm standing inside a one-room makeshift school–community center under a
freeway overpass in one of the poorest sections of Rio. The "school"
was built out of scrap plywood and two-by-fours by Yvonne
Bezerra de Mello and a few of the hundreds of people who live in
this squatters' community called Coqueirinho, "Little Palm."

I'm here because I wanted to come to work with Yvonne.
"Work" is the unpaid, nonstop stream of activity that Yvonne has
taken up on behalf of the street children of Rio. This morning that
means coming here to the school at Coqueirinho. The afternoon
after I arrived in Rio from Buenos Aires, it meant finding and attending a demonstration Yvonne organized in downtown Rio for
the mothers of stolen and disappeared girls, a growing problem, especially for the poor in Rio.

I first heard of Yvonne Bezerra de Mello when the international
press reported on the Candelária Massacre.[1] On July 23, 1993, six
street children, eleven to nineteen years old, were murdered in the
middle of the night when off-duty military police opened fire on
them as they slept on the Candelária church steps, in downtown
Rio. Two others had been abducted earlier that night, shot, and left
to die on the street a few blocks away. Eight altogether died on that

Brazilian mother (*right*) holding photos of missing daughter
and friend, with Yvonne Bezerra de Mello (*left*) and one of
the street children, Rio de Janeiro, Brazil (*China Galland*)

night, and several more were wounded. Sixty children survived.
Yvonne had been working with the street kids who slept on the
steps at Candelária that very day. Five of them had her phone number and the coins in their pockets to call if there was an emergency.
They called right after the police began shooting.

"Aunt Yvonne! Aunt Yvonne!" a terrified child screamed into
the phone at one o'clock in the morning. "Help! They are killing us!
Help! Come quick, come quick!"

She rolled out of bed, dressed, got in the car, and was down at the
square within minutes. Five boys were already dead, but one was
still alive when she got there. The children were terrified. Yvonne
sat up through the night with them, ministering as best she could.
Apparently she was the only adult present who knew them. She was

their protection and the reason their story became known. Their numbers might easily have been added to the growing list of street children reportedly killed in Rio by policemen for extra money. Their pay is so low that apparently it is not difficult to find armed guards, including on-duty and off-duty police for hire, to keep street children out of business districts where merchants don't want them.[2] How to keep them out is up to the individual.

Yvonne stayed until the police came to make an official report and remove the bodies. Since then she has helped in the fight to bring the case to trial, and helped to establish a witness protection program for one of the Candelária survivors who identified four military policemen as the assassins. Wagner dos Santos survived four bullets the night of the massacre, only to be shot twice in the head by the police as soon as he returned briefly to Rio to testify the year after the shootings. Though he was hospitalized, Wagner survived. Two members of the city human rights commission investigating the massacre were assassinated during the investigation.

Yvonne has been both praised and vilified for working with these children. Some people would prefer that all the street children had been killed and she with them. Not everyone is happy about the publicity the case has generated, or about her winning the Jabuti Prize for Literature in Brazil for her book about the Candelária tragedy, *The Lost Sheep and Their Executioners*.

The Candelária case is coming to trial again at the time of my visit, and Wagner will have to testify against the police the following week. To protect him, Yvonne has flown to the capital to call on President Fernando Henrique Cardoso himself on behalf of a witness protection plan. My visit comes at a nerve-wracking time for Yvonne. Still, she remains confident that something will change now. A sculptor, a graduate of the Sorbonne, in Paris, the former wife of a diplomat, married now to one of the most prominent industrialists in Brazil, Yvonne is an insider who won't stay in her place.

She was called in to help in Coqueirinho after the Candelária episode. She agreed to work with the community organizers when they agreed to take in twenty-five of the Candelária survivors.

❦

Children run into the school house under the freeway, squealing and scrambling to grab books that Ayrton, Yvonne's driver, has unloaded from the trunk of her car. They can't be left overnight in the school room or they'll disappear. Ayrton is a slender man of medium height, who goes with Yvonne, helps with the shopping, carries school books, the first-aid kit in the back of the car, whatever is necessary. As we go into the school house, I look back from the doorway and see Ayrton still next to the car, the trunk open, rummaging through the first-aid box for supplies to clean and bandage a cut for one of the children who stands by, waiting patiently for his help.

While the children rush Yvonne and the volunteer helper and teacher, Barbara Harth, who is also with us this morning, Ayrton brings the morning's groceries in to Vera Santos, a strong, serious woman in a blue-flowered dress, behind the kitchen counter of this one-room school. Vera lives here in Coqueirinho. Yvonne has hired her to cook the only hot meal these children eat each day. While Yvonne supervises the children's washups, Ayrton brings the first-aid kit inside and begins to treat the lineup of children that has formed, Vera unpacks the groceries, and Barbara gets reading and writing going at a long green wooden picnic table. I hear Vera singing a haunting song in Portuguese softly under her breath. Her husband is working in the kitchen this morning too, trying to repair one of the two burners on the gas stove they have for cooking.

Yvonne has been working with Rio's street children for more than twelve years. She says that officials now estimate that over ten thousand people in Rio are living under freeway overpasses like this. Though figures vary widely and continue to be debated by the numerous agencies that attempt to serve this population, Yvonne estimates that up to four thousand of these are street children, meaning that they have no home of any kind to go to, only the street.[3]

Chaos prevails as Barbara passes out paper and pencils, yet the noise level doesn't seem to disturb her. She's a tall fifty-five-year-old German woman whose husband works with an overseas aid organization in Rio. Barbara has enormous patience with the children. Once she starts with the day's reading lesson, the noise level in her corner drops perceptibly, though it is never quiet with a Rio freeway directly overhead. The "ceiling" is the freeway roadbed itself.

Some of the young girls have their heads wrapped in plastic bags out of which a dark gray goo oozes at the edges. It takes me a few minutes to realize that this is a hair treatment. One tall young girl approaches me directly. Unlike the others, she has a pink hibiscus behind her left ear, a profusion of unruly, dry black hair, tiny fluorescent-green plastic earrings shaped like hats, and an infectious smile. We connect immediately. Dressed in a short blue skirt, cut-off blue sweatshirt, and blue flip-flops, she watches me making these notes as though the shapes the ink takes on the page is a form of magic.

I write out my name in block print, point to it, and say, *"Mi nombre,"* and hand her my pen and notebook, indicating that she could write her name down too.

"A-l-i-n-e," she writes carefully in medium-size block letters. Suddenly a handful of girls crowd around to proudly write out their names in my notebook, one at a time: "J-o-i-c-e," "A-l-e-s-s-a-n-d-a," "E-d-e-n-e-i-a," and "K-e-l-l-y." All but Aline desert me quickly when they discover that I don't speak Portuguese. Aline insists upon talking to me in Portuguese as though I understand every word she says, despite my repeated *"No comprende."* When I can't answer her questions, she gets frustrated and raises her voice, as if volume will help. I just keep smiling and shaking my head, *"No comprende."* Finally she is so infuriated that she begins to shout at me. I burst out laughing. She stops shouting and begins laughing with me, saying, "Blah, blah, blah." That I understand. She touches to either cheek a piece of bread she's been holding, then kisses it and runs off with a smile.

Yvonne gets my attention. "Come with me," she says, heading for the door. With short brown hair parted on one side, large brown eyes, a full mouth, Yvonne Bezerra de Mello is an attractive woman, a woman of forty-nine who takes care of herself. She wears a yellow cotton T-shirt and modest blue shorts. I hadn't seen her smile much until she saw the children, and then her face lit up. Now they surround her, clamoring, hugging her, hanging on her. Aline and some of the other children follow us. The kids are hugging my waist too. I'm a novelty.

As soon as we're outside, Aline starts pulling on the shoulder strap of my camera—she wants to take pictures. I hesitate for a second—will she break it? I hand it over, showing her quickly how to focus and to advance the film. For the next few minutes she runs around, ecstatically taking pictures. Then other children want a turn. They photograph the bright mural they painted on the front wall of the school; they photograph each other, me, Yvonne.

What would it be like to set these kids loose with this camera and all the film they wanted? What would happen if we could see life from their perspective, under an overpass?

"You need to see where these children live, but don't take pictures now," Yvonne warns me as we cross the pavement into the labyrinth of crude shelters pinned together, propped up with scrap wood, plywood sheets, tin, stray two-by-fours, and bedsheets for doors. Illegal wiring is jerry-rigged into some of the homes, providing a bare-bulb's worth of electricity and power for the ubiquitous television. Freshly laundered clothes flap in the clear, hot morning air to dry, washed in the sour waters of the large open viaduct that flows alongside Coqueirinho. The water supply comes from a city main they've tapped into. Outside of the one toilet in the school room, there is virtually no plumbing, only an open hole for excretion, Yvonne informs me. The faint odor of urine wafts on the air, stronger in some places, as we walk past the shelters.

"It's too dangerous, the camera. There are drug dealers here. They're armed," she explains matter-of-factly, signaling Ayrton to join us as we walk past a row of shacks into a lane that snakes back under the viaduct and opens out into a common area. From here there are a number of directions and tiny alleys we could take. "Make sure the lens cap is on and put your camera back over your shoulder so that it's clear you're not using it.

"We need to get Hernan, he's four. His mother drinks all the time and she won't let him out to come to school unless I come get him. He's very bright, but he lives in a hell-hole with her. This is the only time she lets him out of her sight," Yvonne tells me as we walk up to a shack that has no door, only a latched homemade wooden barricade of sorts.

"Hello!" Yvonne shouts in Portuguese to a woman in the back. "Where's Hernan? It's time for school." A shy blond four-year-old appears in the doorway. He is ready. His mother lets him out. He quickly takes Yvonne's hand, and as we head back toward the school room, several people run up to Yvonne shouting. I don't understand what's happening. Ayrton takes Hernan and heads toward the school; Yvonne takes me deeper into the village, down another back lane. Everyone knows Yvonne and calls out to her as we hurry past, wanting her to stop and visit, but she keeps going. The lanes are full of people coming and going, as well as a number who sit in the sun just visiting.

"They want me to come and break up a fight," Yvonne explains. "Two brothers are going to kill each other," she adds as we come to a house where a small group of worried people stand gathered outside. "Don't come in," she says, "no matter what. Ayrton will be back shortly," she insists as she walks through the sheeted doorway. Those of us standing outside hear all the curses, shouts, and blows of the fight, the makeshift wall is so thin. There's a loud blow, then a crash, and the sound of a body falling, Yvonne's voice rises in authoritative shouts as she yells for them to stop. Suddenly two shirtless young men in their late teens explode through the doorway, rolling onto the ground at our feet, still in each other's grip, landing blows even as they fall. Yvonne follows, shouting and waving her hands. They get up, dazed. One young man is weeping, his eyes crazed and streaming. They stumble. Yvonne seizes the moment and inserts herself between them. The fighting stops, and in moments one of them turns and begins to walk away, talking with Yvonne, while the other goes back into the shack crying. We follow Yvonne, wending our way back to the common area. Just as we arrive there's another row, and more shouts. We turn in time to see the weeping brother running for us with a knife in one hand and a two-by-four in the other. The brother who walked away with Yvonne spins out of her reach and pulls a cut-off knife blade from his pocket, grabs a nearby two-by-four and turns again to face his brother. They circle and stalk each other. People gather around them resolutely. I can't tell if they are fascinated or amused. No one seems to be making a move. I don't know what to do, it's all happening so fast. I start to go forward when Yvonne yells at me to get back.

"They're going to fight to the death and there's nothing we can do," she says, though in a moment both she and Ayrton are trying to stop them again. But the brothers' rage is complete and their hatred so hot that no one can touch them, they are crackling.

I can't stand here and watch this. I can't believe they can't be stopped. I don't believe it, and suddenly I find myself pushing my way back through crowd around them screaming, "Stop, stop, stop! You can't do this!" in English. Ayrton grabs me and pulls me back into the circle. Yvonne confronts me toe-to-toe and forces me back further while the brothers keep circling and swinging at each other.

"The police, I'll call the police," I tell Yvonne as she maneuvers me outside the circle and Ayrton heads in again. "Where is the phone?" I ask, at the same time realizing that the nearest one would be blocks away, I don't speak Portuguese, and there's no time anyway.

"Don't get the police," Yvonne says tersely. "They are worse. Stay back. I can't let you be a witness. If you are, you may be killed. Stay out of this, I know what I'm doing," she snaps and slips through the crowd. Now I can't see anything, there is such a large circle around the men. I stand there for a moment disoriented, not knowing what to do. A couple of men smoking cigarettes across the street are watching the fight. They lean up against an old car and laugh.

Barbara's still in the school room with the children. I turn to make my way there to see if I can at least help her. As I get half the distance across the pavement, Yvonne runs up behind me yelling, "Here! Get rid of these quick so they can't find them!" And runs back into the circle. She has just thrust the brothers' knives into my hands. Relieved to know they can't stab each other to death, I look around quickly, seeing only the waterway to throw them in, too far. Everything is paved and open, the nearest place is someone's open door, or the school room, neither a good solution. I pull off my day pack and zip them inside quickly—no one will think to look there—and turn toward the circle to see the crowd breaking up, Ayrton with one brother going in one direction and Yvonne heading toward the shade under the overpass with the other. He's still weeping in gutwrenching sobs. Yvonne holds him and talks to him softly. Now he listens to her, exhausted, sweating, and crying like a tired child. Everyone walks away, as finally I do, back into the school house, wanting to give the young man the dignity of privacy—so difficult and rare here—in which to recover himself. He is so clearly lost.

Yvonne's response was immediate and strong—fierce—and what I see her giving him now is unqualified compassion, though I doubt that she would call it that. "Understanding" might be her word. When I ask her if she has a guiding faith, she says no, only that she thinks of Christ's words "Do good to one another" every day.

Standing next to the school room and watching her across the way, I see a tender side. A more complicated picture of Yvonne. My expectation that a person doing the kind of work that she does must be sustained by some kind of spiritual practice has been shaken. Beyond her comment about the need to "do good to one another" and a mention of the philosopher Spinoza, she has little to say on the subject. Yet without being religious or spiritual in an identifiable way, Yvonne, like others I've met, seems to fulfill the New Testament's description of practicing "pure religion"—"coming to the help of orphans and widows in their hardships, and keeping oneself uncontaminated by the world" (James 1:27). Perhaps Yvonne is an inadvertent bodhisattva, one who chooses not to enter the promised land or nirvana but stays behind to help others find their way. Yvonne would undoubtedly scoff at such musing, yet, for the moment, her coolness and diffidence have been put aside as she holds the young man and calms him.

"How do I talk about that at a dinner party?" Yvonne asks brusquely, as she walks back into the school-house clamor. I shouldn't be surprised at how quickly she resumes her armor. Life below the freeway is vicious and full of traps.

"Every day it's something, every day. Today we were lucky, we stopped it, but sometimes we're too late and we only find the body after. The children see all this—all of it. See why I don't fit?" she says, half exasperated, half relieved, it seems, for me to have seen close up, first-hand, what she contends with daily besides the excited children in the school room—the violence and chaos that they're left to swim or drown in.

At the end of the day, Yvonne takes a break between Coqueirinho and the world she will enter again in her elegant high-rise apartment at the other end of the city. It's five o'clock and she has a tennis lesson. Ayrton turns the gray sedan into the crunchy gravel drive of a white-walled private club.

We walk through the clubhouse out onto a patio where I can sit in the shade and wait while she takes off for her game. An immaculately dressed waiter appears with a basket of popcorn and asks for my drink order. Ginger ale, I tell him, then sit back to attempt to allow the shift between worlds that I'm making.

Sitting quietly, watching the ocean breeze stir in the towering palm trees, I am consoled by the soothing green of these neatly trimmed grounds, by the sight of well-fed, gurgling toddlers playing with young mothers and nursemaids, by the quiet. I feel guilty about being here. Yvonne enjoys it. She's learned the lesson that flight attendants give on every takeoff: If the cabin loses pressure, put the oxygen mask on yourself before you try to help someone else.

Present moment, wonderful moment, Thich Nhat Hanh says. Yes, but for whom, a voice in me answers, for whom is the present moment a wonderful moment? For me, now. Then the sound of children's laughter breaks through. Can I let in their laughter too, along with Aline's?

When Yvonne joins me after her lesson, her face is flushed from the workout, the white terry-cloth sweatband still around her head. She drinks a glass of water to cool off, and begins to tell me about the philosophy behind her work.

"I want to build a new country, that's my ideal. You saw what we are doing under the bridge. I want to change people's mentality. If you don't change the mentality, you don't go anywhere. And it's very difficult to change anything. I know I'm not going to be successful. I'm a crazy idealist. The problems are getting worse with the increasing concentration of wealth.[4]

"When they asked me to come look at Coqueirinho under the

freeway, to help them with their problems, I said okay. I started to have a plan. There are nearly fifteen hundred people there altogether, mostly black. They had no positive identity, so I started teaching them about Africa. I told them about the lands they came from and that the people they were descended from had been princesses, princes, kings and queens, healers, and priests. I told them that in Angola there are many orphans and sick kids because of war, but there are no street kids. Why? Because kids belong to their community. If there are no relatives, the community takes the children in. A child belongs to everyone."

By teaching rudimentary history as a way to begin to instill pride and a sense of ancestry, and by using Africa as a model for a way of thinking about the street children, Yvonne was able to help community members find their way to taking in the street kids from Candelária. But she didn't ask them to do it alone. She worked alongside them, down to hammering the nails into the used plywood for the school. She seems to function as a more knowledgeable neighbor.

With Yvonne's help, the community-center kitchen was fitted with a two-burner gas stove and a refrigerator. A rudimentary bathroom with a toilet was built in a corner of the school room. The hundred twenty children going to school and being fed two meals a day there have to take responsibility for keeping up the school room and the surrounding area. No work, no food, Yvonne tells me. And she enforces it. Chores are very simple, geared to age, but participation is mandatory. She demands reciprocity, return—relationship. She gives, so must they. Forty children from Coqueirinho are now in the public school system. It's clear that education is their only way out.

While Barbara attends more to basic schooling, Yvonne addresses the life lessons the children need. She often finds herself giving informal lessons in hygiene, behavior, sex education, and general problem solving, just to help the kids survive. Yvonne also provides two teachers in the afternoons to work with the children after she and Barbara leave.

Once a month Yvonne goes into the houses to help the women clean. It took many months for relationships to develop to the point where she could do this. The shelters are tiny—one-room huts—so everyone sleeps together. Often it's a mother and her companion, maybe more than one, so the children are introduced to sexuality early, even if it's only to observe. There's nothing they don't see. Privacy is virtually nonexistent in such close quarters. Kids as young as five or six often have been sexually molested, abused, or raped by some adult, and many have learned to get money by acquiescing. Venereal disease and AIDS are rampant. The Church is still against sex education and contraception. Yvonne is completely frank with the children, trying to provide basic information and helping them understand consequences and options. The only way to protect these children is to face the issue head-on. Teenage pregnancy is high in Rio, especially in this population. More and more babies are being born with AIDS, to girls as young as eleven. Yvonne feels that in the two years she's worked with this community, she's only begun to make the improvements so necessary. Still she feels that there's progress. Yvonne's a realist, she knows that the problems come from all quarters. There is no one solution.

"It's a long-term process. Books, for example, and the Church, they keep talking about the family like it's a mother and a father. These kids don't have that. They lose the kids right there.

"I tell my kids that family is someone who takes care of you. It's more of a tribal concept, like in Africa. Slowly, slowly they begin to understand. But I can't change them. I'm not there twenty-four hours a day. If they sell themselves for a dollar, that's reality."

I can't help but wonder if it wasn't painful for her to face this "reality," if it didn't make her feel small, as though she were up against forces so large that she could never make a difference.

"I would go crazy if I thought I could change that," she says emphatically. "It's not possible. I just have to cope with their reality, try to improve it, and teach them to protect themselves.

"People criticized me for building the school out of used lumber. They said it was terrible. I should have done more. But I say no. At first, it should be just a little better than their house, but not completely different or it will be destroyed. These children have had nothing. They have to learn how to take care of things. Now everyone cares about the school because they built it themselves; they take care of it, with a little help. Every few months we make improvements, slowly, slowly."

Yvonne sits across from me, leaning her forearms on the table, speaking intently.

"We go step by step. You have to start small at the beginning. The kids were dirty, for example—first of all the community didn't have water. How could they be expected to be clean? So we got water coming in. I didn't start to wash the children until I had been there six months, and then only little by little. We wash the hands, then the face, then washing up becomes part of their lives. But this takes time.

"Government has to hurry up and fix things in five years, so they're always in a rush. It's impossible. Many of the changes I've made you cannot see, they're so small, but they mean something for everyday life. I'm in no hurry. My term limit is my life. Big changes come with time, going little by little, consistently. It's a big battle, I fight like a bull."

We finish talking. She signals Ayrton to get the car. Outside the gate, we're stopped at a traffic light. From here I can see that the club is just off the broad avenue that runs along the ocean. Workers stand on the corner waiting for a bus. On the other side of the white-washed wall behind the workers, riders practice jumping on well-groomed horses. I can see only their black-velvet-hatted heads bobbing as their horses leap up and clear the hurdles.

Across the broad avenue are the ocean and the spectacular white sand beaches of Rio, lined by sidewalks with bold curved designs of black-and-white tiles. The coconut-milk stands every few hundred feet are busy; behind them, the surf glints and breaks dark blue into white. On the beach, children run into the shallows screaming, while dark-bodied boys float out beyond the breakers on white surfboards, waiting to catch the next big wave, and women in tiny bright-colored bikinis walk by. In the distance, the mountainous jungle bursts out of the ocean floor, jutting up in a riot of green.

Yvonne is in mid-air, like a trapeze artist flying, having let go of her privilege and wealth and opened herself up to the suffering of children, but I don't see a net under her. She does not have a large community of support to help sustain her, like Mother Teresa's Sisters have, or even a less formal one like that of Aruna, Olga, and Jessie in Asia, or of Laura and the Mothers in Argentina. I would wish that for her. Yet her position is so unusual that I can see that she lives in a world not many would know how to share.

Since her work with street children made the international news after the Candelária Massacre, she says that she's experienced praise, recognition, and jealousies. The effect of her book on the subject has been mixed. She has been accused of using the plight of the street children to catapult herself into politics as a path for a run for political office, she says. She has little to share with her social set, and little to share socially with those for whom she is so impassioned. No wonder she sculpts primarily in stone, I think as I watch her late the next afternoon, in the quiet of her studio, far away from Coqueirinho, on the other side of town. Yvonne's subject is hard, like the marble she's chipping away: cold and intractable. It has to be pounded, blasted, and hammered away in small pieces to make any progress.

Downstairs is a small gallery of her work, all stone: cobalt-blue granite, Carrara marble, black granite—circles and spirals of stone or hard-edged geometric shapes set on cherry wood or dark mahogany, but for one piece. One piece is a human form, cast in bronze. It is a young boy from Candelária, sitting on the church steps after the massacre, his knees drawn up in his arms, his head on his knees, weeping.

CHAPTER 18

An Offering to Jemanjá, Goddess of the Sea

Salvador da Bahia

orns blare as the end-of-the-day traffic slams to a halt in front of us. Red light. A car with two women in it is stopped ahead of us. Suddenly a teenage boy runs up to the driver and asks her something. As he engages her, a younger, smaller boy runs around to the other side of the car, clips a watch off the wrist of the second woman, and dashes away between cars before she even realizes that her watch is missing.

I look at my companions—my translator, Michael Mattis, an American musical ethnographer and percussionist, who has lived for several years in Salvador da Bahia, said to be the most African part of Brazil, and his Bahian friend Gordo, as he is called, Edvaldo José Ferreira Santos. "Always keep your bag in front of you." Gordo laughs. "They're fast!"

Gordo is a social worker by day, working with street children like the ones we just saw; by night, he is a *capoeirista,* a practitioner of an art form that originated uniquely in Brazil. *Capoeira* combines dance with martial arts in which the feet are used as the primary means of attack and defense. *Capoeira* is interwoven into the history of slavery and resistance in Brazil. Three hundred years ago, Africans brought their martial arts tradition with them from Africa and adapted it to their situation in Brazil, disguising it as dance and a form of play. In this way, owners did not suspect that slaves were preparing for an uprising or organizing resistance.[1] Though practiced primarily by men, in the last few years women have taken it up and are advancing rapidly as the form spreads in both the United States and Europe.

Capoeira was also used to protect the ceremonies of the Orishás, the deified ancestors and archetypal forces who are personified as the gods and goddesses of Candomblé, the Afro-Brazilian religion of spirit possession and nature worship that lives just under the surface of Brazilian Catholicism. In general, Orishás are believed to have established control over various forces of nature, such as the wind, thunder, the waters, and over activities such as metalworking and hunting.[2] Orishás also have knowledge of the properties and powers of plants. The power of an Orishá can be transmitted briefly, during possession, to his or her descendant. Possession is a form of communion in Candomblé, though not everyone is capable of experiencing it.

African religions stayed alive in Brazil, unlike in the United States, because of Catholicism. Very quickly Catholic saints and African Orishás became syncretized and roughly equated. St. Jerome with a lion at his feet became Shangô, the powerful thunder god. Oyá-Yansan, goddess of wind and lightning, Shangô's first wife, became identified with St. Barbara because of her association with lightning. Oshossi, the hunter god, was related to St. George, the dragon slayer—at least in Bahia; Jemanjá, goddess of the sea and mother of several other Orishás, was identified as Our Lady of the Immaculate Conception; Nanan Buruku, the oldest water divinity, was St. Ann; Christ was Oshalá, the god of creation; and so forth. Thus on Sundays, when slaves were allowed to meet in groups according to national origins and speak in their own tongues, they could profess Catholicism yet continue their practice of African religions quite easily, claiming their songs were praises to the saints.

Through Gordo, we have been invited to Ilê Axé Apô Afonja Terreiro for the dances for the Orishá Oshossi. These are religious rituals, not open to the public. If I'm fortunate, I'll be able to meet

Mãe Stella, one of the most highly respected *mães dos santos,* mothers of the saints, of the Candomblé tradition in Brazil. But Gordo warns me: It can be difficult to get an appointment with Mãe Stella. One has to go and see and be prepared to wait. The Orishás rule in the *terreiro,* not the clock.

By the time we arrive, at nine o'clock the next morning, the heat is soaring and the sky, though sunny, is starting to cloud over. The *terreiro* is a large rectangular sandy area the size of two long tree-lined playing fields surrounded by single-story brightly painted houses: blue, with brilliant stripes; green, with a red door. These are the houses of the Orishás. The *terreiro* is actually a compound of the Orishás' houses, including a large white assembly hall, the *barracão;* Oshossi's house, where the ceremony will take place and where *capoeira* is taught; and the homes of the "family" members—those who have been initiated into Candomblé—which open into the large, sandy space. The *terreiros* grew out of the nineteenth-century religious brotherhoods formed by the Church according to African ethnicities.

We speak to Cleo, Mãe Stella's secretary. She tells us to wait until later in the afternoon to speak to Mãe Stella. With the feast of Oshossi in preparation and long ceremonies ahead that night, Cleo isn't sure about our timing. Nonetheless, she speaks with me briefly and explains to me that Oyá-Yansan, or Yansan, the first wife of Shangô, is a fierce female Orishá who can spit fire. And there is a story of how she helped save the world when Shangô was on the verge of defeat. Yansan came up with the strategy that confounded Shangô's enemy and assured his victory. She is the archetype of a powerful, audacious woman, a woman very much her own authority. Her nature is voluptuous and sensual, fiery. Africa and Afro-Brasilia, not only India, have a female deity who rises up to defeat demons bent on the world's destruction, Cleo tells me.

As we walk outside across the hot white sands, we see a woman dressed in white coming toward us, dancing by herself, every few moments stopping to shout. She is in a trance, Gordo explains, possessed by a spirit. Just beyond her is Mãe Stella, he tells me, pointing to a tall, stately, gray-haired older woman walking past with a young girl on a bicycle. Her hair is short, brushed straight back from her face. She is a large woman, a substantial woman, at least five-feet-ten, well into her sixties. Suddenly she speeds up, her long skirts swaying as she begins to trot, then she gives the girl a push and the child speeds up and rides off. Mãe Stella and several other women are on their way to Oshossi's house, the feast house, to oversee the preparations. We have been told that she is not to be interrupted or distracted from the preparations, so we wait.

I sit down to paint a watercolor of Oshossi's dark green house with a red door and the brilliant red hibiscus in full bloom next to it while we wait, and in no time, children begin to gather to watch. I tear off sheets of paper, pull watercolor crayons out of my pack, more tubes of paint and more brushes, and lay them out for the children to join me. They dive in. In minutes, with no language between us, only colors and drawings, we are all laughing and teasing one another over our drawings. I am a rank amateur with few skills, the benefit of which is that I'm on the same level as many of the children.

Late in the afternoon there is still no sign of Mãe Stella. Michael and Gordo take me to an old friend who lives on the other side of the terreiro. Descending half a dozen steps out of the heat, I find myself on the cool, covered, cement-floored back porch of Cida Santos's home, where preparations for the feast of Oshossi have been going on all day.

Cida sits in a light brown sundress, a vision of ease, one strap straying off her left shoulder, one foot propped up in the lap of another woman, who's painting Cida's toenails a pearled pink, like the rings on the necks of the doves in the cage next to Cida. Cida cuts up chickens and dips the parts in water to rinse them before handing them to a little girl of four or so at her side. Cida's face is wonderfully shaped, not quite an oval, not quite a square, but something soft in between. Her curly brown hair is piled up on her head, pulled back off the nape of her neck, where a few tendrils have strayed. She wears small gold earrings set with rhinestones. Her smile is warm, her dark eyes direct and inviting, her laughter so infectious that though I cannot join in the conversation going on in Portuguese, Cida makes me feel at home immediately.

The afternoon heat wears on, grinding down the day, until evening will arrive to put it out as if extinguishing a burning cigarette. People come and go down the steps, across the porch into the open door of Cida's family's house, outside of which we sit. Michael, Cida, and Gordo talk on, friends who do not get to see each other that often. Small glasses of beer go round, and cold soft drinks. Michael explains that I am welcome to make myself comfortable here at Cida's house, leave my camera bag, use the bathroom to freshen up before the ceremony and change into fresh, light-colored clothes. No dark colors are allowed in Candomblé. Nothing somber. The gown that Cida will wear tonight is a shade between dawn pink and early-morning lavender. It hangs in her room next to a statue of Our Lady of Aparecida, for whom she is named.

Cida's cousin, Sandra Regina da Cruz Santana, joins us, a young woman in her twenties, thin and dark, with large almond-shaped brown eyes, and an open face full of innocence. I am taken with Sandra's hair, newly cut within an eighth of an inch, showing how elegantly her head is shaped. I tell her how much I like her haircut and mention that I have been thinking of cutting off my hair too.

"Yes, but do you have the courage to do it?" she asks simply, looking me right in the eye. There is no edge to her question, so genuine that it stops me. She waits for my answer.

"Yes," I hear myself say, "yes, I do." She raises her eyebrows in surprise and laughs, holding her hands over her mouth.

"Okay. I'll take you. It's not far," she says. I look at my translator to see if he will go. No, not into a women's beauty parlor. We're on our own.

Sandra takes my hand and off we go, with only my pocket dictionary to help us get back and forth between Portuguese and English. Out the big gate, down the dusty street, past the Reign of God Evangelical Church, Brazil's answer to Jimmy Swaggart, past the shoe store, past the stares of the few who notice us walking hand in hand, a gringa off the beaten track and a young woman from Mãe Stella's. What in the world am I doing?

I feel wildly liberated, wide awake. Argentina left me feeling as though I'd been turned upside down, my head dipped in boiling water. I feel scalded. I have no way to talk about what I've seen and heard. Cutting off all my hair is the only thing that feels appropriate after Argentina. It is an ancient rite, a sign of mourning, of purification. In Salvador da Bahia, women cut their hair as an offering to Jemanjá, the goddess of the sea, and throw it into the waves. I will do the same. I will not keep it.

Our arrival at the tiny neighborhood beauty salon crowds six women into a small shop that might comfortably hold four. The floor is dark red cement, the walls peeling pink stucco. A wobbly plastic fan with blue blades sits on the floor, turning back and forth with steady jerks, keeping the air moving and cooler than the midday heat.

An attractive middle-aged woman sits in front of the window with one hand dipped in solution to soften her cuticles while the manicurist holds her other hand and deftly wields a brush full of red polish onto her customer's long fingernails. Another woman is getting her hair streaked; a third, toothless and slightly tipsy, sits in one of the two salon chairs and waits. When they hear Sandra explain that I want my hair cut off like hers, they all comment and offer opinions. Sandra giggles, they laugh and shake their heads, while I smile and nod emphatically, "*Sí,* yes."

"Okay," Maria, the shop owner, finally says. She'll do it if we are willing to wait. She is busy. We sit down and I field questions—

Where am I from? Do I like Salvador?—as best I can with too little language, until I remember to pull out a thick packet of photos of family, friends, Tibetan lamas, Catholic priests, and various deities, another way to communicate without language, especially with women. They bring out their family pictures too, and together we learn something new about one another's lives. The process is exhausting and slow, but it is an effective way to exchange goodwill and these women have plenty. Now it's my turn to sit in the chair.

Maria begins by cutting off layers of hair with scissors. My heart wells up on the first big cut. I feel a big "yes" inside. I feel lighter with each swatch that falls to the floor. The shape of my skull shows. Finally the electric razor comes out with its loud buzz, and in minutes we are done. I have an eighth of an inch of hair left all over my scalp. Sandra gives me a big hug.

When we return to the *terreiro,* people smile indulgently, rub my near-to-bald head, and laugh. Everyone approves. Cida insists that it looks good, then teases me and ties an elegant long white scarf turban-style around my head, like hers. At least I don't have to see myself. The experience has planted the seed of friendship with Sandra, my hair is cut just like hers, only hers curls attractively against her well-proportioned head and mine looks like the stubble of newly mown brown grass.

Women are dancing in Oshossi's house, I can see them through the open door when we get back, but I can't go in. The house is not yet open, despite the doors swung wide. The women and children are laying down long, leafy branches, cuttings of palms, on the floor as part of the ceremonial preparations.

Finally Mãe Stella comes out of Oshossi's and goes down to the house where women are cooking, preparing food for the feast. Word is passed along. Mãe Stella will see me in an hour in Shangô's house.

When we arrive Cleo seats us on a couch in the waiting room, where a tall floor fan whirs softly in the corner, cooling us. Cleo warns us that Mãe Stella's time is short today, so not to expect much. Within moments, Mãe Stella sweeps into the room, her long skirts softly rustling. I rise to pay my respects. Mãe Stella has a commanding presence, physically commanding because of her size, tall, not heavy, but large, strong, and vital. She sits down on one end of the couch and invites me to sit with her. She has changed clothes and now wears a simple tiny yellow-and-white flower print blouse over her traditional white cotton eyelet underblouse. Her long skirt is a complementary print pattern of pinks and blues. She wears yellow glass beads with coral, the colors of her Orishá. Her head is uncovered, her short, straight silver hair showing. Her presence is intriguing. She looks as though she would be stern, and I half expect that, but what I find is gentleness.

Candomblé is not a religion accessible in the way that Buddhism and Christianity with their emphasis on the text, the word, might be. It is a religion one observes, one experiences, over time. There isn't much Mãe Stella can tell me, I realize as I struggle with my questions about fierce female deities, compassion, transforming anger. Though I had read about Candomblé in preparation for this trip, no mere description could prepare me. Candomblé demands a familiarity with African religions that I don't have. Mãe Stella tailors her remarks to my beginner's level.

"Faith is everything," Mãe Stella explains. "It is the basis for all else. Your teacher can prepare you a great deal, yes, but in the end, what happens depends on the person themself. You have to prepare yourself. I can guide you, yes? But only you can prepare yourself. I can't do that for you. Each person is responsible for themself, for their actions."

There are many initiations in Candomblé, both major and

minor. Some initiations are open, some are so secret that only certain members of the *terreiro* can see them. There is a progression of initiations from the time one first becomes a *filho dos santos,* a child of saints in a *terreiro,* to becoming a *mãe dos santos* or a *pai dos santos.* Only the Orishás can choose a mother or a father of the saints, and they do so through the oracle of the shells. That's how Mãe Stella was chosen as the *mãe dos santos* here. By the Orishás themselves.

Mãe Stella was thirteen years old when her Orishá came to her. She comes from a matriarchy, a line of renowned Afro-Brazilian women *mães dos santos,* starting with the founder of Ilê Axé Apô Afonja, Eugenia Ana. Eugenia Ana was a daughter of Africans who came to Candomblé following the tradition of her family. When she became a *mãe dos santos,* in 1910, eighty-five years before my visit, she bought this land and founded this *terreiro.* I ask Mãe Stella to talk a little about being part of a matriarchy.

"It is very positive. Understand first of all, being head of this *terreiro* doesn't mean only taking care of the Orishás. This whole compound is a community. Having a woman lead is positive because this represents the mother, and the mother's energy is more available to the children. This is the kind of energy that brings a family feeling into the community, it helps pull everyone together. This is good, very good. In Candomblé it is also felt that the feminine has more concentration, also that she gives more. These are important qualities of the feminine."

Mãe Stella explains that the majority of *mães dos santos* sacrifice their own family life and move here to stay within the compound and to be a mother to the whole community, to be able to facilitate the whole process. Mãe Stella has been here twenty years. Though she tells me that she can speak with no authority about any other religion, she knows that this question of sacrifice comes up because it's hard to be head of a religious group or dedicate your life to something and then to have a family. She herself was married once, but had no children. Her husband died. She lived with two sisters after his death, but then came here to dedicate herself exclusively to taking care of this community.

Members of the *terreiro* community come and go in the house as we talk, continuing their preparations for the evening's ceremonies; their momentary presences help create a sense of well-being, carrying us in the flow of events toward evening.

I ask Mãe Stella what to her is the most important thing about Candomblé, what she would like people to know about it. She stops to think for a moment and then tells me.

"There are three important things. The first is to have faith. Next, one must have generosity. This generosity is also a form of selflessness. Third is to have mutual respect and understanding. This is what unites any true religious community and makes it successful. It's important to accept people, not to leave anyone out, and to work to help people grow and expand.

"Candomblé's core comes from Africa. What we're doing here has been modified, because it's Afro-Brazilian, but the essence is the same, because the Orishás have no boundaries, no borders. The Orishás can be anywhere. Where is there no water, where is there no fire, no wind? Nature is everywhere. These are the elements of the Orishás. The Orishás are part of nature, they are throughout the universe. There is no place where they are not."

We are abruptly interrupted with a message for Mãe Stella. An older member is very ill and must be taken to the hospital immediately, explains Cleo, who has been translating. Mãe Stella rises to go. My visit with her is cut short.

When Mãe Stella returns, evening has come and it is time for her to open Oshossi's house. We file in after four honorary members of the *terreiro* are seated up in front, alongside but below Mãe Stella. The painter Carybé is one of them. His wife, Nancy, sits next to me.

Next the women come in and walk around picking up the palm fronds laid out on the floor, then walk by the drums to one side, the *atabaques*, the ritual drums, to touch them, and then go to Mãe Stella's throne, where they bow at her feet, touching their foreheads to her feet or the steps in front of them, similar to Tibetan Buddhists bowing before a revered and precious teacher.

The old women are seated at the front of the room, in a place of honor to the left of Mãe Stella. Those who are going to dance touch the floor, make the sign of the cross, and begin, slowly swaying to the drumbeat. As the first song is chanted, Mãe Stella rises out of her place to join the dancers briefly in a simple rhythmic swaying and graceful circling of the floor. Old women join in too, then the young, each dressed exquisitely in long, full dresses in pastel colors and white eyelet blouses underneath the pastel. Their skirts are long and voluminous and airy, trimmed in yards of elaborate laces. They curve out from the body like rounded bells. A wide band of rich satin is tied around the midriff, flowing down the back and then crossing around to the front again, tying off across the breasts in a big soft bow. Long strands of glass beads in the colors of the Orishás sway, like the skirts, from side to side. The dancers move forward one step and then back in simple, stately movements that combined with the elaborate ceremonial clothes reveal a complicated choreography of color, movement, and song. At the end of each song, the dancers bow low, touch the floor with their foreheads, and make the sign of the cross.

The drumming picks up and now most of the dancers move faster, circling the floor. Out of the thirty or so, seven slow down and begin to shake, a sign of possession by the Spirit. As they go deeper into trance, designated members of the *terreiro* come in and stand beside them to support them, to watch over them. Cida glides and turns, slowly now, swaying serenely in lavender satin. She wears a gold-colored crown with rose-colored beads that hang down in strands, covering her half-closed eyes.

I feel heat rise in waves as the drums speed up. People stand at the edge of the dance floor, their palms held out parallel to the floor, slightly upturned, as though they are holding the energy. There are nearly two hundred more people in the rows behind them. A few go into the circle to greet the dancers gently, giving them bouquets of flowers. As the drums get more insistent, we clap harder and harder, the chanting grows louder, the dancers whirl past, bending and turning, hooting, giving a shout—the Spirit—then the dance slows down and gradually family members, members of the *terreiro,* come in to hug those who are possessed, to receive their blessing, a direct transmission from divine to human. Finally there is only one dancer left on the floor, whom the drums follow. It is Oshossi himself, the hunter, wearing a fur hat and a turquoise skirt.

Now a procession of dancers comes into the hall, turning and chanting, led by a woman who carries on her head an object veiled in gold cloth. She makes her way through the circle to Mãe Stella, to whom she bows and presents this object. Mãe Stella nods, and the gold-clothed object is placed on a table next to her.

The bearer takes a ladle and dips into an unseen opening in the gold veil and fills small cups on nearby trays that are then passed out to everyone. Everyone receives a cup, no matter how long it takes. There are nearly three hundred people in Oshossi's house now, I don't see how there could be enough liquid in that one container, but it does not run out. I am one of the last to be served, as I am in the back row on one side. Cida brings the tray to our section and gives me a smile from another world. She is more than herself. It is a cup of water. I hesitate, will I get sick from it? I forsake my consideration and give my reluctance to the winds. This is communion, this is community, and in this moment I am part of it. I drink the water that Cida gives me. Water as communion. Water as our common union.

I remember Kali Puja at Dakshineswar, in Calcutta, and discovering that night that water, the Ganga, was the source of Kali's strength, the head priest taking the copper pot from the temple to the river to recharge Kali's energy. Sacred ecology. Now our environmental crisis shows us "scientifically" what these ancient ceremonies uphold: Not only is the natural world sacred, it is not separate from us. We are in the web of life *with* it, not *above* it, and these relationships must be honored.

Outside, late at night under the starlit sky, during a break in the ceremony that will go on for several more hours, I am told by one of the honorary members of the *terreiro* that the cult of Oshossi is six thousand years old. I quickly pull out a notepad and pen.

"Then let me ask you—" I begin, when he cuts me off. A handsome man in his forties, tall, erect, with a proud presence, he smiles enigmatically. "The one who learns the most about Candomblé," he says quietly, "is the one who asks the fewest questions."

CHAPTER 19

"Proud Flesh"

Looking at the Scars
San Francisco Bay Area, California

And see how the flesh grows back
across a wound, with a great vehemence, more strong
than the simple, untested surface before.
There's a name for it on horses,
when it comes back darker and raised: proud flesh.

. . . . . .

. . . a single fabric
that nothing can tear or mend.

—JANE HIRSHFIELD, "FOR WHAT BINDS US"

It was easy in Bahia to cut all my hair off, but now that I'm home I have to learn to live with it. People look at me strangely, or pat me on the head constantly. I'm not always quick enough to duck or fend them off. Then come the remarks: "Heat down there get to you?" "Looks awful!" "Fabulous! Wish I had the guts to cut all my hair off, I've always wanted to." "Hmm. Well, at least you've got the bones for it." When asked to explain why I did it, I start to say something about Laura's stories in Buenos Aires, about the Mothers of the Disappeared, the street children of Coqueirinho in Rio. The silence that follows is awkward. I stop trying to make people understand, learn to shrug off comments with a tilt of the head and wry smile. When I offer my hair to the sea, scattering it on the ocean on my birthday, in November, I know I've completed this stage of the journey.

Then, two things happen in quick succession. First, soon after I get home, I open up a newspaper and find a summary of "Walk in the Light," the Conference of Catholic Bishops statement on child sexual abuse issued on October 26, 1996, while I was out of the country. Second, I discover that the priest who telephoned me just before I left for Latin America never delivered my letter to Jim— and that Jim is still alive.

It is a great relief to hear the Catholic Bishops acknowledge that for centuries child sexual abuse "has been cloaked in a conspiracy of silence" and that it's time for the Christian community "to shatter the walls of loneliness, shame, and fear that isolate those who are sexually abused. . . ." It is a welcome balm, after so much silence on and denial of the subject. The Bishops openly acknowledge that "the Church carries a heavy burden of responsibility in the area of sexual abuse. . . ." They express alarm at large numbers of girls under twelve who have suffered sexual abuse. Most important is their statement that justice must play a role in the process of forgiveness and that the community, not only the family, needs to hold the abuser accountable.

Relief, fury, and gratification all follow in a storm of feelings as I read and reread the article in the *National Catholic Reporter*. The contrast between the Bishops' incisive statements and what the priest asked of me is ironic. Further, Jim is still alive. Could this be resolved differently?

The issue of remaining silent troubles me deeply after my journey to Argentina. The clarity of Laura Bonaparte and the Mothers of the Disappeared made the relationship of silence and complicity obvious at a deeper level than I had ever understood before. Argentina was a potent lesson in the way silence can corrode the community. Can I accept my own wound as a gift of life, a way in which I was broken that can open me to the gifts of others, something that might help guide me? Can I make it holy?

"I looked inside and saw my deepest wound and it dazzled me," St. Augustine said.[1] Could this be so? Can I look inside, and then, can I let it go?

A phone call became a catalyst for these thoughts. An older friend and neighbor, a woman in her seventies, called me, a woman who had known a schoolmate of Jim's many years ago. What seemed a random, odd coincidence—our meeting and finding out that we knew some of the same people from long ago and far away—suddenly became another lens through which to view this event. My older friend said that she had recently received a phone call from a former schoolmate of Jim's. The schoolmate was calling to ask her "to talk some sense into her friend China." Apparently he had spoken to Jim within the last few months. Whatever Jim said led him to call my elderly friend, get her involved, and see that I "straightened out."

I was shocked. Not only had I never told my friend about what happened when I was four, it had been more than two years since I had confronted Jim and written to him, offering again to meet with him with a third party. I had never heard from him.

She invited me for tea. When I arrived, not knowing where or how to begin, my friend got right to the matter. A plain-spoken Quaker, she assured me as she had the former schoolmate that she could easily believe that what I said to Jim was true, though she had known nothing about this from me. Jim's friend had gotten off the phone quickly.

I sat on her couch, listening to her recollections, stunned to hear about how my friend had known Jim since he was a teenager and how she had always known that he was troubled. She had also known his older brother, who had confided the family's worries about Jim to her when Jim was a teenager. She remembered that his parents had taken him out of state to try to find help for him; that's when she first met him. He had pulled out all his eyelashes; that was the strongest image of him that stayed with her. It was like a hook that made her remember, it gave him such an odd, astonished appearance.

Then I told her about how, after I confronted Jim, I had found out he was talking to people I knew, and that one of the few people I had confided in, another woman, felt the same way as my older friend did—that Jim had been a troubled young man and that she was not surprised to hear what had happened. She had known Jim in high school, and when I mentioned his name to her, she said that she knew what I was going to tell her before it came out of my mouth, I needed to go no further. When I did, she said that it was as she thought. When I asked her how she knew that's what I would tell her, she would say only that she just did. It fit.

But my mother's response had the most impact and was the strongest. When we talked about the rape some years ago, she had been deeply upset. At first she wanted to deny that such a thing could have happened to me while I was in her care—she had not worked outside the home when I was young. But then I reminded her that this had happened during World War II, and that there had been many times when I was not in her care, when she went to be with my father where he was stationed, and she thought again. Within moments, she was saying yes, she did believe me, for she remembered Jim in high school, where she had known him too, slightly, by reputation. He had gotten into some kind of trouble over a girl, and his family had taken him to a psychiatrist. That was Texas in the late 1930s, early 1940s, not the East Coast or Europe. Seeking psychiatric help was virtually unheard of, that's why she remembered it. She never found out what happened, only that he had some kind of problem that was considered too terrible to talk about.

The next time I went home to visit, my mother suggested calling a meeting to confront this issue head-on with the people involved, at least ones that we knew Jim had contacted. Not only was I surprised by the directness of her suggestion, but two days later, at the meeting, I was thunderstruck to hear my mother take the lead. She told the handful of friends who had gathered that she had called them together to put an end to the talk about what I had done to Jim, as it had been portrayed. She assured them that she had known Jim to have had problems since he was a teenager. She told them that she felt she had to confront this issue not only for my sake, but because her own contemporaries, women in their sixties and their seventies, had begun to come forward and confide their own struggles with childhood sexual abuse that had occurred decades before. They could no longer remain silent, invisible. My mother had been reading and had informed herself on the subject, the existence of it, the denial of it, how people have been falsely accused, how people have falsely denied it. Controversies aside, she knew that child sexual abuse was real and that it was horrifying. It was time to put an end to such abuse. I was a survivor, not a perpetrator, for coming forward, and she supported me.

Never in my life did I so vividly experience my mother's taking up for me, protecting me and siding with me, and it was powerful. She might have done so innumerable times, undoubtedly, but this was the first time that I consciously and fully experienced it, and it made me proud. The one other woman present at this meeting also supported me, completely. But it was the experience of my mother's gathering everyone together, leading the discussion, revealing how much she had informed herself, how much her friends had informed her, her own observations of this man, seeing her courage and her candor, that was the gift of this electrifying experience. I was riveted by my mother's transformation into the embodiment of the fierce feminine, cutting through illusion with fierce compassion, with a furious dignity. She may not have appeared as Durga, with ten hands on a lion, but I have never seen her so powerful, or felt the strength of her love and protection so fully. In that moment, whatever wound there was left between us was healed, sealing the bond between us, irrevocably.

Her response redeemed what had been my private struggle to heal this experience, and it placed it within the context of community, thereby making it shared and meaningful.

"Violence is not the worst thing that can happen," Thomas Bluerganthal, a Holocaust survivor and member of the U.S. Truth Commission on El Salvador, says. "To the victim, the worst thing that can happen is to be told that nothing happened."[2] Words like water after a long, hard thirst.

Memory brings obligation, not solace, as Jewish people have shown us, as Native Americans have shown us, "obligation to bear witness and seek an accounting, even if in that accounting painful memory must prevail against illusions of justice or safety or dignity."[3] It is in this grappling to remain affiliated, to keep the community intact, to include suffering, that we find grace—not hope but grace, and an access to God.

The phone call from my elderly friend settles my resolve. Though I thought this event was long past, it keeps reappearing, like the demon in Durga's story who wouldn't die. Jim is still alive, and I have to grapple with this fact. Maybe there is time for this to turn out differently. I pick up my pen and begin to write a letter to the priest, copying the article on the Bishops' statement to send him as well. I knew when I came back from Latin America that I had to speak out, I tell the priest, only I didn't have the words for what it was I had to say until I read the Bishops' statement. I had wanted to forget this very personal issue. I wanted to think that my letter of forgiveness to Jim, that the meeting my mother called had taken care of what feelings I had left about this matter, but I discovered it had not when I read the Bishops' missive. To then discover that the priest had not given Jim my letter made me furious.

I stop. Here it is again, my anger. I remember Choga's question: Can I have compassion for this priest? I realize that though I might object, mightily, this man had been willing to try to help.

Underneath, love was at work, trying to bring about a healing, reconciliation.

I begin the letter again, asking the priest to help me now. I ask him to read the Bishops' statement. I acknowledge that I am angry, but I don't attack. I ask him to question Jim now as he had me, to ask Jim to search his heart as he had asked me to search mine. Could he invite Jim to apologize as he had asked me to do? I urge him to hold the possibility of both perspectives—Jim's *and* mine—to include the conflict, rather than take only Jim's side.

I ask him to note especially the Bishops' statement that "forgiveness is not forgetting, nor does forgiveness consist in excusing the abuse or in absolving the abuser, which only God can do. . . . Abuse is not the survivor's fault. . . . Justice plays a role in the forgiveness process . . . often a long one. . . . We cannot push the survivor to forgive just because we, the Christian community, feel uncomfortable dealing with the issue. Rather, we need to stand with the survivor, to show the same gentle, loving, patient concern that Jesus showed to those who were hurting."[4] Wise words, well thought out.

The point in writing to the priest now, I explain, is threefold: one, to ask him again to give my first letter to Jim and to let Jim be the one to decide if he wants to read it; two, to let him know about the meeting my mother called; and three, to acknowledge how much the Catholic Bishops' statement on this subject means to me. It gave me words that tasted like honey: "justice," "accountability," "not alone," and above all, "community." In struggling with this dilemma alone for such a long time, then only within a small community, I had been able to gain a certain form of healing, but it was limited. By contrast, in Judaism, in Native American traditions, and in many other non-Western societies, the role of the community in healing is well understood, the memory of past suffering sanctified in rituals shared by all. One moves toward memory, not only resolution, as in modern psychotherapy. The Jewish concept of *tikkun*— repair—includes the reality of brokenness in the world. Some losses can't be healed or cured, but they can be acknowledged. This in it-self is a form of healing. The Wailing Wall in Jerusalem provides a place and a container for the memory of loss, just as the Vietnam Veterans Memorial in Washington, D.C., provides a communal context for veterans and their families in the United States.[5]

I do not want to be angry, I assure the priest. Patience is the anti-dote. I want to accept Jim, the priest, myself, and what happened, but I'm not there yet. It is a great relief to admit this to both him and myself. I let the letter sit, reread it, change it, let it sit again, then fi-nally send it.

Jim died without reading the letter. The priest decided not to give it to him or to let him know about it. He burned both my letters and wrote me a letter of apology for opening up such a painful subject.

Waking in the middle of the night, immersed again in the experi-ence of Argentina, I am unable to sleep, my husband's steady breathing at my side fails to calm me. I try to fall back asleep by imagining that I am laying my head in the lap of Mary, the Black Madonna, but it becomes Claudia Lapaco's lap, her knees—Clau-dia, the daughter of Laura's friend, the one who was taken away to be tortured and never heard from again—not the Madonna's. I get out of bed shaken, I want to scream.

I search my study for books to help me stop this interior free fall. I pull down an annotated edition of the Bible that includes the Apocrypha. At three o'clock in the morning, sitting in front of the altar in my study, I stumble across the story of Esdras.

Esdras cannot sleep either. Awake, in pain, in the middle of the night, he challenges God to explain how He can allow so much evil to exist and let so much good be destroyed. Esdras says that his heart fails him, as I feel mine failing me. I read on, buoyed by his boldness.

God responds by sending the Angel Uriel, "the Fire of God," to answer Esdras. Uriel tells Esdras that he will answer his questions about evil if Esdras can first accomplish certain tasks: gather raindrops already fallen, bring back the bloom of withered flowers. If Esdras is unable to do these things, God will give him yet another chance—bring back one day of the past. Then, Uriel says, he will explain the ways of God to him, he will tell him "why the heart is evil." Still, Esdras does not give up.

Uriel continues. He tells Esdras that he can have yet another chance. He will answer his questions if Esdras will bring him the weight of fire. Then bring him the measure of the wind, can Esdras do that? No matter how impossible the task, Esdras refuses to be intimidated, he stands with dignity in the limitations of his humanity. Then he challenges Uriel. Why, then, was he as a human being given the power of understanding? He had inquired not about the ways above, about what is beyond the human, but only about the experience of everyday life: "Why the law of our fathers has been made of no effect and [why] the written covenants no longer exist; why we pass from the world like locusts, and our life is like a mist, and we are not worthy to obtain mercy. . . . It is about these things that I have asked."[6]

The testimony of Esdras gives me the comfort of shared grief, and the cold, hard stone of no explanation. It is the only pillow I have to sleep on after Argentina.

On December first, the Friday night before the first Sunday of Advent, a friend and I drive to a nunnery for Taize, a Christian service famous for its chanting and meditation, which is modeled after the monks' service at Taize, France. The church is dark, lit only by candles. The floors are covered with thick carpet, making the entire space quiet, open, and comfortable, even for those sitting on the floor. The area around the altar has been opened up as a place for people to put cushions and sit during the simple but moving service, led solely by a small group of singers, and musicians on piano, harp, cello, flute, and violin.

The service begins with a singing of the Magnificat, Mary's prayer of praise, which was outlawed during the military dictatorship in Argentina. Then the Taize chants begin—simple, prayerful chants punctuated by periods of silence.

When we sing the chant "Jesus, when I call on you, answer me; when I pray, answer me," the image of Laura Bonaparte's friend Carmen and her daughter, Claudia, being torn apart in the chambers of torture comes into my mind and won't leave. Surely Claudia and Carmen called out to Christ, to God, to someone. The members of Laura's family—Noni, Irenita, Victor, Adrian, Mario, Jacinta, Santiago—surely every soul who was or has ever been tortured cried out from the depths of their being for help. Even Christ cried out, "My God, my God, why hast Thou abandoned me?" as he hung on the cross. The melodic chanting continues, "Jesus, when I pray, answer me," over and over.

"Answer me!" That one phrase is the clue. It provides the necessary insight for me to go on. I remember the widow before the judge in the New Testament, who will not go away until she is satisfied. Like a night cracked open by lightning, "Answer me!" tells me that God is the name for a very dynamic, fluid process we create by the active interchange between the human and all that is beyond us.

The only way to make God real is to wrestle with God. To make demands. Whether or not Esdras ever understood the problem of evil, he had a relationship with God. Finally I realize that I can pray *because* I have not yet been answered. The tears come, the first since I have been home from Brazil and Argentina. I put my head down in my friend's lap and weep for the Disappeared.

CHAPTER 20

WHO IS THE ENEMY?

The Battleground of the Mind

I was passionate,
filled with longing,
I searched
far and wide.

But the day
that the Truthful One
found me,
I was at home.

—LAL DED, FOURTEENTH-CENTURY (?)

KASHMIRI WOMAN POET

(translated by Jane Hirshfield)

My younger son, Ben, has signed on as a guide for an outfitter in the south of Argentina for the summer. Their summer. Our winter. There was no connection in our traveling to Argentina within months of one another. We were both drawn there out of two very different intentions: mine was to seek fierce compassion and the power of the bond between women, and his was to develop a career after graduating with a degree in outdoor education.

By mid-December, Ben has taken off for Argentina. Over the next few days his periodic faxes assure me that he has arrived as planned, that his new boss has overbooked the trips, there aren't enough boats or guides, the equipment is shoddy, he was almost shot by a ranch guard, and he is working double-time. The guides

WHO IS THE ENEMY?

keep late hours, many drink a lot, and they rise early, in frenzied chaos.

"Still, it is beautiful! The rivers are turquoise green, there are trees like I've never seen before—the mountains are huge! There's one guide who's great, Emiliano. I'll stick with him. I'll be okay, Mom. I love it."

I dream of the truth as an antidote. "Keep looking at the truth," the dream tells me. I am in my grandmother's house with a priest and several other people. I am trusting that the truth, if known, will reveal why the present situation is untenable and, once seen, will allow people to arrive at their own conclusions, eliminate fantasy, and deflate desire naturally. The dream ends as mysteriously as it started.

I need to keep telling the truth, first of all to myself. I don't fit into the life that I lived before I went to Brazil and Argentina. The tectonic plates of my psyche have shifted. Half an inch of movement at that level creates a seismic tremor. I don't know how to be with myself or what will come next.

I am reading the English translation of *Nunca Más* (Never Again), the report of the Argentine National Commission on the Disappeared, the Argentinean government's own official report on the military dictatorship.[1] With bracing clarity, *Nunca Más* outlines how easily this repression began in 1976, when an attempt to re-establish order by the military junta quickly deteriorated into absolute caprice and brutality. The elimination of subversion, the early goal, was quickly superseded by insanity. Nuns, pregnant women, and Jews in particular were subjected to special tortures. Anti-Semitism fueled the so-called "Christian" movement "for the Fatherland." Babies were stolen to be raised by childless military families. "Bored junior officers in the torture squads roamed the streets in their [Ford] Falcons looking only for pretty girls to take back to camp to torture and rape and then kill."[2]

I walk into my office and find a fax from Ben:

"Mom: My boss, Eduardo, was with the police in Buenos Aires during the dictatorship. He said the students being killed were Communists and even anyone closely related to them must be taken out. This is what Eduardo believes.[3] He said he was scared. Lots of bombs. Who knows? Good luck. I love you, Mom. Ben."

I'm stunned. I stand in my office rereading this fax and begin to tremble. It never occurred to me to tell my son not to disclose what I told him about my time with Laura Bonaparte and the Mothers of the Disappeared. I can only conclude that Ben told Eduardo that his mother had recently been in Argentina and is writing about the Mothers. Whatever Ben said apparently made Eduardo defensive. Every cell in my body is firing off warnings of danger.

I immediately pick up the phone and call the number of the lodge in Argentina that Ben had given me. He's there. I ask him if I understood him correctly, that Eduardo was part of the military in Buenos Aires during the dictatorship.

"It isn't clear, Mom, it was a long story. Complicated. I couldn't understand all of it. Eduardo said that his friend was in the military and that he was with him. Raoul, another one of the guides, was in the police. He said I should think of the people who were killed like weak links in a chain or a bad foundation in a building that had to be torn down. Everything was going to collapse. But working for the police made him crazy, Raoul said, that's why he quit.

"Mom, I can't talk. Eduardo's in the car honking for me. We've got to pick up some clients, right now. Gotta go!"

"But Ben! They're talking about *people*, not chains and buildings. My God, don't you understand, Ben?" The horn blares in the background.

"I know, Mom, I know. Look, I can't talk right now! Eduardo's really difficult. I have to go—*now*."

"Got it. Get in touch when you get back from this trip, will you?" I hear the insistent honking.

"Sure, Mom, sure. Listen, don't worry, I'll be back in a week or so. I'll be fine. Love you, 'bye." Click.

Is my son in danger? I struggle to gather my wits about me. One of these men is trying to convince Ben that kidnapping, torture, and murder were acceptable and necessary.

Facts, the illusion of something solid to put my hands on, to send Ben. I need to slow my heart down. Remember my feet on the ground. Remember who Ben is. The maternal instinct is ferociously physical.

I begin what will become a ten-page typed letter, not including the pages I copy from the introduction in *Nunca Más*. I don't know what to do. This feels like the moment you find your child on the edge of an eight-hundred-foot cliff. You don't yell or make a sudden move, or they might lose their balance out of the fright that you as a parent introduce because you know the danger and the consequences of which they are unaware. You approach as calmly and as quietly as you can, taking them by the hand and backing away from the edge. Only later do you tell them what they were in danger of, only when they're older do they begin to understand what happened. Only when they come upon their own child at a cliff's edge do they know how terrifying that moment was. How terrifying this moment is. Only, Ben is not a child. He is twenty-six years old, he has worked as an Outward Bound instructor. I cannot protect Ben, and I have two and a half months to learn to live with this fact.

Meanwhile, I go back to work and fight off the waves of panic, the need to do something, to act. It comes and goes. I weigh each alternative, talk to people in and out of the country, but I always draw the same conclusion. I can do nothing, and nothing is harder. One evening I am given a reprieve when a meditation teacher from the Jewel Heart Center in Ann Arbor visits and leads a meditation on Tara. One evening. A blessing. Though it reminds me of what I know and find so easy to forget—to pray for these men—it is hard for me to hold on to this spiritual axiom in the moment. "Trust," "love," even the words seem far away, and reason tells me that they are useless, foolish, and inappropriate. Aura Glaser, the teacher and a senior student of the Venerable Gelek Rinpoche, is like a magnifying glass, enlarging all the spiritual truth I've been given, but once she is gone it is hard to see my way through all I know about Argentina, to remember. Fear blurs it. Still, I have to find a way. To give in to fear is futile, even dangerous.

In Tibetan Buddhism there is a famous meditation practice promulgated by Machig Ladrop, the major eleventh-century Tibetan woman master and mother of four children. Thousands of people came to Tibet from as far away as India just to hear her teachings, and to learn her meditation practice, called *chöd,* which means "to cut." In this practice, you not only imagine that demons exist but visualize that you are feeding them your own body in order to bring them under control. Embrace what repels you, Machig said, do not reject it or deny it.

Surely there are "demons" loose in the world today, I think, as I continue to work my way through *Nunca Más* (Never Again), struggle with its implications, sit with my fears, tremble. It's as though by imagining that there are no other forces at work in the universe they are given free rein. And yet to imagine that these energies are separate from or independent of us is as dangerous as insisting they don't exist. Our task is alchemical, to transform base material into gold.

Could the failure to understand the power of spiritual forces contribute to the unprecedented horrors of our age? We imagine that we are alone, that the world of the spirit is an outdated superstition, so these energies take over and they will do anything to get our attention, even destroy us.

And what is this energy? It is life and it is sacred. It is a great river flowing, it is Ganga, falling from the Milky Way through Shiva's hair. If you try to stop this enormous force, this flow, it will only break down and destroy whatever lies in its path—not because it in itself is destructive, but because it is powerful and living and, like water, it must have a place to flow. If you block it in one direction, it will flow in another. It does not disappear, only changes forms, and then returns again, to wear our stone hearts down.

I offer the material I face again this morning: the fragments of Laura's stories with the bones of her children, the nameless named, the photograph of the born unborn child, the photograph of Santiago, all these bones and pieces of bodies, these fires and explosions, my own fears, I offer them in this skull cup of my writing. *Chöd*. Come and feast, feed yourself, I say to the Spirit. I acknowledge you. I offer the contents of my mind to you. I offer everything to you. I acknowledge your presence, the presence of the sacred. I demand that you remember that you have promised to be with us, be with me, if we are in heaven, if we are in hell. There is nowhere you are not.

Aparecida, the Mother of the Excluded, is the one who appears. Rise up from the depths of the river, Mother, come to us now, help the Disappeared appear again, in Argentina, in Brazil, in Chile, Uruguay, Paraguay, Peru, Guatemala, El Salvador, Rwanda, Tibet, the former Yugoslavia, in Europe, in North America, in all the places they have disappeared. Bring them back to haunt their tormentors. Ghosts of the Disappeared. Let them wander freely, painlessly, joyfully, strolling arm in arm with one another, visiting their tormentors, whispering to them in their dreams. Let the torturers dream of the people that they murdered. Give them no rest until they confess, until they testify, until they give forth all their knowledge of the people they kidnapped, tortured, and murdered. Let there be a great washing as the waters pour forth out of the breach, no longer blocked, no longer held back, for the truth is sacred and it can wash everyone, lick them clean like Kali's tongue, clean as the bones so long denied. And in this telling of what has been denied, hidden, unknown, let the ghosts of the Disappeared who have haunted their torturers reveal themselves for who they are, angels come to save their souls. For without these ghostly angels, the torturers will be lost, will disappear, and the cycle will repeat itself and instead of the turning being a great *conversión,* a conversion, it will be the spiral of a suckhole, with no opening on the bottom, only an endless, furious turning of the winds: a tornado that destroys everything it touches.

"I Do Not

Rehearse My Anger"

The Teachings of Sister Chân Không

S ister Chân Không, the Vietnamese Buddhist nun who teaches with Thich Nhat Hanh, the renowned Zen master, poet, and peace activist, works for that great turning, the *conversión,* the heart opening that can heal the world. Ben's presence in Argentina as I work my way through stories of the Disappeared compels me to turn back to Sister Chân Không. She is the one who can help me now.

At home, I page through journals, sort through a stack of audio-tapes to find the talk I had with her just before I left for Brazil and Argentina. All the while, in my mind's eye, I see her as I most vividly remember her—standing on a stage in a packed auditorium in the simple brown robes of a Buddhist nun, singing. Thich Nhat Hanh had just finished speaking and had asked her to perform. Ben was with me.

Chân Không sang the song she sang as she stood out in the fields of Vietnam with her shovel, working, burying corpses after the American bombs had fallen. She sang to keep herself alive in the middle of all that death. This is a woman who gives meditation retreats for American Vietnam vets with Thich Nhat Hanh. This is a woman who knows about enemies and sees through them, who loves humanity, who is not fooled by the demons we try to put on one another's faces.

I need her wisdom and her words now. She walked through that

SISTER CHÂN KHÔNG (*China Galland*)

war and came out of it singing with a lion's roar. In the demands of preparing for my trip, I had not read my notes or listened to our conversation again before I left for Brazil and Argentina. Though she lives in France, Chân Không was giving a meditation retreat in the Santa Cruz mountains with Thich Nhat Hanh two weeks before my trip to South America.[1]

Chân Không's teaching echoes Choga's insistence that we have compassion for everyone, no matter what harm they've done. No one is left out of the fierceness of her compassion. Chân Không refused to be a woman without hands.[2] She grew ten thousand hands and twice that in Vietnam, starting to work with the poor as a teenager, organizing a movement of social workers that merged with Thich Nhat Hanh's work.

Listening now, some months later, I realize that I couldn't have absorbed her teachings in the way I can after being with Laura and the Mothers in Argentina and with Yvonne in Brazil. I am being given the essence of what I need to know now more fully: how specifically, in the moment, to be in the wilderness of strong emotion and not get lost; how to experience feelings like anger, rage, grief, frustration, and loss—how to attend to them and how to transform them, step by step; how to maintain a deep awareness of the bond between *all* beings.

Reading my notes, hearing her voice again, I realize that I've found a hidden teaching, a *terma,* in the stack of tapes on the library table. The time is ripe, the need is present, the teaching is revealed.

That unexpectedly cold night in the Santa Cruz mountains, two weeks before I left for Latin America, Chân Không and I sat up late, talking. The sound of crickets hung in the air. Sister Chân Không told me about the Buddha Tara in Vietnam, where she is called Quán Thê Ám, the Great Bodhisattva of Compassion, the one who is "Deeply Listening to the World's Cries."

"Every temple in Vietnam has statues of Quán Thê Ám in both aspects: her 'fierce' form and her 'kind' form, one on either side of the temple. They say that both of them are manifestations of Quán Thê Ám, Tara, because out of compassion, sometimes you have to be very fierce, and sometimes you have to be very kind. Fierceness and kindness go together."

Chân Không wore a thick, soft brown wool scarf wrapped tightly around her neck just above the collar of her simple brown Vietnamese Buddhist nun's robes. Her dark hair was sprinkled with silver and just beginning to grow back after recently being shaved, revealing the shape of her well-proportioned head. She has a strong, distinctive face with a wide forehead and a generous mouth. Her lips were closed in a soft smile, her hands lay folded gracefully in her lap, palms up, right on top of left, open. We sat on meditation cushions on the polished wood floor of an empty music room. The night outside was inky black against large plate-glass panes. It had been a long day, but Chân Không's energy kept us both going.

Sister Chân Không was born on April 9, 1938, the year of the Tiger, in Ben Tre City, in the center of the Mekong Delta. Raised in a large, old-style Vietnamese family of twenty-two people, she was educated in Saigon and Paris, where she studied biology. She became a professor and taught biology at the University of Saigon. She now lives in Plum Village, Thich Nhat Hanh's community in Duras, France. The Tiger energy that she was born with has challenged her, she explained.

"I have a lot of energy. It is the energy of the Tiger. We must know how to make use of, to transform, that energy. Because if we don't know how to handle that Tiger energy, it can be very destructive. It has taken me a lot of time to transform it. I used to react very quickly, and this is harmful. When you react too fast, you have no time to look deeply, and it is easy to react too quickly and hurt people. We must try our best to use the art of mindful living. With mindful living we slow down our acts so we can observe our habit energies, we transform the negative ones and cultivate the positive ones in order to live in harmony with others."

Chân Không, whose family name is Cao Ngoc Phuong, was the eighth of nine children. She was taught to defer to her older sisters, but she could not. Her strong temperament fueled shouting matches with older siblings who tried to tell her what to do: from the time she was a little girl, Sister Chân Không had a mind of her own.

At age fourteen she began working with poor children in the slums of Saigon. She did not meet Thich Nhat Hanh, her teacher, until she was twenty-one. She had no dream of being known by others, she was simply a very devout Buddhist teenager, and she knew that she wanted to help children who were going hungry and becoming delinquents. This is where her Tiger energy was helpful, she said. No one could stop her, though they tried.

A Buddhist teacher she met with told her that working in the slums wasn't "real work," it was "merit work." He advised her to work on her spiritual practice first and become enlightened. When she was enlightened she would see how to help many people. Chân Không disagreed.

"If I wait until I am enlightened, I don't know when I can help," she said cheerfully, "so I decided to do that small work. I went to the slums alone. I helped the children with all my heart, and slowly I moved the hearts of many people around me.

"The war was raging, the whole country was torn apart. I couldn't do anything. All these big political powers—I had no control over them. But I had control over my everyday activities, the power to bring food to these hungry children."

The young Chân Không soon developed a fund-raising technique that proved irresistible: she tailored her requests to what was possible for people. She began with her stingy neighbor, telling her that she had no need for a lot of money, only a little. Chân Không plunged in her stumps—no matter that she had been told she shouldn't do this work, that she wouldn't truly be able to help people or save them—she began.

"Consider me like the bird who eats some leftover rice from your rice pot," she told her neighbor. "In the morning, when you make your rice pot, you take one handful for the bird—that's me. Do this in the afternoon and the evening, three meals a day. You give me three handfuls of rice," she said, handing her a bag to put the rice in.

Her neighbor did as she was told. "Every morning I came and she was very happy to be able to be generous for nothing. So then I asked, Could you give me ten cents? For her ten cents was nothing, it was so easy for her to give ten cents. But I said, You have to promise to give me ten cents every month. So then her daughter, her son, her nephew, her niece said, "Oh, it's so easy to give ten cents, to be generous." When I left her house I had about thirty people who gave me ten cents. So I had more money!" she said laughing, clearly enjoying the success she had organizing people even at a young age.

For three or four years, Chân Không worked alone in the slums. Gradually, volunteers joined her. By the time she met Thich Nhat Hanh, there were between seventy and a hundred people working with her. Thich Nhat Hanh persuaded her to help him organize pioneer villages, self-help models of a nonviolent way to revolutionize and revitalize Vietnam. Thich Nhat Hanh's group was the only organization that worked without being paid by either the Americans or the Communists. They were truly a movement of the people.

This volunteer work Chân Không helped organize in the villages led Thich Nhat Hanh to decide to set up the School of Youth for Social Service in September 1965. By the end of the war in Vietnam it had ten thousand members.

"One person can become ten thousand persons," Chân Không assured me. "From being alone, a small child, determined to do something, much can happen. When you are determined and you have that great desire to really share your time and your energy with those who are in need, you move the hearts of people around you. Then you move the heart of Thich Nhat Hanh and Thich Nhat Hanh brings a lot of friends. We are real collaborators."

Chân Không's work had grown to involve a few hundred friends who would make rounds, collect money, and spend one or two days per week helping in the slums. But when she joined forces with Thich Nhat Hanh, they had three hundred full-time volunteer social workers. These were people who lived like monks and nuns, whether they were or not. For the full-time volunteers, like Sister Chân Không, "that means you forget everything. You are totally, one-hundred percent for the poor." Soon they were reconstructing whole villages, bringing them medical care, plumbing, and schools.

Thich Nhat Hanh had tried to get the Buddhist Church in Vietnam to help and to make a nonviolent revolution to stop the Vietnam War. What Thich Nhat Hanh did was beautiful and difficult in the midst of war, Sister Chân Không assured me. He told the authorities that he had no financial or political backing.

His only support was the Buddha's wise counsel to "stand up and be lamps unto ourselves."

"Our principle is to come to poor people with our love, our care, our understanding, and make the revolution from what we have in our hand, in our ability." This is what he told the Church, she explained. They thought he was a dreamer, a poet, that his plans would come to naught, and they refused to help him initially, though in time, they too were won over by the irresistible success of his teaching.

"Then the bombs arrived. A few guerrillas shot at the sky, and American bombers thought that there were many guerrillas, so they destroyed the area where we had been helping the villagers. We rebuilt. Bombing, and we rebuild. Rebuild houses, rebuild the school. We went on for six months, and then the war came again, guerrillas came, more bombing, and we rebuilt the second time, and then the war came again, then more bombing. Four times.

"I remember at that time I was very angry, very frustrated. Everything was destroyed, ninety-nine percent of a nearby city was destroyed, including our little village. A number of young people who saw the destruction in the village were carried away by anger, and they followed it to one side or the other. They thought that the Communists were evil because the Communists came and provoked the American planes, so they joined the American side; or they thought that the American planes were bad, the government was bad, so they joined the Communist side.

"But this is half a bowl of rice, this situation. When you are angry, you are carried away by your anger. In this training we have to stop thinking, stop acting, go back to our breath to restore the clearness of our mind before making any big decisions. Take no action.

"I released the tension and tried only to dwell in the present moment. And at that moment I saw a little flower make her way through all the ruin of all the bombing. There was a little flower still blooming in the midst of the ruin, and I was truly moved. I could see, 'Oh, the little flower has done her best, why not me?'

275

"So I tried to look deeper. I looked around and I saw so many people who suffered, who cried, who shouted; but there were also very humble people, who silently tried to help the wounded, to bring rice for the sick, for the war victims who had nothing to eat. There were quite a few angels around in the midst of that ruin, hatred, and anger, many bodhisattvas, including that little flower. I had to do my best to go in that direction of beauty. I saw that life is not only cruelty and confusion and ignorance, but life also has many heartful people, wonderful people who are trying to do their best. You don't need to see ten thousand flowers in order to see that so much beauty in life is waving to you and saying hello to you. We try to live in beauty, in that light of goodness."

She begins to sing for me now as we sit in the music room, two women alone on meditation cushions in this large empty room late at night. I recognize the song. I had heard her sing it years earlier and been spellbound. It's about the beauty of the earth, the brightness of the sunflowers. This is the song she sang to herself as she'd buried corpses in a burned-out field in Vietnam. This is the song Ben and I together heard her sing years before. This is the song she had to sing in order to survive:

Waking up this morning, I see the blue sky.
I see the sunshine, I join my palms to give thanks for how
*   wonderful is life,*
For having given me twenty-four brand-new hours.
I vow to live deeply my twenty-four brand-new hours with joy,
*   with understanding.*
I go across the field of sunflowers,
Ten thousand flowers are waving to me, saying hello to me.

"I should not despise the small act. Every small act, if you do it deeply, profoundly, can touch the whole universe. My small act, your small act, her small act, millions of small acts will build a wonderful world. You can move the hearts of thousands of people."

Sister Chân Không does not come by her serenity easily. During the war in Vietnam she witnessed much more pain, frustration, and horror than most Americans have ever known. After the bombing of Saigon, the city was littered with forty thousand bodies, decomposing in the tropical heat. She helped the Red Cross carry away and bury many of the bodies. She could not eat for many days because of the odor.

"I looked deeply into these forty thousand and I saw only suffering dead bodies. I did not see that they were Communist or mercenary. I saw that they were my brothers and sisters. And it made me cry every day."

On June 1, 1966, Thich Nhat Hanh launched the first appeal for peace in Vietnam. One week later, during a twilight gathering at the school, someone threw grenades into the crowd and killed two of Chân Không's friends.

"Love and understanding are beautiful words, but when you see two dead bodies it is very difficult to say that you can love your enemies. I have to be truthful; I did not love the murderer at all. I reminded myself that although I did not love him yet, I had been taught that man is not our enemy. In many of our songs we sing, 'Our enemies are not humans. Our enemies are hatred, jealousy, cruelties, misperceptions. Our enemies are ignorance, our enemies are hatred, our enemies are fame, jealousy, misunderstanding. But our enemies are not humans. If we kill other humans, with whom shall we live?'

"This was a song that we often sang, and then suddenly here we were at the funeral of our friends. We knew we must live in faith with the words we sang, so we said, 'We cannot hate you who killed our friends. We hate only your misunderstanding. And we hope that the death of our friends can remove your misunderstanding. You thought we were aiming only to be a political power, but we were aiming only to remove the suffering, the illiteracy, the disease in this poor area. Our only aim is to bring more happiness to the poor people who live in such miserable conditions. So we hope that the death of our friends will make you understand us better and that you will support us in the future.'

"When we declared that, many good-hearted people who in the past had considered us utopians were very moved. They came and helped from both sides."

A few months later, five of her organization's social workers were arrested and taken to the riverbank. Their captors asked them if they were from the School of Youth for Social Service, and when they answered that they were, they were told, "We are sorry, we are forced to kill you."

"Then they shot five of our friends on the riverbank and pushed them into the river. One survived, and thanks to this person, we knew that they had spoken the words 'We are sorry, we are forced to kill you.' The next day I saw my friends lying slain.

"I was so angry, but I didn't really know who to be angry with— I didn't even know the murderers' faces. I suffered so much, knowing that in four days I would have to conduct my friends' funeral, and to write a eulogy for them. What could I possibly write?

"I had to put *everything* aside. I went back to my breath. I did a little bit of work, cooking, preparing, a number of small things. When I walked, my attention was with my breath and my step. When I gardened, my attention was with the act of gardening and my breath. When I cut carrots I was totally with the cutting of the carrots and my breath. When I washed my face, I was with only that. *Breathing in, breathing out,* I dissociated myself from the anger, for how long, I didn't know. In Buddhism, as I am trained, the first part is calming down the agitation.

"We can calm down when we are carried away by anger because we have the breath. The breath is the link between the body and the mind. The body is here, but the mind is carried away by anger. So I had to dissociate myself from the anger by building into myself that link, which is the breath. I focused on the breath.

"People came and asked to join us in demonstrations. I couldn't allow myself to hear any of it. Instead I kept going back to my breath, and stayed with my breath until the night before the funeral.

"That night while walking I suddenly remembered the words of the person who survived, what the murderers had said before shooting my friends, 'We are sorry, we are forced to kill you.' So I stuck to this one small positive point of the tragedy. My eulogy began, 'Dear brothers who took guns and shot my brothers, thank you for saying that you were sorry before you killed my friends. It seems that you were put in a situation where you couldn't resist the force of your superiors. If you refused you might have been in danger, you might have been put in jail, you might have been killed. In this situation of war, when someone who is ordered to kill betrays that order, he himself could be killed. So I say thank you for saying that you were sorry. We know that in the future you will try your best to support us, because we promised, in front of the bodies of our friends, that we would not hate you, that we would be your brothers. And we need your support.' When I wrote in such a way, I personally did not love them, but I thought that it was necessary to go in the direction of beauty and goodness. Because what will we give to the future generation if they are already bombed, there is already violence, there is already hate, there is already ignorance everywhere? If we can only say, 'I hate you,' what is the use? Our enemies are ignorance, our enemies are hatred, our enemies are fame, jealousy, misunderstanding. Our enemies are not humans. If we kill other people, with whom shall we live?"

"Yes, Sister," I say, "but when your friends were being killed, when your village was being destroyed over and over, it's hard for me to believe that you just took a breath and calmed yourself and went on. I want you to tell me precisely how you did that."

"We walk," she answers. "We focus our attention on the breath and the step. So, on the in-breath, I take one or two steps, on the out-breath, I take one or two steps. I dwell in my breath and in my steps to dissociate myself from the anger. It doesn't mean I surrender and suppress my anger. I will go back to my anger, but when I am quieter, when I obtain more serenity. I do not rehearse my anger. I have to look deep into my anger with a serene mind, and I will see the roots of my anger and the fruit of my action.

"I walked several hours, almost all day long, to calm my anger. Sometimes in the war I was so angry that I walked for several days. But I refrained from doing anything except small things like cleaning, small work, helping people carry wood, distributing food, but not getting carried away by big action like joining that side or the other side or shouting or screaming or doing something very drastic.

"Then I looked deeper, and I saw the decision makers were somewhere else, in the Kremlin, in Peking, in the White House. They were not the soldiers of both sides. These soldiers were only victims of the big machine of confusion and ignorance.

"One day during the war someone said to Thich Nhat Hanh, 'I cannot understand your attitude, why you do not join Hanoi. In this Vietnam War there are two sides to choose from: One is the rapist and the other is the little girl raped on the highway—the rapist is the American army and the little girl raped is the Vietnamese people. I cannot understand your attitude. You stand between the rapist and the little girl. You do not take sides with the little girl.'

"And Thich Nhat Hanh said, 'Yes, I do side with the little girl against the rapist. But I want to invite you to look deeper. Who is the rapist? The rapist is men who sit quietly in the Kremlin Palace, in Peking Palace, in the White House. And the little girl raped is not only the voiceless Vietnamese person but also the soldiers of both sides, North and South Vietnam. She is also American soldiers who are victims of wrong propaganda and wrong information; they are also the girl raped.' When I remember these words I know I cannot take sides."

Sister Chân Không continues. "When I am angry, I first focus on the breath to calm myself. When I feel my heart is less agitated, I go to the second part, which is mindfulness, looking deeply into oneself and into the cause of the anger. Why am I so angry, I ask myself. Is there a physical problem—do I have a headache, an unhappy body? Next I consider my feelings. Sometimes I am angry for nothing, I'm irritated by things that have happened before this; anger just comes out as the last straw. The other person who is supposed to be my enemy brings out the last drop of all the anger I have felt in the past. When I have gone through my body and my feelings, I go next to my perception. This is very important, because my perception is my outlook, the way I see things. The Buddha explained that in the dark, if you see a snake, you scream. But when you have a light, you see it is a rope. Sometimes we see a person as a snake, whereas she is only a rope. When I change my perception of the situation, my anger is transformed.

"Next I examine stored consciousness. Since I get so easily irritated, do I have a lot of hidden pain? First I look deeply into my whole being, second I try to look deeply into the object of my anger. If it is anger concerning a person, I try to see all her difficulties, then I can understand and accept her misbehavior toward me. So looking deeply into myself, into the cause of the anger, and when I understand, I can release the anger on my own. Nobody can force me to repress my anger. The anger is transformed. I can have some clearness of mind. I am willing to look deeply at one side and then at the other. And the most important part is to question my perception: Is this a snake or a rope?"

The practices of breathing and meditation can bring Sister Chân Không clarity and understanding, but they do not make her a saint. I am relieved to know that she feels deeply, that she struggles with her feelings every day. "But I am a stubborn woman," she says, "very determined," and fiercely committed to compassion.

"Even if you cannot go yet in the direction of beauty, please try to turn yourself in that direction, because it is the only way for the future to be possible. This is the most important message. You don't need to be a saint or a bodhisattva, but try to go in that direction only. You don't need to be an angel; try to go in the direction of the angel only."

We sit in silence for a little while. Then she says, "We see ourselves like a stream of life from no-beginning to no-end. We say, 'I am here, but at the present moment I am also the mountain, the river, the air. I am also all these small creatures who suffer, who are joyful. I am at the same time those who are in jail; I am at the same time the dictator who puts people in jail; I am at the same time the frog; I am at the same time the snake who eats this frog; I am at the same time the poor people who are exploited; I am at the same time the person who exploits people; I am at the same time all these bodhisattvas who are holy persons, like Mother Teresa, like many Buddhist nuns in Vietnam I know, who worked during the war until now for the poor, the suffering, for the maimed. So I feel that I am them, and I am at the same time those who are suffering. I am one."

Sister Chân Không helps me remember that meditation and prayer are the deepest relief from anger and fear. I walk, I pray, both for my son and for these men in Argentina whom I do not know and whom it would be so easy to make into my enemy. I understand viscerally how easy it is to fall into the terrible assumptions we can make about each other. At least one of these men did so: people became "weak links," part of a "bad foundation" that had to be torn out if there was to be an Argentina. I have to avoid a similar trap. In meditation, while observing and watching the thoughts arise, then deconstructing them, I see that the greatest danger is the idea of an enemy, the torturer that I've projected in my own mind.

Listening to my conversation with Chân Không reminds me that these men too are my brothers. I decide not to send the letter with the pages from *Nunca Más* to Ben in Argentina. I give it to him after he comes home, safely, many weeks later. He tells me that though he loves Argentina and many of the people that he met, he will never again work for Eduardo.

CHAPTER 22

"WE CAN ALWAYS USE
SOMEONE TO SERVE"

Mother Teresa's, San Francisco, California

Without action, one perishes.

—*THE DEVI-MAHATMYA*

I had gone to Mother Teresa's in Kathmandu and in Calcutta, now it was time to go to Mother Teresa's soup kitchen for the homeless in San Francisco. This was the place to which I had been most afraid to go, Mother Teresa's in my own community, to see the homeless in front of me, not at the safe remove of a foreign country.

The Missionaries of Charity, Mother Teresa's Sisters, run several projects in San Francisco, but I knew from a conversation with the Sister in charge that the place where I could be immediately useful was at their soup kitchen. It operates out of a decommissioned firehouse near the docks of Hunter's Point, in one of the roughest parts of the city. Every morning there are vegetables to be chopped, meal preparation to be done. No training required. Just show up. Every evening there's serving the homeless and then there is the cleanup. Except Thursday. On Thursdays, Mother Teresa's Sisters all over the world take the day off for prayer and reflection.

I drive down to the waterfront looking for the firehouse, out over a little bridge to a part of the city I've passed through only once before. I can't find the street number I've been given, but I find an old fire station nearby. It looks deserted. I make a U-turn and drive by slowly, turning at the corner, where I discover a large fire-truck door partially open. There are a handful of homeless men standing around outside, arranging their belongings on grocery carts, getting ready to roll away. Through the open garage door I can see a very bad oil painting of Mary with her hand on her heart, hanging on a wall inside. There are lights on. This has to be it.

I park across the street, facing the main thoroughfare, a little nervous in this neighborhood of abandoned buildings, old buses, and trucks with windows painted out. I stand on the sidewalk, change shoes, take off my suit jacket, grab an apron I'd thought to bring, and stuff it in my purse, and lock everything else in the car. It is late afternoon, a clear, warm day. The men standing outside are friendly enough, but not too friendly. We smile at each other and nod.

I enter the large room bustling with the ongoing cleanup.

"Hello, Sister," I say to the nun in charge, "I've come to help."

With no formalities, she shows me a bucket and hands me a string mop. The dining room and the serving room need to be cleaned, she tells me. There are two other volunteers already mopping the linoleum dining room floor and the cement block of the larger hall, two middle-aged men who come whenever they can to help the Sisters. A handful of older women are putting away the leftover food. In another part of the firehouse, a young novice Sister is cleaning the kitchen. Though the nuns are not allowed to cook there, they had used the sink and are scrubbing it clean. All food preparation and cooking must be done at the mother house in another part of the city, then the food transported to this fire station to be served. It is a Sisyphean labor. The city doesn't pick up trash here, so every night, all traces of the Sisters' good work—food, dishes, pots, pans, garbage, everything—vanish, down to the last paper wrapper. It's all loaded up into a volunteer's van and carted back across the city to the mother house. A couple of men from outside wander over to the open door and look at us working inside. "Thank you," one of them says sheepishly, staring at his feet, "thanks a lot, Sister. Hey, good night," he calls as he turns to roll away his grocery cart and belongings across the sidewalk to find a place to sleep for tonight.

Before we finish the cleanup, someone asks if I can give Lita a ride to the Civic Center area.[1] Lita is a thin African-American woman, well into her sixties, with silvering hair, a narrow face, and a beaming smile. She is a staunch supporter of the Sisters and has been working with them as a volunteer for three years. Yes, I say, it's right on my way home. Lita wants to bring the leftover boxes of glazed doughnuts to the homeless down on Market Street and had planned to take the bus, but she's happy for the ride.

On Market Street, where Lita asks me to stop, a crowd of at least two hundred people mill around. "This is just fine, honey, why, thank you," she says. But now I'm curious and I get out to follow her. I quickly lose her in the crowd—she's busy handing out dough-nuts—but I see people in lines and a man ladling out hot soup into cups. I go up to the landscaped ledge where he sits next to a large plastic bucket, serving. "Need any help?" I ask.

"Sure," he says, "salad needs to be served. Open the bucket next to me. We don't have any utensils, you'll have to use a cup to serve it with. Go ahead and serve it until we run out of cups. Then people can use their soup cups when they're done and come back for salad."

The soup is steaming hot as he carefully ladles the vegetables into a tall Styrofoam cup and hands it to the next person in line. I pop open the big white plastic bucket, full of fresh mixed greens and currants, scoop up a cup full of salad and ask the man in front of me if he would like some. Yes, he would, please, "Thank you," he says. Next. "Salad tonight?" "Why, yes, please." "No." "Yes." "Umm-huh." I'm surprised by the large number of people. It's six-thirty in the evening and they are hungry.

One by one we serve them. People stand in two lines now, one for the soup and one for the salad. The evening is balmy and pleasant. Each person I hand a cup of salad to further breaks down whatever stereotype I might have had about homeless people on Market

Street. People are polite, they look me in the eye, they are calm and pleasant. The mood is subdued. It isn't fun to find oneself in that line. Suddenly a large, ebullient woman bursts through the line wanting seconds. "I am hungry, darlin'!" she exclaims. Everyone tolerates her without making trouble. Finally someone tells her to take her place in line. A young couple have brought a plastic container to take food home for their children. My fellow server says that's fine and fills it up too.

Though I keep looking for Lita in the crowd, I don't see her again. I find myself feeling inexplicably light, and happy to be here. There are a few young girls with dyed black hair, tattoos, and chains, but for the most part, these are middle-aged people, men and women, but more men. One older woman wears a silver hard hat, clear welder's goggles, and several layers of clothes. She's smart. The street's a hard place, especially for older women. She looks prepared for the night.

I ask my fellow server his name. Sean. He's a handsome Pakistani man. No one can pronounce his Pakistani name, so he's ended up with Sean, he explains.

I ask him what organization he works with, who made this good food we're serving. "I'm with Food Not Bombs," he tells me. "We're here every night at six-thirty."

A young woman arrives and tells me that it's her time to serve, I can go now. She's a regular volunteer. Apparently another volunteer had not shown up that evening and I had come at just the right time to fill in. Now it's her turn.

"Come back anytime. We can always use help," she says as she takes the Styrofoam cup I've been using to serve the salad. "We can always use someone to serve."

CHAPTER 23

Because I Saw
the Women Dancing

Coming Home at Last

Listen.
Listen to the women
They are arriving
over the wise distances
on their dancing feet
Make way for the women
Listen to them.

—CORINNE KUMAR

I walk out of the packed "Peacemaking, the Power of Nonviolence" conference in San Francisco, out of the cavernous auditorium, and the press conference with the Nobel Peace laureates the Dalai Lama, Anita Menchú Tum, standing in for her sister, Rigoberta Menchú, and Dr. José Ramos-Horta.[1] It is now June 1997. José Ramos-Horta had just announced the formation of an association of Nobel Peace laureates to lend their moral weight to the cause of peace and justice where needed, to help countries struggle through the reconciliation process, and to keep the focus on cases such as that of the indomitable woman and leader of the democratic movement in Burma, Aung San Suu Kyi, a living embodiment of fierce compassion, another Nobel Peace laureate who was still under close military surveillance after years of house arrest in Burma. Nelson Mandela, Elie Wiesel, Oscar Arias Sánchez, the Dalai Lama, Rigoberta Menchú, Ramos-Horta himself, and Carlos Ximenes Belo, the Bishop of East Timor in Indonesia, with whom he shared the 1996 Nobel Peace Prize, all had discussed and agreed to the association and had begun to work together. The commitment of these Nobel laureates to the power of compassion is recognized the world over. To have them banding together in association can only strengthen its reach into international politics.

The Dalai Lama points out that developing loving-kindness and compassion is the only practical option we have in this increasingly small world we live in. "Unbiased compassion, irrespective of others' attitudes towards us, this is what we need," he says. "Kindness, maybe this is the best religion.

"Destroying your enemy, this is a very old-fashioned idea, left over from ancient time," he tells us, laughing. "Today our modern, global economy, the environment we live in, they show us how interdependent we are, how completely our interests are intermingled. How important nonviolence is."

Anita Menchú, wearing a handwoven Guatemalan cloth skirt, a brilliantly colored embroidered-flower top, her long, shiny straight black hair falling halfway down her back, speaks on behalf of her sister Rigoberta. She recalls the vast experience indigenous people have in nonviolent conflict resolution. This is a wisdom we can draw upon today, she tells us, ". . . the wisdom of the ancestors, the elders of indigenous people. It has worked for thousands of years in Guatemala.

"The elder, an honorable, wise person dedicated to serving the community, presides over an assembly where each person is taken into account, no matter how great the differences. The elder and the assembly stay in dialogue until a solution is reached that is definitive and acceptable to all parties. Tolerance, mediation, and dialogue," this is what we must have today, she tells us.

Afterward I have a conversation with José Ramos-Horta. He speaks of spending days with the Dalai Lama in India and envisioning the power of compassion to help us bring about world peace. Yes, I tell him, fierce compassion. He says that Tibet, if allowed to be free, could help China. Tibet could be the bridge and a model that could help settle world conflicts.

The people of East Timor, his country, have survived tremendous suffering and continue their demands for peace, too. "Force is not capable of resolving humanity's problems. No amount of weapons or oppression will ever be able to subjugate the spirit of our people."

Standing in the crowded hallway outside the auditorium, it becomes impossible to continue talking. We retreat and find a corner in an office that's not in use, where we can close the door, shut out the noise and crowds of people. We find two gray folding chairs to sit down. It's late in the day, Horta's heavy beard is showing. He's tired, but he wants to finish telling me about his recent visit to South Africa, which he was just starting to tell me of in the hallway. His dark, curly hair is sprinkled with silver, his circular horn-rimmed glasses give him the look of a scholar. He wears a dark gray Nehru-style jacket, no tie. He sits erect.

"About South Africa," he says, explaining that this episode happened while the Truth Commission was collecting testimony everywhere they could about what happened under apartheid.

Horta was out walking with his friend Robert, a black man. Suddenly a white man came up to Robert, greeted him warmly and embraced him, then went on. After the white man left, Horta asked Robert if the man was a friend from the African National Congress. Oh, no, Horta's friend Robert explained, the white man had been his jailer, his warden.

"Amazing!" Horta exclaimed, taken by surprise, but Robert told him that he and his former warden had spoken of what happened with one another during Apartheid, spoken truthfully, and they had been reconciled.

"Mandela had his jail warden present at his inauguration," Horta reminds me. "This is *amazing,* yes?!" He tells me now, his eyes lighting up, "but this is true, and this is what can happen when the truth comes out."

I ask him about situations such as those in Argentina, Brazil, and the former Yugoslavia, Rwanda, Guatemala, about amnesty.

"It is opportunistic to just grant blanket amnesties," he says, "politically motivated. I don't think it helps. There has to be real courage, by all sides, to face the ugly truth, the tragedies. This is the only way for true reconciliation. You cannot just by a decree declare that a crime is no longer a crime, that genocide is no longer genocide.

"There have to be trials, the truth has to come out. Because reconciliation and peace can come about only if justice is done. People seek justice, but justice cannot be confused with revenge. There has to be extreme caution. I have lost three brothers and a sister in my country, in East Timor, I know of these difficulties, but one must forgive—absolutely—though it is a struggle. Violence is no answer. Making peace, this is the only answer we have."

I leave the long crowded corridors and take off into the early evening, eager to be outside.

I recognize some of the young people from the conference standing in line, on the grass in the city park across the street, clapping their hands, singing, and swaying to drumbeats: African-American, Latino, European, Asian, Polynesian, Native American, a true American mix. At first I stand and watch with a smile, feeling the warmth and the fun they're having from across the street. What's happening? I see a woman friend, she wants to see too, so we go across together. We stand at the edge of the circle that's forming, next to an older man with short gray hair in a suit, who's grinning widely, tapping his feet, and clapping his hands. My friend and I move in closer, glad to find someone nearer our age. A handful of others from the conference like me, women I know, join the crowd too with a knowing smile, *This* is what's happening, these young people from the conference, coming together from all parts of the country, city kids, country kids, some former gang members, newly exposed to peacemaking and nonviolence training. Some of the young people in the group work with MOSAIC, a multicultural group that uses community ritual with young people to transform violence. The line has come full circle now, and the circle turns into dancing. Soon I am standing on the edge of the circle, clapping too, the drumbeat is so insistent, their rhythm so good. There are several people in their forties and fifties now. It feels right for us to be on the perimeter, clapping, watching, being present, one of the many it takes to hold the circle. Dancers flash in and out, spin, hop, and twist, roll around, jump up, flap their arms, and shout. The drumbeat shifts, the rhythms get faster, the intensity in the faces of the drummers grows as the beat takes over.

There is a small pile of smooth blue-gray stones in the center on the sidewalk—river stones, softened and polished by water, no hard edges. The dancers take turns dancing around the stones, jumping over them, circling, bowing low, then leaping, spinning and laughing. People take turns moving in and out of the center to dance around them, while the rest of us clap, sing, hoot, and encourage them, support them, give a shout. A young Latino man comes up, pulls me away from the edge, says, "You too, come on, dance!"

I shake my head, too shy, too old.

"No, no!" he says. "You dance too, it's for everyone! It's fun, here, I'll go with you," he says, gently pulling me from the outer circle into the center, coming with me to dance, then leaving me as soon another white woman enters, a woman also in her fifties, who comes out to dance, and for a brief moment we dance together around the stones, not touching, and the young people cheer, then I move back into the circle, while she continues, swiveling her hips freely, turning, delighting in the sinuousness she has still in her body. She is a plain blond woman, not attractive, but in the dance she becomes a beautiful woman, a dignified woman, a stately woman, drawn up to her full height. Then she moves back into the larger circle and a big young African-American man is called out, his name chanted, until finally he enters, awkward, a former gang member, shy now, but happy. I watch his face change as he dances around the stones, his smile spreading, his arms reaching up to the sky, his head thrown back, I want to cry, but I don't, I clap and shout louder, encourage him, "*YES!*" A young Latina woman sidles in with slow, smooth moves that flow like water. She wears heavy leather work boots, jeans, and a white Mexican shirt with a riot of red, blue, yellow, and green flowers to adorn her. Her short brown hair is smoothed back behind her ears, then it curls. She moves effortlessly, flowing, her head cocked back slightly, smiling with her eyes half closed, she knows she's good, and she's enjoying it. A young white woman with a mop of frizzy red hair, wearing a brown velvet shirt and jeans, jumps into the circle with a young black man with a dazzling smile in a bright blue African shirt. They freeze. A martial-arts pose, fists closed, arms drawn and ready. Fierce. Then they break, whirl, and kick high into the air, and come down into splits on the sidewalk. We all shout. Then up, another kick, and back on their feet. I recognize their dance from Salvador da Bahia, they're doing *capoeira,* the Brazilian martial-arts dance that's played low to the ground with the feet as a weapon, or with sticks like the sugar canes or machetes used by the people in slavery who made up this dance. This is a dance of disguise. The masters thought they were playing and celebrating, that people in slavery were happy and harmless. They did not know that this dance was an African martial art adapted to the conditions of slavery in Brazil. Did not know this dance protected the ceremonies of the Orishás, the gods and goddesses of their people, did not know that each step was choreographed code, was a way of organizing, maintaining resistance, mounting the uprisings that led to whole cities of runaways, free people, in the mountains of Brazil, twenty thousand in New Palmares alone. *Capoeira* Angola, the style played low to the ground because the power is in the root, in the earth, in the stone, in the water, in the drum, and in the people dancing and singing. *Capoeira,* now an art form, a street form, a fierce acrobatic dance with feet flying, high kicks, upside-down turns and flips, a low squatting, hands planted on the ground, the kick powerful, rising up as it does, drawing on the energy of the earth. The spirit is rising, cannot be suppressed or broken, rises to the beat of the drum, the heartbeat. Because I saw Indramaya dancing Durga's story in Nepal, because I saw the women dancing by the Ganges in India, because I saw the dances of Candomblé in Bahia, because I saw the Mothers demonstrating, circling, in the center of Buenos Aires, because I saw my mother rise up, because I have a daughter, because my sons taught me to drum, drummed for me when I turned fifty, I am willing to join this circle, to join these young people now. I see the fire of Yansan, the whirlwind Orishá, goddess of wind and fire in Candomblé, I see the movement of Nanan Buruku, the oldest Orishá, the divinity of water who refused to revere Ogun when he was declared the most important Orishá of all—Ogun, the lord of iron and all metals, without which no one could make war. Nanan Buruku proved that metal was not necessary, she used hardwoods and bone, clay, bamboo, and hides, for hunting, gathering, protection, and farming. She has joined us. The spirit of Nanan Buruku, divinity of waters, the oldest one, ripples through the crowd, washes over the sidewalk river stones, breaks over us with her spirit. Now the young woman in the workman's boots dances out again, her body moving like water, her face serene and concentrated, she flashes a smile at me, a young man beckons, and this time I go, slower, step into the circle because I love to dance, I want to join them, and for a moment I let go, let my body move as it will, loosen up, turning and turning around the stones—a *stupa,* a city *chorten,* a momentary shrine. This is the way, this is the way, the drumbeat is saying. I step out of the circle now, the wave washes me back up onshore, another steps in, then another, then another, then young people link hands and pull us all together dancing in a circle. This is how we are—black, white, brown, yellow, red, older, younger, male, and female. This is the practice of rejoicing.

I know the steps now; this is unlike my time at Durga Puja in Nepal, when I didn't know the dance, when I was not invited, when I was a foreigner, when I had no way to join in. Tomorrow these young people will feed the homeless in whose park they dance, will invite us to join them. They leave no one out, these young people, they show us the way.

My camera sits to the side now, on the sidewalk, I have put it down. I no longer struggle to capture this story, I have joined it.

Humbly welcome the word that has taken root in you,
with its power to save you.
Act on this word.

—JAMES 1:21–22

NOTES

A Prologue in Three Parts

1. In Anne Carolyn Klein, *Meeting the Great Bliss Queen* (Boston: Beacon Press, 1995), 172–73. Klein quotes the Dalai Lama writing on the basic nature of the mind. Her comments on the implications of "a passionately happy female deity" in her description of the Great Bliss Queen, Yeshey Tsogyel of Tibetan Buddhism, 181ff, deserve serious study.

2. This compressed retelling of the seven-hundred-verse *Devi-Mahatmya* is compiled from several sources: the essential work of Thomas B. Coburn in *Encountering the Goddess: A Translation of the Devi-Mahatmya and a Study of Its Interpretation; Hindu Goddesses: Visions of the Divine Feminine in the Hindu Religious Tradition* and *Goddesses' Mirror* by David Kinsley; *Kali: The Feminine Force* by Ajit Mookerjee; and the lectures of Elinor Gadon and Andrew Harvey on Hindu goddesses at the California Institute for Integral Studies in San Francisco.

3. See Coburn, *Encountering the Goddess* (Albany: State University of New York Press, 1991), 1. For a fuller discussion of the meaning of *mahatmya* see pages 102–3. It can refer both to the verbal *account* of the activity of the Goddess and to the *activity* itself (italics Coburn's).

4. The import of this detail was pointed out to me during a conversation with Gangaji, a Western woman teacher in the lineage of the great Indian saint Ramana Maharshi.

   "How did Durga defeat the Buffalo Demon?" Gangaji asked me.

   "By piercing his heart with a dagger," I replied.

"That's it!" she said laughing. "Don't you see? That's what always has to be done, the heart has to be pierced, broken open, for real change to happen."

Her insight pervades this book.

5. Helen Hunt at Union Theological Seminary pointed out the significance of the fact that four of the five planners of the historic Seneca Falls Convention of July 1848 were church women. The roots of the women's movement in North America are spiritual. Hunt's research suggests that a re-examination of this nineteenth-century history might help bridge the gap that exists between many church women and women who are politically active today. Also see Margaret Hope Bacon, *Mothers of Feminism* (New York: Harper and Row, 1986), 184–85.

6. This narrative is not only the story of the journey, it is also a ritual invocation of Durga, a re-membering, a calling forth, a rudimentary telling of her story in Western form and a devotional act. Thomas B. Coburn notes evidence that bookmaking was undertaken as a devotional act in association with the Goddess in the sacred Hindu texts of the *Devi Purana* and the *Nilamata Purana,* 103–4.

Chapter 1: The Return of the Fierce Goddess

1. *Encountering God: A Spiritual Journey from Bozeman to Banaras*, Diana L. Eck (Boston: Beacon, 1993). See her discussion "Shakti, Energy for Life," 136–43. Eck's book probes the meaning of Banaras as well as arguing for the necessity of interreligious dialogue and religious pluralism. Informed by years of study and travel in India, Eck's book is important not only for its scholarship but also for her explication of religious pluralism. *Encountering God* is essential reading for an informed understanding of America's rapidly changing religious landscape. Her thinking on this subject helps form the underpinnings of this book. Also see *On Common Ground: World Religions in America,* Eck's new work, a groundbreaking CD-ROM (New York: Columbia University Press, 1997), the result of the Pluralism Project, a Harvard-based research project on the changing religious landscape of America. Eck is Professor of Comparative Religion and Indian Studies at Harvard University.

2. Diana L. Eck's *Darśan: Seeing the Divine Image in India* (Chambersburg, PA: Anima Books, 1981) is an excellent guide to "seeing," and understanding Hinduism.

3. "Problems of the Girl Child, Devikiis" by Dr. Pushpa Bhatt, Ellon Coon, and Rita Baldhya, *Quarterly Development Review*, vol. IX, no. 12, 10–11.

4. From *Grace and Mercy in Her Wild Hair: Selected Poems to the Mother Goddess* by Ramprasad Sen. Translated by Leonard Nathan and Clinton Seely (Boulder: Great Eastern Book Company, 1982), 55.

Chapter 3: Pages on Fire

1. Carroll Dunham and Kristina Carlson's article "Sex Slavery," *Marie Claire,* UK, November 1994, gives a fuller treatment of Gita's story.
2. *Rape for Profit: Trafficking of Nepali Girls and Women to India's Brothels,* Human Rights Watch Asia Report, June 1995. Human Rights Watch, 485 Fifth Ave., New York, NY 10017-6104. "The Dangers of Dissent," p. 62ff, recounts others' experiences of similar threats. The report also explains the relationships of gangs, police, and political corruption that make this such an intractable problem. The appearance of AIDS makes this situation a time bomb, with over 50 percent of the brothel workers in Bombay alone being infected.
3. Ibid.
4. Dunham and Carlson, "Sex Slavery."
5. From *Sisters and Daughters Betrayed,* a documentary film by Chela Blitt, 1995, for the Global Fund for Women's Project, the Circle Against Trafficking and Forced Prostitution. For copies of this half-hour documentary film ($25) or more information, contact the Global Fund for Women, 425 Sherman Avenue, Suite 300, Palo Alto, CA 94306-1823.
6. Ibid. I heard stories of this as well. Marcia Anderson introduced me to a young woman who had been rescued from this situation.
7. Ibid.
8. *The San Francisco Examiner*, April 6, 1997. Seth Rosenfeld's article on the "Global Sex Trade" gives a good summary of the problem: "Victim tells story of being kidnapped at age nine, ordeal lasted eighteen years."
9. The English title of the film is *Throwaway Children,* a term coined by the Rev. Shay Cullen, an Irish Catholic priest who had worked with street children in the Philippines for over twenty years at the time the film was made, in the late 1980s. Street children are especially vulnerable to this kind of abuse and crime. The film was the collaborative work of author Alf G. Andersen, on whose book it was based, photographer Jan Erik Winther, and writer/filmmaker Edvard Hambro, all three young fathers at the time. They produced the film for the Norwegian Ministry of Justice, the Norwegian Red Cross, and World City Corporation, a private corporation. Norway's leadership in this arena helped get legislation passed in home countries to prosecute citizens who might travel abroad for such purposes. The film was aired in the Scandinavian countries on most major television channels. It helped heighten public awareness and bring about changes in procedures and prosecution of this problem. The film is distributed through Jane Balfour Films in London. To order, contact Jane Balfour Films, Ltd., Burghley House, 35 Fortess Road, London NW5 1AQ, England. Tel: +44-171-267-5392, Fax: +44-171-267-4241, or E-mail: JaneBalfourFilms@compuserve.com.

In September of 1994, a new Crime Bill was passed in the United States that made it illegal for U.S. citizens and legal aliens to travel abroad with the intent to engage in sexual acts with minors, that is, anyone under eighteen years of age. It also rendered the production of child pornography in other countries with the intent to bring such materials into the United States illegal as well. In August of 1996, a World Congress Against Commercial Sexual Exploitation of Children met in Stockholm, Sweden. Governments of 119 countries around the world, in conjunction with ECPAT-USA (End Child Prostitution in Asian Tourism), UNICEF, and other agencies within the United Nations, committed themselves to "a global partnership against the commercial sexual exploitation of children." The presence and support of Queen Silvia of Sweden, who addressed the congress, was an important element in the success of the congress, providing a symbol of the governmental leadership necessary at the highest levels. For further information, contact ECPAT-USA, Inc., who helped organize the 1996 World Congress: 475 Riverside Drive, Room 621, New York, NY 10115, Tel: 212/870-2427, Fax: 212/870-2055.

Chapter 4: "Whose Anger Is It?"

1. This well-known story from the *Jataka Tales* is discussed by the Dalai Lama in his book *The Good Heart,* 107–9. The translator and scholar Dr. Joe Loizzo helped me understand some of the complexities of this concept and also referred me to Jeffrey Hopkins, ed. and trans., *Compassion in Tibetan Buddhism, Tsong-ka-pa.*
2. Gangaji, the Western woman teacher from Ramana Maharshi and Papaji's lineage, also pointed this out in our conversation.

Interlude: "Only in a Woman's Body"

1. The Wisdom tradition runs through world religions. Wisdom is feminine in Buddhism, as was the Greek Sophia. Sophia, like Isis in Egypt, was called upon as a Divine Saviour, as is Tara in Tibetan Buddhism. The Jewish Wisdom tradition with its idea of Chokmah is important as well. There is more to be said on the parallels among Tara, Wisdom, and Sophia. One of the many starting points is Elisabeth Schüssler Fiorenza's excellent work *Jesus: Miriam's Child, Sophia's Prophet.*
2. The story of that search became the book *Longing for Darkness: Tara and the Black Madonna* (New York: Viking/Penguin, 1990/1991).

Chapter 5: Earth's Heart Beating

1. I Peter 2:6 and I Peter 2:5, *New Jerusalem Bible.*
2. Author's adaptation of the traditional *Twenty-one Praises to Tara*, from a text translated and published by Kagyu Shenpen Kunchab, 751 Airport Road, Santa Fe, NM 87501.
3. Kunsang Lama Shelung.

Chapter 6: Mopping the Floor

1. For more information on Mother Henriette Delille and her cause for canonization, contact the Sisters of the Holy Family, 6901 Chef Menteur Highway, New Orleans, LA 70126.

Interlude: Tara Grows

1. This list was compiled primarily from Martin Willson's book *In Praise of Tara* and from the Twenty-one Tara initiation given by the great Tibetan woman Sakya lama, Her Holiness Sakya Jetsun Chimey Luding, whose center is Sakya Tsechen Thubten Ling, 7340 Frobisher Drive, Richmond, BC V7C 4N5, Canada.
2. The Eight Great Fears are traditionally spoken of as the fears of drowning, thieves, lions, snakes, fire, demons, captivity or chains, and elephants. These are symbols for the internal states that Tara can rescue one from (in corresponding order): attachment, wrong views, pride, envy, anger, doubt, avarice, and delusion. The Eight Great Fears in Tibetan Buddhism are in turn a summation of the Sixteen Great Fears. See Taranatha's *Golden Rosary*.
3. (London: Wisdom, 1986), 148. See Willson's "Commentary" on the Twenty-one Praises, 123–66. Sadhanas vary as to the colors of the Twenty-one Taras.
4. I have also drawn on Atisha's tradition of the Twenty-one Forms of Tara in this listing of Taras, combining it with Martin Willson's work, and my own research in the Library of Tibetan Archives in Dharamsala, India. Atisha's tradition is used extensively by the Sakyas. H. E. Jetsun Kusho Chimey Luding relies on Atisha's tradition. Descriptions vary from tradition to tradition. Famed for his devotion to Tara, Atisha often had visions of her and, according to biographical accounts, often spoke with the Buddha Tara directly.

Chapter 7: Nakedness Is the Hard Part

1. From *Women in the Wilderness* (New York: Harper and Row, 1980).
2. Michel Henry died in December 1995.

Chapter 8: The Ganges Holds Everything

1. *Encountering God,* 116.
2. This statue has also been identified as Shiva's devoted wife, Parvati, who bore their son, Ganesha, the elephant-headed Hindu god of good fortune.
3. Crabgrass is the name of the organization that has grown out of their work. See Appendix.
4. Mahant-ji, Dr. V. B. Mishra, was later awarded a Global 500 Award by the United Nations Environmental Program.
5. "Women, Water, and Wood: Resource Managers in the Commons Crisis" by Mairi Dupa. *Earthlight,* Summer-Fall, 1994, 10.

Chapter 9: Life Revered Is Life Revealed

1. Anthropologist Mary Douglas writes of this in *Hindu Goddesses* by David Kinsley. Kinsley, 129.
2. See Rani's story (York Beach, ME: Nicolas-Hays, Inc. 1993), 159–68.
3. Ibid., 163.
4. Ramakrishna's chief disciple, the learned and gentle Vivekenanda, came to Chicago, Illinois, in 1893 to represent Hinduism at the world's first Parliament of Religion. He was an overnight success, brilliant in his presentation of the complexities of Hinduism, cutting through to the heart of the matter to the ways in which Hinduism helps one know God. Vivekenanda founded the Vedanta Society and was instrumental in bringing Hinduism to the West. Also see *The Great Swan: Meetings with Ramakrishna* by Lex Hixon (Boston: Shambala, 1992).
5. Harding, *Kali,* 47.
6. Ibid., brackets mine.
7. John Todd, "The Meaning of Water," *AquaTerra, Metaecology & Culture,* vol. 1, ed. by Jaqueline Froelich with Barbara Harmony (Eureka Springs, AR: The Water Center, 1995), 82–83.

Interlude: Holy Ground

1. Kinsley, *Hindu Goddesses,* on Sati, 38–40, on *pithas,* 186.

Chapter 10: The Lesson of the Forest

1. *Staying Alive: Women, Ecology, and Development* (Atlantic Highlands, NJ: Zed Books, Ltd., 1989). First published in India and Asia by Kali for Women Press

in Delhi. Vandana is also the founder and director of the Foundation for Science, Technology and Natural Resource Policy, in Delhi and Dehradun, India, and active in the Third World Network. See Appendix.

2. Ibid., 81–82.
3. *Monocultures* (London: Zed Books, Ltd., 1993), 9.
4. This was the focus of our conversations in San Francisco in 1995 and 1996.
5. *Staying Alive,* 77.

Chapter 11: "I Had to Do Something"

1. Through Antioch College's Buddhist Studies Program, Yellow Springs, Ohio. See Appendix.
2. Massihi Gyanodaya Abhiyan. See Appendix.
3. (St. Paul, MN: Yes Publishers, 1994), 23–24. Johnsen's book is a good companion, both for the traveler in India and the student of the Indian Goddess tradition. This telling is taken from Johnsen's story of Adi Shankacharya and the low-caste widow. The quotes are from her text.
4. Reports of the day claimed that "thousands of women patrol the streets of Imphal, the capital, and the surrounding towns and villages at night, and the movement is quickly spreading. . . . ," *San Francisco Chronicle,* "Women Warriors Patrol Indian State," 7/15/93.

Interlude: The Handless Maiden

1. This telling was inspired by Linda Cutts, a Buddhist teacher at San Francisco Zen Center's Green Gulch Farm. Cutts gave a *dharma* talk, a Buddhist lecture, on the Handless Maiden, and when I read it, I knew that this story was medicine for healing. It was published in *The Windbell,* a publication of San Francisco Zen Center, vol. XXVII, no. 1, Spring 1993, 18–24. Versions of this tale vary from country to country, from Italy to Russia and beyond. Herein is my own retelling.

Chapter 12: Learning to Roar

1. See *Sisters and Daughters Betrayed,* Chela Blitt's documentary film, and the Norwegian documentary film by Edvard Hambro, et. al, *Throwaway Children* referred to in the notes to Chapter 3.
2. Tsultrim referred me to Miranda Shaw's book, *Passionate Enlightenment: Women in Tantric Buddhism* on the subject of ferocity, Buddhism, and the fem-

inine. Shaw talks about the classes of women who were considered suitable for tantric practice, a particular form of meditation practice which Tsultrim also teaches. "One class was women who were always truthful and proud of their strength, they didn't hide it," Tsultrim noted. "The next category was women whose minds were powerful and energetic. After that were fearless women who 'revel in ferocity.' And then, the most qualified women of all, according to Shaw's study, were the women who 'derive pleasure from the fact that they are untamable.'" See *Passionate Enlightenment*, 54–55.

3. See Tsultrim Allione on the *khatvanga, Women of Wisdom,* 34–36.

4. *Tantra* is also often described as meaning "to weave" from its Sanskrit root. "Integrate" is another word used to describe tantra, a spiritual path that includes the world, the body, and the senses, one might say is "continuous with" them. In the tantric view, there is a single energy that pulses throughout the universe "dancing in various patterns and forms" (see *Passionate Enlightenment*). It is neither negative nor positive, it simply is.

5. *The Myth of the Goddess: Evolution of an Image* by Anne Baring and Jules Cashford (Arkana/Penguin Books, 1991), 204.

6. Allione, *Women of Wisdom,* 25.

7. Miranda Shaw, *Passionate Enlightenment,* 30.

8. Ibid., on dakini language, 104.

9. Allione, *Women of Wisdom,* on the language of dakinis, 42–43.

10. A *terton* is one who discovers and reveals a *terma.*

11. A mind treasure is called a *gongter,* one of the several kinds of *termas.* See *Women of Wisdom* for more of A-Yu Khadro's story, which is told briefly here.

Chapter 13: Stonecutting

1. In Ellen Bruno's documentary film, *Satya: A Prayer for the Enemy.* Available from the Film Library, 22D Hollywood Ave., Ho-Ho-Kus, NJ 07423, 800-343-5540.

Interlude: The Story of Inanna

1. There are many tellings of the Inanna-Ishtar story, Diane Wolkstein and Samuel Noah Kramer's work being one of the most accessible and reliable, *Inanna, Queen of Heaven and Earth* (San Francisco: Harper and Row, 1983). For this telling I also consulted *The Myth of the Goddess* by Anne Baring and Jules Cashman (New York: Arkana/Penguin Books, 1991) and *The Descent to the Goddess* by Sylvia Perrara (Toronto: Inner City Books, 1981).

Chapter 14: "Raise Up Those Held Down"

1. There are numerous tellings of this famous legend. I draw primarily on Ivone Gebara and Maria Clara Bingemer's *Mary: Mother of God, Mother of the Poor* (Maryknoll, NY: Orbis Books, 1989), 154–58.

2. Gebara, one of the most esteemed feminist theologians of liberation in Latin America, an Augustinian nun who lived with the poor in Recife in the northeast of Brazil, also a professor of theology, philosophy, and anthropology with a doctorate from the Louvain, in Belgium, was silenced by the Vatican for two years in the summer of 1995 for her outspoken views on women and the poor. See *Mary: Mother of God* for more on the Madonna of Aparecida in the context of liberation theology.

   Through Gebara's friend, anthropologist and professor Safina Newbery in Argentina, I was able to write to Gebara during her "silence." Newbery had told me about Gebara's talk on Susanna in the Old Testament that she was having translated for publication, on how important it is for women to "scream" like Susanna, not to be quiet.

   Gebara answered my letters, despite the sentence of silence, and gave me her permission to cite her letter herein.

   "The author of this biblical book forgot to glorify the strength and resistance of Susanna. Resistance is very important in women's lives. It is very important for women to 'scream' when there is injustice, not to be silent when life is threatened or killed. I think we are living in a 'culture of obedience,' as Dorothy Sölle likes to say. In the culture of obedience, it is very difficult to be responsible, to have responsibility, to give your personal 'response.' I was never invited to dialogue with some of the representatives of the Vatican in Rome about my situation. They sent letters only to my general superior, and they talked with a Brazilian bishop and a Jesuit priest about me, but never directly to me.

   "Responsibility in this patriarchal culture is reduced to a kind of submission to authority. You submit to the system, you are obedient to the system. That means you are not allowed to be creative, to ask questions, to critique, to have doubts. . . .

   "In Latin America, different groups of women are waking up to responsibility, to their own historical responsibility, and because of that, some of them are not accepted in the Church, in the universities, and so forth.

   "Maybe I am wrong, but I think that I was silenced not only because of my personal ideas, but because Roman Catholic authority is afraid of 'women's power' in Latin America. We women are working very well in different popular organizations and also inside Roman Catholic institutions. Now we are able to criticize the 'sacred' patriarchal power and we are doing that in different ways.

"I was punished because I am a kind of representative of all these 'revolutionary' women working particularly in Church institutions. I am helping them think by themselves, to make their own choices, to say clearly yes and no. And they are helping me be what I need to be. It is very hard, but it is very nice."

3. Slavery was abolished in Brazil in 1888.

4. Palmares, a city of twenty thousand people in the mountains, was the largest of the *quilombos*, communities of freed and runaway slaves; hence Palmares is like Zion, the promised land where all are free.

5. See Mary Judith Ress's essay, "After Five Centuries of Mixing, Who Are We? Walking with Our Dark Grandmother's Feet," in *Women Healing the Earth: Third World Women on Ecology, Feminism, and Religion*, ed. Rosemary Radford Ruether, 51–61. Ress is part of the Con-spirando collective in Santiago, Chile, a network of Latin American women interested in feminist theology, spirituality, and ecofeminism. They are looking again at the profound devotion to Mary in Latin America and asking, "Why is she rather than Christ the principal source of prayer and devotion? What relationship does she have to indigenous cosmologies?.... Is she the Mother of God or the Mother Goddess?"

6. See *Longing for Darkness: Tara and the Black Madonna* (New York: Viking/Penguin, 1990/1991) for a fuller discussion of this subject.

Chapter 15: "A Hiroshima Inside Her"

1. *Nunca Más: The Report of the Argentine National Commission on the Disappeared,* with an introduction by Ronald Dworkin (New York: Farrar, Straus & Giroux, in association with Index on Censorship, London, 1986), xi–xiii.

2. The capriciousness of the process can be glimpsed in a comment by General Videla, one of the three generals who ruled during the military dictatorship. During a press conference not long after the takeover, he told English journalists that to be considered a subversive, an enemy of the state, was a broad category. "A terrorist is not just someone with a gun or bomb, but also someone who spreads ideas that are contrary to Western and Christian civilization." The case in point was that of a young disabled girl, Claudia Ines Grumberg, who had been "detained" by the military and who is still among the Disappeared. *Gente,* 22 November 1977, *Diario Popular, Clarín, La Opinión, Crónica,* and other national newspapers dated 18 December 1977, cited in *Nunca Más: The Report of the Argentine National Commission on the Disappeared,* 333.

3. *The Report of the Argentine National Commission on the Disappeared.*

4. This same photo of Laura Bonaparte appeared in *Time* magazine, November 1995.

5. These specific comments on Laura's fantasies of revenge, her insights into how damaging such thoughts were, and her decision to go to the legal system were take from Louis Dubose's interview with Laura Bonaparte, "Family Reunion." Dubose's interview took place in San Antonio, Texas, at a human rights conference at St. Mary's University. It was published in *The Texas Observer*, October 15, 1993 (Austin, TX), and was part of what strengthened my conviction to go to Argentina directly. All other comments are from our conversations in Buenos Aires.

6. By William R. Long, March 3, 1995. Scilingo's interview with the journalist Verbitsky was published as a book, *The Flight*. He was arrested shortly after its publication. He has since been released.

Chapter 16: Isis in Argentina

1. Filmmakers John Knoop and Susanna Muñoz, with a grant from the Soros Documentary Fund, are producing a film about the Disappeared, *The Legacy,* from the point of view of HIJOS and a broad range of other Argentines, in the lineage of the classic film on the Jewish Holocaust, *Shoah*.

2. Reportedly sixty thousand Latin American military officers have been trained at the School of the Americas (SOA). Of the twenty-six officers in El Salvador cited by the UN Truth Commission for the murder of six Jesuit priests and two women co-workers, nineteen were trained at the School of the Americas. There has been a public outcry and growing movement to close the school since the Defense Department released several Spanish-language training manuals used at SOA that recommended the use of such tactics, among others, as torture and execution. A bill currently is pending in the U.S. Congress to close the school and begin a new era in U.S.–Latin American military relations. Copies of declassified documents on this subject are available from the National Security Archive in Washington, D.C. Information also is available from SOA Watch, P.O. Box 3330, Columbus, GA 31903, or 1719 Irving St., NW, Washington, D.C.

3. María Adela Gard de Antokoletz was awarded the Goldman Foundation's prestigious International Activist Award, in April 1997, for her work with the Madres de la Plaza de Mayo Línea Fundadora. The International Activist Award is a $100,000 award presented every other year to two outstanding individual activists in the international community, awarding them $50,000 each for their exceptional perseverance, selflessness, and leadership in combating social injustice.

4. This is not the translator's actual name.

Interlude: Isis and Osiris

1. There are many tellings of the Isis myth which I consulted, including Ann Baring's and Jules Cashford's in *The Myth of the Goddess* (New York: Arkana/Penguin Books, 1991) as well as Jean Houston's retelling in *The Passion of Isis and Osiris* (New York: Random House, 1995) and others. In Houston's telling, Isis says that her grief was so strong that "I have found another kind of strength. I have turned myself into a man," 59.

2. In Joan Chamberlain Engelsman, *The Feminine Dimension of the Divine*, 65–66.

Chapter 17: "Help, They Are Killing Us"

1. My friend Otis Kriegel, a young teacher and student of Latin American studies who works with inner-city youth, saw the story of the massacre, tore it out of a newspaper, and brought it to me, encouraging me to meet Yvonne since I was going to Latin America.

2. The year before the Candelária massacre, more than fifteen hundred youths, most of them street children, were assassinated by hired gunmen in Rio alone.

3. Estimates of the number of actual street children vary from seven hundred to five hundred thousand or more. See *Invisible Action: A Guide to Nongovernmental Assistance for Underprivileged and Street Children of Rio de Janeiro*, by Licia Valladares and Flávia Impelizieri (Rio: Instituto Universitário de Pesquisas do Rio de Janeiro, 1992) for a discussion of this problem. Research coordinator Professor Licia Valladares uses a figure of fifteen hundred to identify those children who live on the streets in Rio as opposed to the nearly nine hundred thousand children identified as needy in Rio as of 1990.

   The United Nations Children's Fund estimates that there are one hundred million children worldwide who have been abandoned to the streets. For the first time in human history, humankind will soon be an urban rather than a rural species. In 1975, only one-third of the world population lived in cities and towns. By 2025, two-thirds of the world population will do so. Currently at least five hundred million people live in the world's slums "and every day fifty thousand people, mainly women and children, die as a result of poor housing, water or sanitation." (Figures from "Fatigue Takes Toll on U.N. Habitat II Conference" by Geoffrey Lean, London *Independent,* in the *San Francisco Examiner,* June 10, 1996.)

   Accurate numbers of street children in Rio aside, the problem grows dramatically. Accounts in the press often fail to distinguish between street children and needy children, lumping them all together as "one million street children." There are over six hundred agencies attempting, with very modest success, to help the street children, while government programs remain extremely limited. In Brazil a girl is considered an adult at age fourteen and there are no laws to protect her thereafter. Twenty-three percent of the births in Rio are to girls between the ages of eleven and sixteen, many of whom have AIDS. AIDS is spreading rapidly in this Catholic country, where the Church continues to outlaw birth control, including condoms. AIDS is making vast inroads into the heterosexual community, Yvonne assured me, as more and more married women become infected as a result of the machismo culture. Unlike the homosexual community, the middle- and upper-class women are as of yet unidentified and isolated, separated by their choice to suffer in silence. The Brazilian government and Church prefer to portray the problem as an isolated phenomenon within the gay community.

4. The concentration of wealth is happening in the United States as well, where children are hit the hardest by the increase in poverty. Poor children in the United States are poorer than children in almost any other industrialized country in the West according to an extensive study of eighteen industrial nations released in 1995. The United States ranks sixteenth among the eighteen nations studied. ("Poor Children in U.S. Are Among Worst Off in Study of 18 Industrialized Countries," by Keith Bradsher, *The New York Times*, August 14, 1995, p. A7.)

Chapter 18: An Offering to Jemanjá, Goddess of the Sea

1. The themes of resistance and liberation run deep in Brazil. December of 1995 marked the three-hundred-year anniversary of the death of Zumbi, the revolutionary black leader who was killed at Palmares, the largest town of the *quilombos* movement, the movement of free people who lived in sanctuaries of secret villages and towns in the mountains and jungles. Palmares, the largest such settlement with its population of up to twenty thousand, flourished throughout most of the seventeenth century. People who lived in the *quilombos* were people who had either run away from slavery, bought their way out, or had somehow been freed. More attention needs to be paid to this important subject of the history of the *quilombos* movement, especially the legendary Palmares.

Capoeira became so powerful as a tool of insurrection that it was outlawed in the slave quarters of Brazil in the eighteenth century and practiced surreptitiously in the forests. It was illegal to practice it until the 1930s, when Mestre Bimba changed the focus from martial arts to artistic expression and opened up his school in Bahia. Today it has become an international art, with schools in the United States and Europe as well as in Brazil.

2. *African Gods in the Candomblé of Bahia,* illustrated by the painter Carybé, with an introduction by Jorge Amado, and text by Pierre Fatumbi Verger and Waldeloir Rego (Salvador-B.A. Brasil: Bruno Furrer, 1993), is an important, beautiful text on the organization of the *terreiros,* Candomblé in Bahia, and the Orishás, 235–61.

Chapter 19: "Proud Flesh"

1. Richard Rohr, O.P., cites this quote from St. Augustine in his talk "The Theology of Brokenness and the Descent," Liturgical Conference, March 1997.
2. "Walls for Wailing," by Jeffrey Jay, Ph.D., *Common Boundary*, May/June 1994. Jay is the director of the Center for Post-Traumatic Stress Studies and Treatment in Washington, D.C. This is an excellent article on the role of the community in healing using the Jewish approach to trauma as an instructive model, 30–35.
3. Ibid., 32.
4. *Walk in the Light, A Pastoral Response to Child Sexual Abuse. A Statement by the Bishops' Committees on Women in Society and in the Church and Marriage and Family, Affirmed by the General Membership of the National Conference of Catholic Bishops.* Publication No. 5-000, United States Catholic Conference, Washington, D.C. Copies can be ordered from 1-800-235-8722.
5. "Walls for Wailing," by Jeffrey Jay, Ph.D., *Common Boundary,* May/June 1994.
6. 2 Esdras 4:1–22, *The Oxford Annotated Apocrypha*, The Apocrypha of the Old Testament, ed. Bruce M. Metzger (New York: Oxford University Press, 1977), 29–30.

Chapter 20: Who Is the Enemy?

1. Farrar, Straus & Giroux is the North American publisher, in association with Index on Censorship, London, introduction by Ronald Dworkin, 1986. The report was first published in 1984, in Buenos Aires. Farrar, Straus & Giroux is to be commended for publishing this extraordinary document and keeping it in print. It is a devastating historical record of depravity.

In 1982, President Raúl Alfonsín of Argentina campaigned and won his presidency on the issue of human rights. He had immediately appointed a distinguished commission to investigate the disappearances, investing them with full authority to issue the report, *Nunca Más* (Never Again), after painstaking, methodical study. Commission members went to the actual sites of torture and imprisonment, mass graves, and detention centers. They interviewed first-hand witnesses and survivors of torture and detention (most did not survive), cross-checked witnesses' stories, viewed original photographs, created detailed flow charts of events, and confirmed the worst fears for the fate of many thousands who disappeared. *Nunca Más* includes photographs of the detention centers, hospitals, and police quarters that were used for torture. It is a remarkable document which Robert F. Drinan, S.J., says should be required reading. "It is a warning of what horrors can occur when a ruling elite declares war on the people in the name of defending Western or Christian civilization."

2. See John Simpson and Jana Bennett, *The Disappeared and the Mothers of the Plaza* (New York: St. Martin's Press, 1985).

3. The names in this passage have been changed.

Chapter 21: "I Do Not Rehearse My Anger"

1. The Santa Cruz mountains retreat was one of the Mindfulness retreats that she and Thich Nhat Hanh also give through the Community of Mindful Living. (See Appendix.)

2. *How I Learned and Practice Social Change in Vietnam* by Chân Không (Cao Ngoc Phuong) (Berkeley, CA: Parallax Press, 1993), 249. Chân Không means "True Emptiness." *Emptiness,* as Buddhists use it, does not mean void of meaning but empty of a separately existing, independent self. Sister Chân Không describes it as a word that celebrates our interconnectedness, the reality of "interbeing" with each other and with all being.

Chapter 22: "We Can Always Use Someone to Serve"

1. Her name has been changed.

Chapter 23: Because I Saw the Women Dancing

1. Organized by Tibet House in New York, in association with the California Institute for Integral Studies.

SELECTED BIBLIOGRAPHY

Abram, David. *The Spell of the Sensuous: Perception and Language in a More-Than-Human World.* New York: Pantheon Books, 1996.

Allione, Tsultrim. *Women of Wisdom.* London: Routledge & Kegan Paul, 1984.

Almeida, Bira (Mestre Acordeon). *Capoeira: A Brazilian Art Form.* Berkeley: North Atlantic Books, 1986.

Anderson, Victor. *Beyond Ontological Blackness: An Essay on African American Religious and Cultural Criticism.* New York: Continuum, 1995.

Argentine National Commission on the Disappeared. *Nunca Más: The Report of the Argentine National Commission on the Disappeared.* Introduction by Ronald Dworkin. New York: Farrar, Straus & Giroux, in association with Index on Censorship, London, 1986.

Ashe, Geoffrey. *The Virgin.* London: Routledge & Kegan Paul, 1976.

Aung San Suu Kyi, *Freedom from Fear.* New York: Penguin Books, 1995.

Bacon, Margaret Hope. *Mothers of Feminism: The Story of Quaker Women in America.* New York: Harper and Row, 1986.

Baldwin, Christina. *Calling the Circle: The First and Future Culture.* Newberg, OR: Swan, Raven & Co., 1994.

Barber, Janey, IHM. "The Sacred Image Is a Divine Codex," and the "Codex That Breathes Life." In *Handbook on Guadalupe.* New Bedford, MA: Franciscan Friars of the Immaculate, 1996.

Baring, Anne, and Jules Cashford. *The Myth of the Goddess: Evolution of an Image.* New York: Arkana/Penguin Books, 1991.

Barndt, Joseph. *Dismantling Racism: The Continuing Challenge to White America*. Minneapolis: Ausberg, 1991.

Batstone, David, Eduardo Mendieta, Lois Ann Lorentzen, and Dwight N. Hopkins, eds., *Liberation Theologies, Postmodernity, and the Americas*. New York: Routledge, 1997.

Benard, Elizabeth Anne. *Chinnamasta, the Aweful Buddhist and Hindu Tantric Goddess*. Delhi: Motilal Banarsidass Publishers, 1994.

Berry, Thomas. *Dream of the Earth*. San Francisco: Sierra Club Books, 1988.

Birnbaum, Lucia Chiavola. *Black Madonnas: Feminism, Religion, and Politics in Italy*. Boston: Northeastern University Press, 1993.

Bolen, Jean Shinoda, M.D. *Crossing to Avalon: A Woman's Midlife Passage*. San Francisco: Harper San Francisco, 1994.

Boner, Alice. *Alice Boner, Artist and Scholar*. Georgette Boner and Eberhard Fischer, eds. Varanasi, India: Alice Boner Foundation for Research on Fundamental Principles in Indian Art, 1982.

Boner, Georgette, Luitgard Soni, and Jayandra Soni, eds. *Alice Boner Diaries: India 1934–1967*. Delhi: Motilal Banarsidass Publishers, 1993.

———— and Eberhard Fischer, eds. *Alice Boner: Artist and Scholar*. Varanasi: Ratna Printing Works (Offset Division), [1982].

Brenner, Anita. *Idols Behind Altars*. Cheshire, CT: Biblo-Moser, (1929) 1967.

Brown, Karen McCarthy. *Mama Lola: A Vodou Priestess in Brooklyn*. Berkeley: University of California Press, 1991.

Bruno, Ellen. *Satya: A Prayer for the Enemy*. A documentary film.

Calvino, Italo. *Italian Folk Tales,* comp. New York: Harcourt Brace Jovanovich, 1980.

Cannon, Katie Geneva. *Katie's Canon: Womanism and the Soul of the Black Community*. New York: Continuum, 1995.

Carybé, António Carlos. *Os Deuses Africanos no Candomblé da Bahia. African Gods in the Candomblé of Bahia*. Salvador, Brazil: Editora Bigraf, 1993.

Coburn, Thomas B. *Encountering the Goddess: A Translation of the Devi-Mahatmya and a Study of Its Interpretation*. Albany, NY: State University of New York Press, 1991.

Cox, Harvey. *Fire from Heaven: The Rise of Pentecostal Spirituality and the Reshaping of Religion in the Twenty-first Century*. Reading, MA: Addison Wesley, 1995.

Cunneen, Sally. *In Search of Mary: The Woman and the Symbol*. New York: Ballantine Books, 1996.

Danaher, Kevin, and Michael Shellenberger. *Fighting for the Soul of Brazil: A Project of Global Exchange*. New York: Monthly Review Press, 1995.

David-Neel, Alexandra. *My Journey to Lhasa*. Introduction by Diana N. Rowan. Boston: Beacon Press, 1993.

Dubose, Louis. "Family Reunion," in *The Texas Observer,* October 15, 1993. Austin, Texas.

Dowman, Keith. *A Buddhist Guide to the Power Places of the Kathmandu Valley.* Kathmandu, Nepal: Diamond Sow Publications, 1984.

Eck, Diana L. *Encountering God: A Spiritual Journey from Bozeman to Banaras.* Boston: Beacon Press, 1993.

————. *Darśan: Seeing the Divine Image in India.* Chambersburg, PA: Anima Books, 1985.

————. *Banaras, City of Light.* Princeton: Princeton University Press, 1982.

Elizondo, Virgilio. *The Future Is Mestizo, Life Where Cultures Meet.* Bloomington, IN: Meyer-Stone Books, 1988.

Engelsman, Joan Chamberlain. *The Feminine Face of the Divine.* Wilmette, IL: Chiron Publications, 1994.

Erndl, Kathleen M. *Victory to the Mother: The Hindu Goddess of Northwest India in Myth, Ritual, and Symbol.* New York: Oxford University Press, 1993.

Feagin, Joe R., and Melvin P. Sikes. *Living with Racism, the Black Middle-Class Experience.* Boston: Beacon Press, 1994.

Fortune, Marie Marshall. *Sexual Violence, the Unmentionable Sin: An Ethical and Pastoral Perspective.* Cleveland, OH: Pilgrim Press, 1983.

Gadon, Elinor W. *The Once and Future Goddess: A Sweeping Visual Chronicle of the Sacred Female and Her Reemergence in the Cultural Mythology of Our Time.* San Francisco: Harper and Row, 1989.

Galeano, Eduardo. *Open Veins of Latin America: Five Centuries of the Pillage of a Continent.* Cedric Belfrage, trans. New York: Monthly Review Press, 1973.

Galembo, Phyllis. *Divine Inspiration.* Foreword by David Byrne. Essays by Robert Farris Thompson, Joseph Nevadomsky, Norma Rosen, Zeca Ligièro. Albuquerque: University of New Mexico Press, 1993.

Gates, Henry Louis, Jr. *Loose Canons: Notes on the Culture Wars.* New York: Oxford University Press, 1992.

Gebara, Ivone, and Maria Clara Bingemer. *Mary: Mother of God, Mother of the Poor.* Phillip Berryman, trans. Maryknoll, NY: Orbis Books, 1989.

Gilbert, Sandra M., and Susan Gubar, eds. *Shakespeare's Sisters: Feminist Essays on Women Poets.* Bloomington: Indiana University Press, 1979.

Gimbutas, Marija. *Gods and Goddesses of Old Europe 6500–3500 B.C.: Myths and Cult Images.* Berkeley: University of California Press, 1982.

Golden, Marita, and Susan Richards Shreve, eds. *Skin Deep: Black Women and White Women Write About Race.* New York: Nan Talese/Doubleday, 1995.

Guider, Margaret Eletta. *Daughters of Rahab: Prostitution and the Church of Liberation in Brazil.* Harvard Theological Studies 40. Minneapolis: Fortress Press, 1995.

Gyatso, Tenzin, the Dalai Lama. *The Good Heart.* Boston: Wisdom Publications, 1996.

Habito, Ruben L. F. *Total Liberation: Zen Spirituality and the Social Dimension.* Maryknoll, NY: Orbis Books, 1989.

Hanh, Thich Nhat. *Living Buddha, Living Christ.* New York: Riverhead Books, 1996.

———. *Old Path, White Clouds: Walking in the Footsteps of the Buddha.* Berkeley: Parallax Press, 1991.

———. *The Blooming of a Lotus: Guided Meditation Exercises for Healing and Transformation.* Annabel Laity, trans. Boston: Beacon Press, 1993.

Harding, Elizabeth U. *Kali: The Black Goddess of Dakshineswar.* York Beach, ME: Nicolas-Hays, Inc., 1993.

Hennelly, Alfred, S.J. *Liberation Theologies: The Global Pursuit of Justice.* Mystic, CT: Twenty-Third Publications, 1995.

Herman, Judith Lewis, M.D. *Trauma and Recovery: The Aftermath of Violence, from Domestic Abuse to Political Terror.* New York: Basic Books, 1992.

Hirshfield, Jane, ed. *Women in Praise of the Sacred: 43 Centuries of Spiritual Poetry by Women.* New York: HarperCollins, 1994.

———. *Of Gravity and Angels.* Middletown, CT: Wesleyan University Press, 1988.

Hixon, Lex. *Great Swan: Meetings with Ramakrishna.* Boston: Shambhala, 1992.

Hopkins, Jeffrey, ed. and trans. *Compassion in Tibetan Buddhism, Tsong-ka-pa.* London: Rider, 1980.

Houston, Jean. *The Passion of Isis and Osiris.* New York: Ballantine Books, 1995.

Human Rights Watch Women's Rights Project. *The Human Rights Watch Global Report on Women's Human Rights.* New York: Human Rights Watch, 1995.

Isherwood, Christopher. *Ramakrishna and His Disciples.* Calcutta, India: Advaita Ashrama, 1990.

Johnsen, Linda. *Daughters of the Goddess: The Women Saints of India.* Minnesota: Yes International Publishers, 1994.

Johnson, Elizabeth. *She Who Is: The Mystery of God in Feminist Theological Discourse.* New York: Crossroads, 1992.

Jones, Alexander, gen. ed. *Jerusalem Bible.* Reader's Edition. New York: Doubleday, 1968.

Không, Chân (Cao Ngoc Phuong). *Learning True Love: How I Learned and Practiced Social Change in Vietnam.* Berkeley: Parallax Press, 1993.

Kinsley, David. *Hindu Goddesses: Visions of the Divine Feminine in the Hindu Religious Tradition.* Berkeley: University of California Press, 1986.

———. *The Goddesses' Mirror: Visions of the Divine from East and West.* New York: State University of New York Press, 1989.

Klein, Anne Carolyn. *Meeting the Great Bliss Queen: Buddhists, Feminists, and the Art of the Self*. Boston: Beacon Press, 1995.

Kumar, Corinne. Cited in Catherine Allport. *We Who Believe in Freedom: Pictures and Stories from the Greatest Gathering of Women on Earth*. Berkeley: Work in progress.

Lerner, Gerda. *The Creation of Feminist Consciousness*. New York: Oxford University Press, 1993.

May, Herbert G., and Bruce M. Metzger, eds. *The New Oxford Annotated Bible with the Apocrypha*. Revised Standard Version. New York: Oxford University Press, 1973.

McGinn, Bernard, ed. *Meister Eckhart and the Beguine Mystics*. New York: Continuum, 1994.

Mookerjee, Ajit. *Kali: The Feminine Force*. New York: Destiny Books, 1988.

Morrison, Toni. *Playing in the Dark: Whiteness and the Literary Imagination*. New York: Vintage Books, 1993.

Moss, Leonard P., and Stephen C. Cappannari. "In Quest of the Black Virgin." In *Mother Worship: Theme and Variations*, James Preston, ed. Chapel Hill: University of North Carolina Press, 1982.

Munro, Eleanor. *On Glory Roads: A Pilgrim's Book about Pilgrimage*. New York: Thames and Hudson, 1987.

Neihardt, John G. *Black Elk Speaks: Being the Life Story of a Holy Man of the Oglala Sioux*. Lincoln: University of Nebraska Press, 1961.

Nelson, Gertrud Mueller. *Here All Dwell Free: Stories to Heal the Wounded Feminine*. New York: Doubleday, 1991.

Norris, Kathleen. *Little Girls in Church*. Pittsburgh: University of Pittsburgh Press, 1995.

Oda, Mayumi. *Goddesses*. Berkeley: Lancaster Miller Publishers, 1981.

Pannikar, Raimon. *The Intra-Religious Dialogue*. New York: Paulist Press, 1978.

Peavey, Fran. *By Life's Grace: Musings on the Essence of Social Change*. Philadelphia: New Society Publishers, 1994.

———. *Heart Politics*. Philadelphia: New Society Publishers, 1986.

Perera, Victor. *The Cross and the Pear Tree: A Sephardic Journey*. New York: Knopf, 1995.

———. *Unfinished Conquest: The Guatemalan Tragedy*. Berkeley: University of California Press, 1993.

Plath, Sylvia. *Ariel*. New York: Harper and Row, 1966.

Puleo, Mev. *The Struggle Is One: Voices and Visions of Liberation*. New York: State University of New York Press, 1994.

Rahula, Walpola. *What the Buddha Taught*. New York: Grove Press, 1974.

Rhie, Marylin M., and Robert A. F. Thurman. *Wisdom and Compassion: The Sacred Art of Tibet.* New York: Asian Art Museum of San Francisco and Tibet House in association with Harry N. Abrams, Inc., 1991.

Rolland, Romain. *The Life of Ramakrishna.* Translated by E. F. Malcolm-Smith. Calcutta, India: Advaita Ashrama, 1992.

Ruddick, Sara. *Maternal Thinking: Toward a Politics of Peace.* New York: Ballantine Books, 1989.

Ruether, Rosemary Radford, ed. *Women Healing Earth: Third World Women on Ecology, Feminism, and Religion.* New York: Orbis Books, 1996.

Savvas, Carol, and Tulku Lodro, trans. *Transformation into the Exalted State: Spiritual Exercises of the Tibetan Tantric Tradition,* "Prayers of Request to the Lady Tara Who Is Inseparable from the Guru, Including All the Points of the Path," Fasc. 18. *Opuscula Tibetana,* Peter Lindegger, ed. Rikon-Zurich: Tibet Institute, 1987.

Schell, Jonathan. "Reflections: A Better Today." *The New Yorker,* February 3, 1986.

Schüssler Fiorenza, Elisabeth. *Jesus: Miriam's Child, Sophia's Prophet.* New York: Continuum, 1995.

Sen, Ramprasad. *Grace and Mercy in Her Wild Hair: Selected Poems to the Mother Goddess.* Leonard Nathan and Clinton Seely, trans. Boulder: Great Eastern Book Company, 1982.

Shaffer, Carolyn R., and Kristin Anundsen. *Creating Community Anywhere: Finding Support and Connection in a Fragmented World.* New York: Tarcher/Putnam, 1993.

Shaw, Miranda. *Passionate Enlightenment: Women in Tantric Buddhism.* Princeton: Princeton University Press, 1994.

Shiva, Vandana. *Staying Alive.* London: Zed Books Ltd., 1989.

———. *Monocultures of the Mind: Perspectives on Biodiversity and Biotechnology.* London: Zed Books Ltd., 1993.

———, ed. *Close to Home: Women Reconnect Ecology, Health and Development Worldwide.* Philadelphia: New Society Publishers, 1994.

Smith, Catherine F. "Jane Lead: The Feminist Mind and Art of a Seventeenth-Century Protestant Mystic," in *Women of Spirit: Female Leadership in the Jewish and Christian Traditions.* Rosemary Ruether and Eleanor McLaughlin, eds. New York: Simon & Schuster, 1979.

Sölle, Dorothy. *Creative Disobedience.* Translated by Lawrence W. Denef. Cleveland, OH: Pilgrim Press, 1995.

Spretnak, Charlene. *States of Grace.* San Francisco: Harper San Francisco, 1993.

Swami Amritasvarupananda, trans. *Awaken Children! Dialogues with Sri Mata Amritanandamayi,* vol. 3. San Ramon, CA: Mata Amritanandamayi Centers, 1991.

Thubten Chodron, ed. *Spiritual Sisters*. Seattle: Dharma Friendship Foundation, 1990.

Valeriano, Antonio. *Nican Mopohua*. Janet Barber, trans. In the Catalog of the Exhibit "Nuestra Senora de Guadalupe: Mother of God, Mother of the Americas." Edwin E. Sylvest, Jr., Curator. Dallas: The Bridwell Library, Southern Methodist University, 1992.

Valladares, Licia, and Flávia Impelizieri. *Invisible Action: A Guide to Non-Governmental Assistance for Underprivileged and Street Children of Rio de Janeiro*. Rio de Janeiro: Instituto Universitário de Pesquisas do Rio de Janeiro, 1992.

Vardey, Lucinda, comp. *Mother Teresa: A Simple Path*. New York: Ballantine Books, 1995.

Vogelsanger, Cornelia, curator. *Kali, Visions of the Dark Mother*, exhibit at the Folk Museum, University of Zurich (Völkerkundemuseum der Universität Zürich), 1994.

Wagoner, David. *Who Shall Be the Sun?* Bloomington: University of Indiana Press, 1978.

Warner, Marina. *Alone of All Her Sex: The Myth and the Cult of the Virgin Mary*. New York: Vintage Books, 1983.

Willson, Martin. *In Praise of Tara: Songs to the Saviouress*. London: Wisdom Publications, 1986.

Woodman, Marion, and Elinor Dickson. *Dancing in the Flames: The Dark Goddess in the Transformation of Consciousness*. Boston: Shambhala, 1996.

Wolkstein, Diane, and Samuel Noah Kramer. *Inanna: Queen of Heaven and Earth*. New York: Harper & Row, 1983.

APPENDIX

Following are brief descriptions of the organizations with which the women written about in this book are affiliated, provided in many cases by the women or the organizations themselves, should the reader want further information.

AMNESTY INTERNATIONAL USA
322 Eighth Avenue
New York, NY 10001 USA
Tel: (212) 807-8400
Fax: (212) 627-1451
E-mail: aimember@aiusa.org

Amnesty International works with individuals and organizations around the world to fight human rights abuses, free prisoners of conscience, ensure fair and prompt trials for political prisoners, and end all use of torture, political killing, "disappearance," and the death penalty. They also work with the Mothers of the Disappeared in Argentina. See *Madres de Plaza de Mayo Línea Fundadora.*

BUDDHIST STUDIES PROGRAM
Antioch Education Abroad
Antioch College
795 Livermore Street
Yellow Springs, OH 45387 USA
Tel: (800) 874-7986; Tel: (513) 767-6366

Fax: (513) 767-6469
E-mail: AEA@college.antioch.edu

Antioch Education Abroad weaves the diverse resources of Bodh Gaya, India, the site of the Buddha's enlightenment, into a fall semester study program for college students. Emphasis is placed on a comparative approach to both theory and practice, so that participants may reach their own understanding of that essence which is common to all the varieties of Buddhism while learning to appreciate the many cultural and historical environments in which it has flourished. Bodh Gaya, India, is a pilgrimage site sacred to many traditions.

COMMUNITY OF MINDFUL LIVING
P.O. Box 7355
Berkeley, CA 94707 USA
Tel: (510) 527-3751
Fax: (510) 527-7129
E-mail: parapress@aol.com

Sister Chân Không works closely with Thich Nhat Hanh, teaching and assisting at many of his retreats. Thich Nhat Hanh has lectured and led many retreats in North America and around the world on the art of mindful living. Thousands of people have been inspired to take up the practice of mindfulness to refresh themselves, reduce stress, renew the depth of their understanding, and find real happiness in their lives.

The Community of Mindful Living was formed in 1983 to help support the practice of mindfulness for individuals, families, and societies. Their work includes organizing and conducting mindfulness retreats; publishing and distributing books, tapes, and a newsletter on mindful living; establishing a rural residential retreat center; and developing and conducting programs for the greater community, including veterans of war and those who are in real need in Vietnam and elsewhere.

Sister Chân Không and Thich Nhat Hanh are part of a community of Zen Buddhist monks and nuns of the Order of Interbeing living in a retreat center in Plum Village, France. Retreats are open to guests during certain times of the year. Contact the Community of Mindful Living for information on retreats at Plum Village.

CRABGRASS, WORKING FOR SOCIAL CHANGE
3181 Mission St., #30
San Francisco, CA 94110 USA
E-mail: crabgrass@igc.apc.org

Fran Peavey and Tova Green created the nonprofit organization Crabgrass. The work of Crabgrass is based on relationship, on creating and strengthening bonds that deepen understanding and reduce fear and prejudice. Our work in the former Yugoslavia and in India (where Fran has been involved in cleaning the Ganges for fifteen years) is one part of the whole; the other is linking our communities in the United States with these places so that all of us can renew our energy for cleaning the rivers and building relationships that bridge differences wherever we are.

Crabgrass projects include cleaning the Ganges River in Varanasi (Banaras), India (working with Friends of the Ganges U.S. and with the Sankat Mochan Foundation in India), organizing the 2nd Women and Water Conference in Kathmandu, Nepal, in September 1998, and working to support refugee women's and anti-war groups in the former Yugoslavia.

Fran and Tova also facilitated the U.S. publication of *I Remember: Writings by Bosnian Women Refugees* (San Francisco: Auntie Lute, 1997).

HEDGEBROOK
Women Writers Retreat
2197 East Millman Road
Langley, WA 98260 USA
Tel: (360) 321-4786
Fax: (360) 321-2171

Hedgebrook is a private, nonprofit organization and retreat center, open to all women writers, published or not. Founded in 1988 by Nancy Nordhoff to support and strengthen women's voices and the written word, Hedgebrook's thirty-three acres on an island off the Washington coast overlook wetlands and Puget Sound, and provide space for six writers at a time. Each resident has a private timber-frame cottage, fully furnished, including a small bathroom and kitchen, heated by a wood-burning stove. There are no phones in the cottages. Hedgebrook provides the rare gift of nature's quiet and the opportunity to work uninterrupted. Interaction with the land is integral to the experience of Hedgebrook. Trails through the woods and fields, and ponds and nearby beaches provide ways to explore this small island environment.

There are no fees for residents at Hedgebrook. All meals are provided. Women writers can stay from one week up to three months. Write for notice of deadlines for submission of application for residency.

IMAGES OF DIVINITY RESEARCH PROJECT (IOD)
Sponsored by the Center for Women and Religion
The Graduate Theological Union
2400 Ridge Road
Berkeley, CA 94709 USA
Website: www.imagesofdivinity.org

The Images of Divinity Research Project (IOD), an independent project founded in 1987, seeks to reclaim living traditions of the enlightened feminine, re-establish their connections to earth-based traditions, bring them into mainstream culture, promote religious pluralism, and dissolve the barriers of race and gender.

MADRES DE LA PLAZA DE MAYO LÍNEA FUNDADORA
Perón 1671 - Piso 11 - Dpto. "J"
(1037) Capital Federal
ARGENTINA

The Madres de la Plaza de Mayo Línea Fundadora maintains a cordial, cooperative relationship with all human rights organizations in Argentina and also with Amnesty International. We are willing to be contacted and will respond to everyone who wants to know more about us. There is material to send.

MOTHER TERESA'S MISSIONARIES OF CHARITY
333 East 145th Street
Bronx, NY 10451 USA
Tel: (718) 292-0019

The Missionaries of Charity is an international religious family composed of active and contemplative branches with perpetual, public vows of chastity, poverty, and obedience, and wholehearted and free service to the poorest of the poor all over the world. Our religious family started when our foundress, Mother M. Teresa Bojaxhiu, was inspired by the Holy Spirit with a special charism on September 10, 1946. In addition to this branch, there are branches in many other cities around the world where one can easily volunteer. (Mother Teresa died in September 1997.)

NEPALESE YOUTH OPPORTUNITY FOUNDATION (NYOF)
Olga Murray
203 Valley St.
Sausalito, CA 94965 USA
Tel: (415) 332-4589
Fax: (415) 331-5029
E-mail: nyof@well.com

The Nepalese Opportunity Foundation (NYOF) supports and educates impoverished and disabled children in Nepal. Its objective is to provide these youngsters with what is every child's birthright—adequate food, clothing, housing, and medical care—and to educate them as far as their abilities will take them. It aims to imbue the children with a sense of social responsibility so that they will become useful citizens of their country and go on to lead happy and productive lives. The Foundation views the support and education of these children as a gift to the future of Nepal. NYOF also has a small pen-pal program with school children in the United States to help promote international understanding.

GABINETE DO DR. RAMOS-HORTA
Rua São Lazaro n°16, 1°
1150 Lisboa
PORTUGAL
Tel: +351-1-886-3727
Fax: +351-1-886-3791
E-mail: np98g@mail.telepac.pt

Source for information on East Timor and Dr. Ramos-Horta's work.

RESEARCH FOUNDATION FOR SCIENCE,
TECHNOLOGY, AND ECOLOGY
A-60 Hauz Khas
New Delhi-110016
INDIA
Tel: +91-11-6968077
Fax: +91-11-6856795/4626699
E-mail: vandana@twn.unv.ernet.in

The Research Foundation for Science, Technology, and Ecology has been involved for more than a decade in issues of biodiversity conservation emerging from a concern for people's rights to natural resources and sustainable livelihoods. This involvement has led to pioneering in linking trade issues with issues of ecology and gender equity. Through participatory research, the Foundation has given scientific support to social movements like Chipko, farmers' movements, and movements for the conservation of biodiversity.

The Foundation has made significant contributions to discussions related to the Biodiversity Convention in Rio in 1992 and its implementation. It has also informed the debates on Intellectual Property Rights and Agriculture in GATT. Through partnership with grassroots movements and participation in international dialogues, the Foundation has developed the concept of Community Intellectual Rights as the countervailing system to Intellectual Property Rights encoded in GATT and the national legislation emerging from it. Dr. Vandana Shiva is the founder and director of the Foundation.

RURAL HEALTH EDUCATION SERVICE TRUST (RHEST)
P.O. Box 355
Ga-1/258 Dilli Bazaar
Kathmandu 2, NEPAL
E-mail: startup@ventures.mos.com.np

Rural Health Education Service Trust (RHEST) is a not-for-profit trust (guthi) established in March 1993 for the benefit of the disadvantaged rural women and children of Nepal with the help of Dr. Aruna Uprety. It conducts TBA (Traditional Birth Attendant) trainings in rural areas, sponsors the education in government schools of rural girls who would not otherwise go to school, and runs health and education camps in rural areas.

TARA MANDALA
P.O. Box 3040
Pagosa Springs, CO 81147 USA
Tel: (970) 264-6177; Fax: (970) 264-6169
E-mail: tara_mandala@compuserve.com

Tara Mandala is a nonprofit religious organization that supports spiritual activities oriented toward teachings of innate wisdom, specifically in the Tibetan Buddhist tradition. Our principal purpose is the development of the Dzogchen tradition in the lineage of Chögyal Namkhai Norbu Rinpoche. We are a repository for the preservation and development of Buddhist traditions and wisdom lineages. Our primary goal is to develop the Tara Mandala Retreat Center on our wild and beautiful land of five hundred acres in southwestern Colorado for personal and group retreats.

TIBET HOUSE INC.
22 W. 15th Street
New York, NY 10011 USA
Tel: (212) 807-0563; Fax: (212) 807-0565
E-Mail: TIBETKB@aol.com; Website: www.tibethouse-ny.org

Tibet House is a not-for-profit cultural institution founded under the auspices of His Holiness the Dalai Lama. Its purposes are to help preserve Tibet's cultural and religious heritage; to present Tibet's ancient traditions of philosophy, art, and science; and to share Tibet's unique contributions to spiritual understanding and human development.

SISTER JESSIE UPADHAYA
Campaign for Awakening Wisdom
Burmese Vihar
Bodhgaya, Gaya 824231
Bihar, INDIA
Fax: +91-631-400873

Sister Jessie works to bring about Gandhi's lifelong dream of a kingdom where all live together in harmony. The Campaign for Awakening Wisdom (Massihi Gyanodaya Abhiyan) has been endeavoring to continue this effort of Gandhi's to bring about total unity of all castes, creeds, and religions. Toward this end, Sr. Jessie and her co-workers have started an education program. "The ultimate aim is education of the heart as well as the head. There are millions of children who never get a chance for an education; we hope to reach some of them."

ACKNOWLEDGMENTS

Gratitude for the help I've received in working on this book is owed to many. Most often the acknowledgment given here is for support that is substantial, tangible, material. Yet sometimes it is for something as seemingly small as a conversation upon which a crucial insight turned. Help has come in all forms, material and immaterial. The day I completed the manuscript a letter arrived from Tarapith, in Bengal, the most sacred site to Tara in India. It was a letter in Hindi with flower petals and a blessing enclosed, but I know not from whom. Writing this book often has been an experience like receiving the letter from India—goodness intervened, help was provided, but I knew not from where. Blessings and prayers of friends far and wide have sustained me. Their goodwill, kind thoughts, fierce encouragement, and generosity have kept me going time and again when I thought the way I was traveling had ended or become impassable. Writing this book has been what I call "Riding the Lion," my original title, a title that rests now on new work. The greatest challenge has been to stay with this lion energy, so much greater than mine, not be devoured by it, *and* keep writing. The mouth of God is wide and full of teeth.

Some who helped are acknowledged within the pages of this story, their roles clear, their influence obvious, such as my friend, Tara Doyle. Others are mentioned in the notes. Still others could hardly be thanked adequately, no matter how lengthy my acknowledgments. Nonetheless, I embark upon this risky business. Should anyone be left out who should have been included, the oversight comes from my own limitations, not their contribution.

I am grateful to the Graduate Theological Union (GTU) of Berkeley, California, and their Center for Women and Religion for my appointment as a Research

Associate for the last ten years. The sponsorship of the Center for Women and Religion has helped my work with the Images of Divinity Research Project (IOD) grow, the ongoing work of which this book is but one part. Dean Margaret Miles's belief in how independent work such as IOD's might help broaden theological education has been essential. I am grateful as well to Glenn Bucher, the President of the Graduate Theological Union, whose support has helped provide a base and a context in which I could work.

The Sister Fund, the Tara Fund, the Foundation for a Compassionate Society, an anonymous donor-advised fund of The San Francisco Foundation, the Philanthropic Collaborative, the Deep Ecology Foundation, and the Tara Foundation all have provided the critical, essential, and timely support needed to complete this phase of the work and to continue the ongoing work of the Images of Divinity Research Project.

Friends and colleagues who have believed in this work from the start deserve special thanks. Their constancy and support have grounded me time and again in the possible. I am especially grateful to Helen Hunt, Miriam Ella Alford, Nancy Nordhoff, Margaret Schink, Isabel Allende, Kathy Barry, Ph.D., Ann R. Roberts, Genevieve Vaughn, Tracy Gary, Diana N. Rowan, Marx Cazenave, Mary Ann McGuire, Marion Hunt-Badiner, Mimi and Peter Buckley, Bokara Legendre, Maja Ramsey, Linda Zidell, Trish Kubal, Marcia Anderson, Ann Sonz Matranga, Tabra Tunoa, Rose Boyle, Patty and Dennis Burke, Kathleen Burgy, Gail Thomas, and Elizabeth S. Wally. My friendships with Miriam Ella Alford and Helen Hunt have been particularly meaningful and sustaining. The dialogues and remarkable exchanges, the length of history I share with many of these women is part of the ground out of which this book grows.

The support of Mary Cross and the Rev. Pamela Cooper-White, Ph.D., both former Directors of the Center for Women and Religion; Marta Vides, M. Div., Ph.D., who served as Interim Director of the Center for Women and Religion; and now the Rev. Cheryl Kirk-Duggan, Ph.D., the current Director, has been essential. All of these women have been advocates and allies, and continue to help advise, shape, and develop IOD. Rebecca Parker, Director of the Starr King School of Theology at the GTU, and Professor Claire Fischer, Ph.D., the Aurelia Rinehardt Professor of Religion and Culture at Starr King, have helped hone my thinking and have given me a sense of how much more work there is to be done. Ideally a project such as the Images of Divinity will continue to help bridge the distance between academia and the larger community, for rarely before in history, if ever, has the need to understand one another's religions and faith traditions been so necessary to our survival and that of the world around us.

Theological education has a critical leadership role to play in the twenty-first century. My friend and colleague Helen Hunt's recent move from the world of social action into Union Seminary's doctoral program is a sign of the times and of the conclusion to which she has come: we need a return to the roots of the women's movement in this country, to the spiritual foundation—not religious, spiritual—upon which it rests, a re-uniting of faith-based women and women of action. It is in this spirit that I affiliate and remain in conversation with those more formally engaged in the business of theology. My work as a writer has required me to move beyond the bounds of formal academia; nonetheless, I believe strongly in being in dialogue with those who are within those bounds, especially those involved in theological education. This is why I am grateful to the GTU for my affiliation. We may not always be in agreement, but we are in conversation. My association with the GTU/CWR is not in any way to be construed as an endorsement by the Graduate Theological Union or the Center for Women and Religion of the thinking I put forward in this book. IOD is an independent project that has grown out of my research, thus I am responsible for whatever limitations, errors, or shortcomings are contained herein.

I remain grateful to Robert Thurman, Ph.D., who holds the Jey Tsong Kapa Chair of Indo-Tibetan Buddhist Studies at Columbia University and who started me down this path of "fierce compassion" with his incomparable, lively, ongoing translation of Tibetan Buddhism into Western culture years ago. I owe him much appreciation for his early help on this subject. I thank Nena Thurman and Tibet House for their help as well. My thanks to Elinor Gadon, Ph.D., of the California Institute for Integral Studies, for the extensive knowledge of Hinduism and Hindu art that she shared.

Rachel Fell McDermott, Ph.D., also of Columbia University, provided crucial information in order for me to get to Kali Puja, in Calcutta, and Tarapith, in Bengal. Cornelia Vogelsanger, Ph.D., the Director of the Folk Museum at the University of Zurich who curated the Kali Exhibit there in 1994, helped with visual materials on both Durga and Kali, and the Black Madonna. She also introduced me to the work of Manuel Bauer. Bettina Baumer, Honorary Coordinator of the India Gandhi National Center for the Arts of Banaras, and Curator at Baranas Hindu University, was of great help in Banaras.

My appreciation goes to Harvey Cox, Ph.D., Victor S. Thomas Professor of Divinity at Harvard University, for introducing me to his student Margaret Elleta Guider, Ph.D., whose experiences of living in Brazil as a Catholic nun working with prostitutes and whose knowledge of the Black Madonna at Aparecida proved decisive in turning my work toward Latin America. Little did we know that day at lunch how far our meeting would take me. Barbara Holifield, whose friendship has long sustained me, connected me with Gerry Maretzski in Rio, whose hospitality and introductions made all my work there and in Salvador possible. I owe Gerry and her assistants a great many thanks. I am also grateful to José Geraldo Rocha of the Centro de Estudos, Cultura e Teologica Negra, in Rio de Janeiro, Brazil, whose community and inspired ministry made me feel profoundly welcomed. His position as a leading exponent of Black Theology in Brazil has much to teach us in North America. Otis Kriegel, a young, innovative teacher of inner-city students, brought the story of the Candelária massacre of street children in Rio to my attention. Rebecca Wunderlich introduced me to *capoeira* and to the Brazilian woman *capoeira* master Marcia Treadler, whose support has also been important. The Rev. Bernardino Andrade's generous help and that of his family in Brazil made travel to Aparecida possible. Father Bernardino's deep love and understanding of the Mother of God and his openness helped guide me. The Rev. Joe Bravo, the Rev. Joe O'Connell, and the Rev. Charles Murphy— Dom Bede Griffiths' students—all encouraged me and gave me ways to connect to my own cultural tradition and to Catholicism.

The Rev. Raimun Pannikar of Spain has had an abiding influence on my work. The ongoing interreligious dialogue which he helps lead continues to be a decisive, if unseen, influence. Christina Feldman, the vipassana Buddhist meditation teacher, the Venerable Gelek Rinpoche of the Jewel Heart Center in Ann Arbor, Michigan, one of my own teachers to whom I am particularly grateful, his senior student Aura Glaser, the scholar/translator Joe Loizzo, M.D., and vipassana teacher Jack Kornfield, of Spirit Rock Meditation Center, in Woodacre, California, have provided aid at key moments in the life of this book.

I am also immensely grateful to the women with whom I spoke about the concept of fierce compassion and whose wisdom, which penetrates these pages, I had the benefit of: Ammachi, Mata Amritanandamayi, the living saint and holy Mother of India with whom I was fortunate enough to have a private interview; the Tibetan Buddhist teacher, Her Holiness Sayka Jetsun Chimey Luding of the Sakya Center in Vancouver, B.C., one of my own generous and most important teachers; Gangaji, the Western woman teacher in the tradition of Ramana Maharshi; Yvonne Rand of the Goat-in-the-Road Center in California, Zen priest and student of Tibetan Buddhism; Mayumi Oda, painter of Goddesses, meditation teacher and cofounder of Plutonium Free Future; Safina Newbery, Professor of Anthropology at the University in Buenos Aires; Jane Sieh, founder of Primavera, the girls' program in Campinas, Brazil; Pat Cane of Capacitar; and Linda Tillery, founder of the Cultural Heritage Choir in Oakland and one of the country's great voices. Each of these women has had a profound influence on this book.

Many friends and colleagues commented on the various drafts of this book, or parts of it, and gave me important criticism. Professor Anne Klein, Ph.D., Chair of Buddhist Studies at Rice University, read the manuscript and was especially helpful. My appreciation goes to Helen Stoltzfus, whose friendship, encouragement, and critical eye as an artist I would find it hard to work without. Nina Wise's intelligence and candor have been important influences and have helped shape my work significantly. The Rev. Pamela Cooper-White, Connor Sauer, Heather Byrne, Ellen Gilbert, Solace Sheets, Miriam Ella Alford, Lynn Hayes,

Nancy Nordhoff, Susan Scott, Mark Cenac, Sandra Lopez, Doyle Barnes, Anita Weissberg, Louise Gund, Dr. Cesar Chelala, John Knoop, Marilyn Yalom, Ph.D., and Edgar Jenkins were important readers as well. Jean Bolen, M.D., Toni Trieste, and Pauline Tessler helped me to see the challenges that would present themselves because of this book. Walks with Katy Butler helped me understand this too. Karen Geiger not only read the book but traveled with me on portions of this journey. I thank her for the continuing journey.

Yeshi Sherover-Neumann, Maxine Wyman, Bonnie Lundberg, and Sala Steinbach read the manuscript or portions thereof at critical moments and gave essential feedback. Alice Walker gave me a transfusion of fierceness when it was most needed and has continued to be an important, quiet influence. Evelyn White has had an abiding effect on my work as well as helping me learn how to recognize what is in front of me and call it by its true name. Elizabeth Kelly, Lois Ann Lorentzen, Dominique Mazeaud, Lucia Chiavola Birnbaum, and the Black Madonna group have given critical support and shared generously too.

Thanks also to Venise Wagner of the *San Francisco Examiner,* Cecile Holmes, Religion Editor of the *Houston Chronicle,* Bill Marvel of the *Dallas Morning News,* and Rebecca Newhall of the *Contra Costa Times* for their interest and understanding of my material on the Black Madonnas and the positive implications they hold for our society. My appreciation too to Noah Griffin for his continued support and enthusiasm for this subject and to James Noel, Assistant Professor of American Religion and member of the Black Theological Forum at the GTU.

I owe a special debt to Betty Simmons, whose love and support have been a lifeline. I remain grateful for the wisdom of Noelle Poncelet, Ph.D., and the deep, abiding friendship of Linda A. Lucy, who helped hold my life together during the years of travel, research, and writing. Thanks also to Christine Calliway, Rachael Steinberg, and Sybill Schmidtt. Pat Perini, Judy Irving, Sherry Reson, Doug Kyle, Michael Grogan, Ph.D., Judith Gilbert, and Pat Morgan all have been generous friends and helped keep me moving forward through all kinds of weather. Many thanks to Heather Byrne for her ready, generous assistance and her boundless enthusiasm for this work.

My thanks to Shana Chrystie of Inner Asia/Geographic for her assistance with travel arrangements, as well as Sonam Gyalpo of Great Escapes in Kathmandu, Nepal, and Marmot Mountain outfitters. Carroll Dunham, of Kathmandu, and Irene Taylor provided invaluable help, as did Haydi Sowerwine.

Diana Schweickart has walked with me through the challenges of helping coordinate this project in all its phases. Rarely have I been involved in a book whose requirements were as extensive and complicated as this one's. Her help has been essential and I am grateful for all that she has done. Additionally, I want to thank Gari Thompson for her capable assistance, as well as Linda Smith. Desne Border provided skillful photo editing and introduced me to the work of Mary Ellen

Mark. Shoshana Alexander helped with editorial feedback at a turning point in the life of this book, as did Naomi Lucks, whose sound cuts helped begin to focus the story. My husband, Corey Fischer, provided ongoing, excellent editorial assistance as well.

I am grateful for the continuing support of my Tuesday night prayer and meditation group. My absence during this writing has been a challenge for all of us. The love and patience that continued to be extended are gratefully received and valued. The same is true of all my friends. Their love and patience have been extraordinary. Certain friendships, such as that of Barry Lopez, manage to survive no matter what. I am mindful of and humbled by these many gifts.

Isabel Allende not only helped me find Laura Bonaparte again but helped to translate Laura's stories when I returned from Argentina. Her own family's experience in Chile helped broaden my understanding of military dictatorships in Latin America. I am immensely grateful for the help Isabel has given me. Carolyn Holmes and Toni Palmer also helped with Spanish translation.

I also owe special thanks to the poet Jane Hirshfield for the quiet witness she has been in my life, and for giving me the words "proud flesh" in her poem "For What Binds Us." They have been a great teaching.

My time at Hedgebrook Farm, the women's writing community, retreat center, and thirty-five-acre organic farm on Whidbey Island, off the coast of Seattle, led to a breakthrough in the writing of this book. Founded and designed with great care by Nancy Nordhoff, Hedgebrook provided the quiet, privacy, and atmosphere that allowed me to dive deeply into this material in a way that would have been otherwise impossible. Meals appeared in a wicker basket at my cottage door; no one asked questions or found my need for solitude strange—in fact, they shared it. To live in a community committed to a diversity of women writers and storytellers, to be cared for with the respect and sensitivity that the Hedgebrook staff offer, created a container for the heat this material generated, allowed it to cook, brought the pressure up so that the alchemy of writing could happen. There were woods to walk in, big Douglas firs, flower gardens, ponds to sit by and ponder. Fresh food from the gardens and the sound of the water on the nearby shore made a place where we could experiment with voice, find it, allow it, and have enough quiet around to hear it, our own and others. One's only responsibility was to write. I could not have written this book without my time there and the support of both the excellent Hedgebrook staff and the Tara Mandala community on Whidbey Island, especially Lynn Hays.

Special thanks is owed to my publisher, Riverhead Books, a member of Penguin Putnam Inc., and especially to Susan Petersen, who first believed in the importance of this work and gave it into the able hands of my editor, Amy Hertz. Amy's intelligence, confidence, and enthusiasm helped me get through the process of writing. Her rigorous editing has made this a better book. From the jacket designer, Lisa Amoroso, to the head of copy editing, Coral Tysliava, and production editor Elizabeth Wagner; from Claire Vaccaro, the head of interiors, to free-lance book designer Deborah Kerner; from production manager Lisa Ferris to Amy's indefatigable assistant, Jennifer Repo, this book has been in the hands of extraordinarily talented, committed women who only know how to give their best.

My agent, Sandra Dijkstra of Dijkstra Literary, has been not only an ally and advocate, she has given important editorial comments and has been invaluable throughout this process.

Honor is due to Ethel Fischer, whose keen interest in and support for my work was boundless. I am only sorry that she did not live to see the book reach publication. My husband, Corey Fischer, gave both to me and to this book on top of his own demanding work as a writer, teacher, and performer. This book would not have come into being without his steady help, careful criticism, and collegiality. The understanding of the artistic process that he brings to bear is all that a writer could wish for. I was blessed to have his support in every way throughout this book. I have no words to express my appreciation to him, only my life.

I am grateful to my family. They saw less of me than ever, received fewer calls, visits, gifts, and letters, and yet stayed steady, full of love and support throughout. My children, Matthew, Madelon, and Ben, have been unstinting in their support, as have been those closest to them, Annamaria Carenzi, Bud Grant, and Rebecca Wunderlich. All helped contribute to the atmosphere needed to birth this book.

I give thanks for the love and confidence of my large family, the broad weave of kin and cousins that helps sustain me. My mother, Ruth, of whom I write in these pages, can never be thanked for all that she has made possible for me. I remain always grateful. I owe thanks to my stepfather, Bob, as well.

The support for my writing and the understanding of my father, C.R., toward the end of his life, was especially meaningful. Though he died just before I formally began this book, he knew the direction I was going in and was very much with me as I made the journey. I took some of his ashes mixed with clay and hardened, Tibetan style, with me to the mountains of Switzerland, Nepal, and India, to be left as *tsa-tsas,* thanks to the kindness of my teacher, Her Holiness Sakya Jetsun Kusho Chimey Luding. But that, dear reader, is another story.

Mother Teresa's death, on September 5, 1997, came as this manuscript was going into production, giving a finality to the brief time I spent with her Sisters. It also gave rise to the realization that though Mother Teresa and her Sisters had been a source of inspiration for this book, her nineteenth-century predecessor Mother Henriette Delille of New Orleans, a free woman of color, was even more so. Mother Henriette's dedication to the poor was profound, and the obstacles she faced as a woman of color in the 1840s in the American South, the racism, still lie at the root of American sorrows, North and South. Her legacy is kept alive by the

Catholic order of nuns she founded, the Sisters of the Holy Family. Whether overseas or in the Americas, these women and all the women in this book walk a path of compassionate action, showing us the many faces of fierce compassion.

When I wanted to interview Mother Teresa's Sisters, they invited me to work with them rather than listen to them talk about what they do. This is the spirit with which she imbued them: "Just come and do." Buddhism challenges us to do no harm; Christianity challenges us to act. Even Christ said that we could perform miracles as great as His, if we had but the faith and acted upon it. Buddhism and Christianity are only the traditions with which I am most familiar. Each of the great faith traditions, including the earth-based indigenous traditions, challenges us to see one another anew, to hold up a light, to extend a hand in help and service, to hold the world sacred.

May the example of all the great teachers, known and unknown, show us the power of doing small things with love. May we behold the presence of the Divine in all Its disguises—beautiful and distressing—and let that be what binds us, women and men, as we walk together into the next millennium, for the benefit of all and for the generations to come.

PERMISSIONS

Author gratefully acknowledges permission to reprint the following:

Excerpt from "Lost" from *Who Shall Be the Sun?* © 1978 David Wagoner. Reprinted by permission of the poet.

Excerpt from poem #47 from *Grace and Mercy in Her Wild Hair: Selected Poems to the Mother Goddess* by Ramprasad Sen, translated by Leonard Nathan and Clinton Seely. © 1982 Shambhala Publications.

Excerpt from "Stings" from *Ariel* by Sylvia Plath. © 1963 by Ted Hughes. Copyright renewed. Reprinted by permission of HarperCollins Publishers, Inc.

Excerpt from "A Letter to Paul Carroll, Who Said I Must Become a Catholic So That I Can Pray for Him" from *Little Girls in Church* by Kathleen Norris, © 1995. Reprinted by permission of the University of Pittsburgh Press.

Excerpt from *The Feminine Dimension of the Divine* by Joan Chamberlain Engelsman © 1994 Chiron Publications.

"I was passionate . . ." from *Women in Praise of the Sacred* by Lal Ded, translated by Jane Hirshfield. © 1994 Jane Hirshfield. Reprinted by permission of the translator and HarperCollins Publishers, Inc.

Excerpt from "What Binds Us" from *Of Gravity and Angels* by Jane Hirshfield. © 1988 by Jane Hirshfield, Wesleyan University Press by permission of University Press of New England.

Grateful acknowledgment is also made for permission to reproduce art on the following pages:

$\mathscr{I}$ N D E X